FOURTH

Going Public

NEW STRATEGIES OF PRESIDENTIAL LEADERSHIP

Samuel Kernell
University of California, San Diego

CQ PRESS

A Division of SAGE, Washington, D.C.

CQ Press
1255 22nd Street, NW, Suite 400
Washington, DC 20037

Phone: 202-729-1900; toll-free, 1-866-4CQ-PRESS (1-866-427-7737)

Web: www.cqpress.com

Photo credits: 20, Franklin Delano Roosevelt Library; 137 (left) CBS/Landov; 137 (middle) Kevin Lamarque/Reuters/Landov; 137 (right) Reuters/Fred Prouser/Landov; 185, Reuters.

Cover design: Lorraine Doneker

∞ The paper used in this publication exceeds the requirements of the American National Standard for Information Sciences—Permanence of Paper for Printed Library Materials, ANSI Z39.48-1992.

Printed and bound in the United States of America

10   2   3   4   5

Library of Congress Cataloging-in-Publication Data

Kernell, Samuel
   Going public / by Samuel Kernell. -- 4th ed.
      p. cm.
   Includes bibliographical references and index.
   ISBN-13: 978-1-56802-899-6 (alk. paper)
   ISBN-10: 1-56802-899-7
      1. Presidents—United States. 2. Presidents—United States—Press conferences. 3. Communication in politics—United States.   I. Title.
   JK554.K47 2006
   352.23'60973—dc22

                                                                                        2006032005

Nothing is so unbelievable that oratory cannot make it acceptable.
—Cicero

One thought receiving wide expression [is] that the politician of tomorrow must become an "actor."
—Jack Gould, *New York Times*, June 25, 1951

Too many good people have been beaten because they tried to substitute substance for style.
—Adviser to Jimmy Carter, December 1976

A President doesn't just need a majority on Election Day. The President needs a majority every day of the week behind every bill that he has.
—Adviser to Bill Clinton, February 1997

In my line of work you got to keep repeating things over and over and over again for the truth to sink in, to kind of catapult the propaganda.
—George W. Bush, March 2005

CONTENTS

Going public is a class of activities that presidents engage in as they promote themselves and their policies before the American public. Some examples are a televised press conference, a special prime-time address to the nation, a speech before a business convention on the West Coast, a visit to a day-care center, a White House ceremony to decorate a local hero that is broadcast via satellite to the hometown television station, and a paid issue commercial promoting some policy or nominee currently under consideration in Congress. What these various activities have in common is that they are intended principally to place the president and his messages before the American people in a way that enhances his chances of success in Washington. Going public draws heavily upon techniques developed over the years in election campaigning; but in going public, the ultimate object of the president's designs is not the American voter, but rather fellow politicians in Washington.

The possibility that the president might at times appeal for the public's support in dealings with Congress occurred to James Madison. In *Federalist* No. 49 Madison argued against a constitutional provision that would allow any of the branches of the federal government to redress constitutional imbalance by appealing "to the people" for reform. Citing recent occurrences in various state legislatures, Madison began by stipulating that if any branch were likely to be guilty of "aggrandizement," it would be the popular one, Congress. Though presidents "are generally the objects of jealousy; *and their administration is always liable to be discolored and rendered unpopular*" [emphasis added]; members of Congress by virtue of being "more numerous," and having "connections of blood, of friendship, and of acquaintance, embrace a great proportion of the most influential part of society." Simply stated, Congress can trump any effort by the president to enlist public opinion.

Near the end of *Federalist* No. 49, Madison allowed the possibility that "the executive power might be in the hands of a peculiar favorite of the people." Against this he reverted to the distinction, common in his day, between the public's *passions* and its *reason*. Public appeals excite the passions so that the outcome, he concluded, "could never be expected to turn on the true merits of the question." In short, Madison had nothing much good to say about going public. Of course, his extraordinary precognition concerned political circumstances far different from those today.

Today, more than two hundred years later, the matter warrants reassessment. No longer a subject only of speculation, going public is a strategy modern presidents routinely enlist. Like Madison, I find the most interesting appeals to be those that involve the president's dealings with Congress. Because the president's success in publicly advancing his policies presupposes his own strong standing in the country, I also give considerable attention to the things presidents do to gain the public's favor.

The fourth edition further explores the use and effectiveness of going public, by drawing heavily from Presidents Clinton and Bush's media strategies. I also grapple with the strategic implications of increasingly polarized political parties in Washington and the growth of cable and satellite television in liberating viewers from their former captivity to presidential television addresses.

THE PLAN OF THE BOOK

I begin by examining presidential power in the context of political relations in Washington. The president's influence with other, more or less autonomous politicians depends upon his ability to satisfy their needs and exploit their vulnerabilities. In the first chapter I develop a rationale for the rise of going public as a presidential strategy tailored to the ever-changing political relations in Washington. As other politicians' needs and expectations are changing, so too must the president's.

Alternative models of political relations in Washington that should be the most conducive to bargaining and going public are set forth in chapter 2. It is not too surprising to find that different forms of influence thrive in quite different kinds of political communities. Paying special attention to changes in Congress and its relations with the presidency, I argue that within the past half century, political Washington has come to look less like institutionalized pluralism (which is conducive to bargaining) and more like individualized pluralism (which is conducive to going public). Presidents more freely go public nowadays because it is a strategy better adapted to modern politics. Since the emergence of going public as a familiar strategy during the 1970s, the Washington community has continued to evolve in ways that challenge the president's ability both to marshal public opinion and to enlist opinion to influence Washingtonians.

In chapter 3 I continue to explore the basis for going public by examining the kinds of politicians who enter the White House and the likelihood that when they arrive in Washington they will find one or both chambers of Congress controlled by the opposition party. Neither the arrival of "outsiders" nor divided party control of government appear to be abating any time soon. Consequently, in this edition I introduce and give special consideration to a particular kind of presidential rhetoric—the veto threat.

Chapter 4 continues to look at presidential leadership as a function of evolving community relations, this time by chronicling presidential-press relations throughout the twentieth century. This inquiry reveals some of the specific political circumstances that gave rise to presidents adopting technologies of direct communications between the White House and the country—the *sine qua non* of going public. At each moment new technologies for gathering and reporting the news have been introduced, and their effects have shaken standard routines of presidential-press relations. Nowhere is this more apparent than with the many altered states of the press conference.

Having established a rationale for the going public phenomenon, I next present the evidence that presidents do indeed increasingly rely upon public relations to build support for their policies in Washington. Chapter 5 presents sixty-year trends that document the growing practice of going public, highlighting President Reagan's use of the televised address and President Clinton's unprecedented level of political travel across the nation. I also consider the effects of pervasive cable subscriptions on presidents' declining ability to speak directly to the American public.

To appreciate the extent to which going public is altering the character of presidential leadership, one must examine firsthand the president's choice to go public or to bargain and its ramification on the choices of others. As with Clinton and Bush, President Reagan was ideally suited by experience, temperament, and ideology to capitalize on going public, and in chapter 6 I analyze the strategies he employed in promoting his budgets in Congress during his first three years in office.

As presidents rely more heavily upon public strategies, their success in Washington will depend vitally upon the reactions of ordinary citizens. In chapter 7 I shift the discussion from Washington relations to public opinion—specifically, public opinion about foreign policy and events. I begin by considering the rally phenomenon, in which the public frequently responds to international crises by upgrading its assessment of the president's job performance. Typically, however, the president's public leadership rests on more than job performance ratings. Additionally, it requires that the approval of the president's performance be transferred to support for his policies. In chapter 7 I consider a model of this type of opinion change and then examine the effects of one specific presidential appeal—the Truman Doctrine speech of 1947. The way the American public did (and did not) respond to President Truman's appeal for emergency aid for Europe offers instruction to present-day presidents similarly interested in molding public opinion.

In chapter 8 I close by considering the implications of recent developments for going public. With polarized parties and an increasingly fragmented communications media portending difficulties for the president's ability to mobilize and employ public opinion, one might suspect that presidents would be reluctant to undertake public strategies. Yet Presidents Clinton and Bush plunged into massive public relations campaigns to promote major reforms of America's health care and Social Security systems. That they tried, rather than that they failed, are encouraging signs that presidents will not shrink away from tackling tough national problems.

ACKNOWLEDGMENTS

The proximate motivation to sit down and write the first edition of this book was Ronald Reagan. It was his success in 1981, coming on the heels of Jimmy Carter's defeat a year earlier, that so confirmed and clarified my own views on the direction of presidential leadership. A fellowship at the Hoover Institution (and in particular the cookie-hour banter there) gave me the needed time and additional inspiration to write *Going Public*. Subsequent revisions have been prompted as much by the thoughtful comments and criticism generously offered by numerous colleagues over the past decade and a half as by the strategic adaptations of our presidents and those who deal with them in an ever-changing communications environment. I am especially indebted to several colleagues at CQ Press—namely, Brenda Carter, Charisse Kiino, and Talia Greenberg—for prodding me to rethink this leadership strategy in light of major changes in technology and in politics and for ushering the manuscript through revision.

Much of the text assumes the form of argument, but more of it is engaged in presenting statistical analysis and marshaling other kinds of evidence. Hardly any of these data originate with me. At various times I have called upon colleagues for assistance in obtaining hard-to-come-by facts and figures. The following individuals, some of whom I have never met, were most charitable in helping me obtain important material to sustain my argument: Sula Richardson and Steven Rutkus at the Congressional Research Service; Laura Kapnick and Mark Knoller at CBS News; Diane Buono at A.C. Nielsen Company; and fellow scholars Richard Brody, Roger Davidson, Joe Foote, Michael Baruch Grossman, Susan Webb Hammond, Martha Joynt Kumar, William Lammers, Richard W. Steele, and Jeffrey Tulis. Matt Childers, Nicole Fox, Delynn Kauffman, and Justin Vaughan provided prompt and accurate research assistance.

chapter 1

Introduction: Going Public in Theory and Practice

When President George H. W. Bush delivered his State of the Union address to the joint assembly of the mostly Democratic Congress on January 28, 1992, he assumed what was becoming a familiar stance:

> I pride myself that I am a prudent man, and I believe that patience is a virtue. But I understand that politics is for some a game. . . . I submit my plan tomorrow. And I am asking you to pass it by March 20. And I ask the American people to let you know they want this action by March 20.

> From the day after that, if it must be: The battle is joined.

> And you know when principle is at stake, I relish a good fair fight.

Once upon a time, these might have been fighting words, but by the 1990s presidents had so routinely come to appeal for public support in their dealings with Congress that Bush's rhetoric scarcely caused a stir among his Washington audience. Presidential appeals for public support had, in fact, become commonplace. Two years later Bill Clinton would use the same forum to launch a six-month public relations campaign to persuade Congress to expand coverage of federal health care beyond Medicare to include everyone not covered by employer insurance. What raised eyebrows was not the announcement or even the scope of the plan. Rather it was the bravado—some would say hubris—with which Clinton warned the assembled legislators that if they failed to give him a fully comprehensive program "I will take this pen and veto it." Two days after his 2004 reelection George W. Bush held a press conference in which he outlined an ambitious policy agenda headed by overhaul of the Social Security system. He matter-of-factly told reporters, "I earned capital in the campaign, political capital, and now I intend to spend it. It is my style." [1] Six weeks later he unveiled in his State of the Union address his partial privatization scheme for Social Security and announced a "sixty cities in sixty days" campaign to push it through Congress.

I call the approach to presidential leadership that has come into vogue at the White House "going public." It is a strategy whereby a president promotes himself and his policies in Washington by appealing directly to the American public for support. Forcing compliance from fellow Washingtonians by going over their heads to enlist constituents' pressure is a tactic that was known but seldom attempted during the first half of the century. Theodore Roosevelt probably first enunciated the strategic principle of going public when he described the presidency as the "bully pulpit." Moreover, he occasionally put theory into practice with public appeals for his Progressive Party reforms. During the next thirty years, other presidents also periodically summoned public support to help them in their dealings with Congress. Perhaps the most famous such instance is Woodrow Wilson's ill-fated whistle-stop tour of the country on behalf of his League of Nations treaty. Equally noteworthy, historically, is Franklin D. Roosevelt's series of radio "fireside chats," which were designed less to subdue congressional opposition than to remind politicians of his continuing national mandate for the New Deal.

These historical instances are significant in large part because they are rare. Unlike Richard Nixon, who thought it important "to spread the White House around" by traveling and speaking extensively,[2] these earlier presidents were largely confined to Washington and obliged to address the country through the nation's newspapers. The concept and legitimizing precedents of going public may have been established during these years, but the emergence of presidents who *routinely* did so to promote their policies outside Washington awaited the development of modern systems of transportation and mass communications. Going public should be appreciated as a strategic adaptation to the information age.

The regularity with which recent presidents have sought public backing for their Washington dealings has altered the way politicians both inside and outside the White House regard the office. The following chapters present numerous instances of presidents preoccupied with public relations, as if these activities chiefly determined their success. Cases are recounted of other Washington politicians intently monitoring the president's popularity ratings and his addresses on television, as if his performance in these realms governed their own behavior. We shall also examine various testimonials of central institutional figures, including several Speakers of the House of Representatives, citing the president's prestige and rhetoric as they explain Congress's actions. If the public ruminations of politicians are to be believed, the president's effectiveness in rallying public support has become a primary consideration for those who do business with him.

PRESIDENTIAL THEORY

Going public has become routine. This was not always the case. After World War I Congress refused to support President Wilson's League of Nations, a peace treaty the president himself had helped negotiate. In this instance Congress determined to amend the treaty and a president equally determined to finalize the agreement the other countries had ratified left him with little choice but to go public to try to marshal public opinion to force the Senate's agreement. Today our information-age presidents opt to go public regardless of the political climate in Washington.

There is another reason to systematically study this leadership strategy. Compared with many other aspects of the modern presidency, scholarship has only recently directed its attention toward this feature of the president's repertoire. Although going public had not become a keystone of presidential leadership in the 1950s and 1960s, when much of the influential scholarship on the subject was written, sufficient precedents were available for scholars to consider its potential for presidential leadership in the future.

Probably the main reason traditional presidential scholarship short-changed going public is its fundamental incompatibility with bargaining. Presidential power is the "power to bargain," Richard E. Neustadt taught a generation of students of the presidency.[3] When Neustadt published his definitive study of presidential leadership in 1960, the "bargaining president" had already become a centerpiece of pluralist theories of American politics. Nearly a decade earlier, Robert A. Dahl and Charles E. Lindblom had described the politician in America generically as "the human embodiment of a bargaining society." They made a special point to include the president in writing that despite his possessing "more hierarchical controls than any other single figure in the government . . . like everyone else . . . the President must bargain constantly."[4] Since Neustadt's landmark treatise, other major works on the presidency have reinforced and elaborated this theme.[5]

Going public violates bargaining in several ways. First, it rarely includes the kinds of exchanges necessary, in pluralist theory, for the American political system to function properly. At times, going public will be merely superfluous—fluff compared with the substance of traditional political exchange. Practiced in a dedicated way, however, it may displace bargaining.

Second, going public fails to extend benefits for compliance, but freely imposes costs for noncompliance. In appealing to the public to "tell your senators and representatives by phone, wire, and Mailgram that the future hangs in balance," the president seeks the aid of a third party—the public—to force other politicians to accept his preferences.[6] If targeted representatives are lucky, the president's success may cost them no more than an opportunity at the bargaining table to shape policy or to extract compensation. If unlucky, they may find themselves both capitulating to the president's wishes and suffering the reproach of constituents for having resisted him in the first place. By imposing costs and failing to offer benefits, going public is more akin to force than to bargaining. Nelson W. Polsby makes this point when he says that members of Congress may "find themselves ill disposed toward a president who prefers to deal indirectly with them [by going public] through what they may interpret as coercion rather than face-to-face in the spirit of mutual accommodation."[7] This senator may echo the sentiments, if not the actions, of those on Capitol Hill who find themselves repeatedly pressured by the president's public appeals: "A lot of Democrats, even if they like the President's proposal, will vote against him because of his radio address on Saturday." [8]

Third, going public entails public posturing. To the extent that it fixes the president's bargaining position, posturing makes subsequent compromise with other politicians more difficult. Because negotiators must be prepared to yield some of their clients' preferences to make a deal, bargaining proverbially proceeds best behind closed doors. Consider the difficulty Ronald Reagan's widely publicized challenge "My tax proposal is a line drawn in dirt" posed for subsequent budget negotiations in Washington.[9] Similarly, during his nationally televised State of the Union address in 1994, President Bill Clinton sought to repair his reputation as someone too willing to compromise away his principles by declaring to the assembled joint session of Congress, "If you send me [health care] legislation that does not guarantee every American private health insurance that can never be taken away, you will force me to take this pen, veto the legislation, and we'll come right back here and start all over again." [10] Not only did these declarations threaten to cut away any middle ground on which a compromise might be constructed, they probably stiffened the resolve of the president's adversaries, some of whom would later be needed to pass the administration's legislative program.

Finally, and possibly most injurious to bargaining, going public undermines the legitimacy of other politicians. It usurps their prerogatives of office, denies their role as representatives, and questions their claim to reflect the interests of their constituents. For a traditional bargaining stance with the president to be restored, these politicians would first have to reestablish parity, probably at a cost of conflict with the White House.[11]

Given these fundamental incompatibilities, one may further speculate that by spoiling the bargaining environment, going public renders the president's future influence ever more dependent upon his ability to generate popular support for himself and his policies. The degree to which a president draws upon public opinion determines the kind of leader he will be.

PRESIDENTIAL PRACTICE

Bargaining and going public have never been particularly compatible styles of leadership. In the early twentieth century, when technology limited presidents' capacity to engage in public relations, they did so sparingly. On rare occasions, presidents might enlist public support as their contribution to bargains with politicians for whom their position was potentially risky. But generally, these two leadership strategies coexisted in a quiet tension. In modern times, though, going public is likely to take the form of an election campaign. George W. Bush's "sixty cities in sixty days" Social Security reform tour in 2005 is a recent example to which we shall later return. When presidents adopt intensive public relations as their leadership strategy they render bargaining increasingly difficult. The decision to go public at one juncture may preclude and undermine the opportunity to bargain at another, and vice versa. All this means that the decision to bargain or to go public must be carefully weighed.

The two case studies below reveal that modern presidents and their advisers carefully attend to this strategic issue. As we shall do throughout this book, we compare instances of presidential success and failure in order to understand the potential gains and losses embedded in presidents' choices.

Ronald Reagan Enlists Public Opinion as a Lever

No president has enlisted public strategies to better advantage than did Ronald Reagan. Throughout his tenure, he exhibited a full appreciation of bargaining and going public as the modern office's principal strategic alternatives. The following examples from a six-month survey of White House news coverage show how entrenched this bifurcated view of presidential strategy has become. The survey begins in late November 1984, when some members of the administration were pondering how the president might exploit his landslide victory and others were preparing a new round of budget cuts and a tax reform bill for the next Congress.

November 29, 1984. *Washington Post* columnist Lou Cannon reported the following prediction from a White House official: "We're going to have confrontation on spending and consultation on tax reform." The aide explained, "We have somebody to negotiate with us on tax reform, but may not on budget cuts." [12] By "confrontation" he was referring to the president's success in appealing to the public on national television, that is, in going public. By "consultation" he meant bargaining.

January 25, 1985. The above prediction proved accurate two months later, when another staffer offered as pristine an evocation of going public as one is likely to find: "We have to look at it, in many ways, like a campaign. He [Reagan] wants to take his case to the people. You have a constituency of 535 legislators as opposed to 100 million voters. But the goal is the same—to get the majority of voters to support your position." [13]

February 10, 1985. In a nationally broadcast radio address, President Reagan extended an olive branch, inviting members of Congress to "work with us in the spirit of cooperation and compromise" on the budget. This public statement probably did little to allay the frequently voiced suspicion of House Democratic leaders that such overtures were mainly intended for public consumption. One Reagan aide insisted, however, that the president simply sought to reassure legislators that "he would not 'go over their heads' and campaign across the country for his budget without trying first to reach a compromise." [14] In this statement the aide implicitly concedes the harm public pressure can create for bargaining but seeks to incorporate it advantageously into the strategic thinking of the politicians with whom the administration must deal by not forswearing its use.

March 9, 1985. After some public sparring, the administration eventually settled down to intensive budget negotiations with the Republican-led Senate Finance Committee. Failing to do as well as he would like, however, Reagan sent a message to his party's senators through repeated unattributed statements to the press that, if necessary, he would "go to the people to carry our message forward." * Again, public appeals, though held in reserve, were threatened.

March 11, 1985. In an interview with a *New York Times* correspondent, a senior Reagan aide sized up his president: "He's liberated, he wants to get into a fight, he feels strongly and wants to push his program through himself. . . . Reagan never quite believed his popularity before the election, never believed the polls. Now he has it, and he's going to push . . . ahead with our agenda." [15]

May 16, 1985. To avoid entangling tax reform with budget deliberations in Congress, Reagan, at the request of Republican leaders, delayed unveiling his tax reform proposal until late May. A couple of weeks before Reagan's national television address on the subject, White House aides began priming the press with leaks on the proposal's content and promises that the president would follow it with a public relations blitz. In the words of one White House official, the plan was to force Congress to make a "binary choice between tax reform or no tax reform." [16] The administration rejected bargaining, as predicted nearly six months earlier by a White House aide, apparently for two strategic reasons. First, Reagan feared that in a quietly negotiated process, the tax reform package would unravel under the concerted pressure of the special interests. Second, by taking the high-profile approach of "standing up for the people against the special interests," in the words of one adviser, tax reform might do for Republicans what Social Security did for Democrats—make them the majority party. [17]

During these six months, when bargaining held out promise—as it had during negotiations with the Senate Finance Committee—public appeals were held in reserve. The White House occasionally, however, threatened an appeal in trying to gain more favorable consideration. On other occasions, when opponents of the president's policies appeared capable of extracting major concessions—House Democrats on the budget and interest groups on tax reform, for example—the White House disengaged from negotiations and tried through public relations to force Congress to accept the president's policies. Although by 1985 news items such as the preceding excerpts seemed unexceptional as daily news, they are a recent phenomenon. One does not routinely find such stories in White House reporting twenty years earlier when, for example, John Kennedy's legislative agenda was stalled in Congress.

---

*Jonathan Fuerbringer, "Reagan Critical of Budget View of Senate Panel," *New York Times*, March 9, 1985. Senate Majority Leader Bob Dole told reporters that if the president liked the Senate's final budget package he would campaign for it "very vigorously … going to television, whatever he needs to reduce federal spending." Karen Tumulty, "Reagan May Get Draft of Budget Accord Today," *Los Angles Times*, April 4, 1985, 1.

President Clinton Snares Himself by Bargaining

Shortly after assuming office, Bill Clinton received some bad news. The Bush administration had underestimated the size of the next year's deficit by $50 billion. The president's campaign promises of new domestic programs and a middle-class tax cut would have to be put on hold in favor of fulfilling his third, now urgent pledge to trim $500 billion from the deficit over the next five years. On February 17, 1993, President Clinton appeared before a joint session of Congress and a national television audience to unveil his deficit reduction package. The president's deficit-cutting options were constrained by two considerations: he wanted to include minimal stimulus spending to honor his campaign promise, and he faced a Congress controlled by fellow Democrats who were committed to many of the programs under the budget ax. Even with proposed cuts in defense spending, the only way the budget could accommodate these constraints was through a tax increase. The package raised taxes on the highest-income groups and introduced a broad energy consumption tax. During the following weeks, the president and his congressional liaison team quietly lobbied Congress. He would not again issue a public appeal until the eve of the final vote in August.

The president soon learned that Republicans in both chambers had united in opposition to the administration proposal. Led by Newt Gingrich in the House of Representatives and Bob Dole in the Senate, Republicans retreated to the sidelines and assumed the role of Greek chorus, ominously chanting "tax and spend liberals." This meant that the administration needed virtually every Democratic vote to win. Democratic members appreciated this, and many began exploiting the rising value of their votes to extract concessions that would make the legislation more favorable to their constituents.

By June the president's bargaining efforts had won him a watered-down bill that even he had difficulty being enthusiastic about. Meanwhile, the Republicans' public relations campaign had met with success: the American public had come to regard President Clinton as a "tax and spend liberal." Whereas shortly after the February speech, the *Los Angeles Times* had found half of its polling respondents willing to describe the president's initiative as "bold and innovative" and only 35 percent of them willing to describe it as "tax and spend," by June these numbers had reversed. Now, 53 percent labeled it "tax and spend" and only 28 percent still regarded it as "bold and innovative." [18] Given this turnaround in the public's assessment of the initiative, it was not surprising that the public also downgraded its evaluation of the initiative's sponsor. During the previous five months, President Clinton's approval rating had plunged from 58 to 41 percent.

This was the situation when several of Clinton's senior campaign consultants sounded the alarm in a memo: in only six months the president had virtually exhausted his capacity for leadership. If he did not turn back the current tide of public opinion, he would be weakened beyond repair. In response, the president assembled his senior advisers to evaluate current strategy. This set the stage for a confrontation between those advisers who represented the president in bargaining with other Washingtonians and those staffers who manned the White House public relations machinery. The argument that erupted between these advisers should disabuse anyone of the notion that bargaining and cultivating public support are separate, self-contained spheres of action that do not encroach on one another.[19]

The president's chief pollster, Stanley Greenberg, opened the discussion by stating his and his fellow consultants' position: "We do not exaggerate when we say that our current course, advanced by our economic team and Congressional leaders, threatens to sink your popularity further and weaken your presidency. . . . The immediate problem," he explained, "is that thanks to the Republican effort no one views your economic package as anything other than a tax scheme. You must exercise a 'bold zero option,' which is consultant talk for 'rid your policy of any taxes that affect the middle class.' " (In fact, the only tax still in the bill was a 4.3-cent-per-gallon gasoline tax that would raise a modest $20 billion.) Greenberg then unveiled polling data that found broad public support for such a move. He closed by warning everyone in the room, "We have a very short period of time. And if we don't communicate something serious and focused in the period, we're going to be left with what our detractors used to characterize our plan. . . . Don't assume we can fix it in August." This concluded the case for going public. And in order to use this strategy, Clinton had to change course on taxes.

According to those present, the economic and congressional advisers had listened to this argument "with a slow burn." Finally, the president's chief lobbyist, Howard Paster, blurted out, "This isn't an election! The Senate breaks its ass to get a 4.3-cent-a-gallon tax passed, and we can't just abandon it." Besides, they needed the $20 billion provided by the tax to offset other concessions that would be necessary to get the bill passed. "I need all the chips that are available," Paster pleaded. "Don't bargain them away here. Let me have maximum latitude."

From here, the discussion deteriorated into name calling and blame assigning that stopped only when Clinton started screaming at everyone—"a purple fit" is how one participant described it. In the end the president decided that he had to stay the course but that he would begin traveling around the country to explain to the public that his economic package was the "best" that could be enacted. In mid-August, after a concerted public relations campaign that concluded with a nationally televised address, the legislation barely passed. (In the Senate, Vice President Al Gore cast the tie-breaking vote.) The new administration's first legislative initiative had drained its resources both in Congress and across the nation. From here, the Clinton administration limped toward even more difficult initiatives represented by the North American Free Trade Agreement (NAFTA) and health care reform.

Clearly, as both case studies show, going public appears to foster political relations that are quite at odds with those traditionally cultivated through bargaining. One may begin to examine this phenomenon by asking, what is it about modern politics that would inspire presidents to go public in the first place?

NOTES

1. Dan Froomkin, "Bush Agenda: Bold but Blurry," *Washington Post*, November 5, 2004.
2. Robert B. Semple Jr., "Nixon Eludes Newsmen on Coast Trip," *New York Times*, August 3, 1970, 16.
3. Richard E. Neustadt, *Presidential Power* (New York: John Wiley and Sons, 1980).
4. Robert A. Dahl and Charles E. Lindblom, *Politics, Economics, and Welfare* (New York: Harper and Row, 1953), 333.
5. Among them are Aaron Wildavsky, *The Politics of the Budgetary Process* (Boston: Little, Brown, 1964); Graham T. Allison, *The Essence of Decision: Explaining the Cuban Missile Crisis* (New York: HarperCollins, 1987); Hugh Heclo, *The Government of Strangers* (Washington, D.C.: Brookings Institution, 1977); and Nelson W. Polsby, *Consequences of Party Reform* (New York: Oxford University Press, 1983).
6. From Ronald Reagan's address to the nation on his 1986 budget. Jack Nelson, "Reagan Calls for Public Support of Deficit Cuts," *Los Angeles Times*, April 25, 1985, 1.
7. Nelson W. Polsby, "Interest Groups and the Presidency: Trends in Political Intermediation in America," in *American Politics and Public Policy*, ed. Walter Dean Burnham and Martha Wagner Weinbey (Cambridge: MIT Press, 1978), 52.
8. Hedrick Smith, "Bitterness on Capitol Hill," *New York Times*, April 24, 1985, 14.
9. Ed Magnuson, "A Line Drawn in Dirt," *Time*, February 22, 1982, 12–13.
10. William J. Clinton, *Public Papers of the Presidents of the United States: William J. Clinton, 1994*, vol. 1 (Washington, D.C.: Government Printing Office, 1995), 126–135.
11. See David S. Broder, "Diary of a Mad Majority Leader," *Washington Post*, December 13, 1981, C1, C5; David S. Broder, "Rostenkowski Knows It's His Turn," *Washington Post National Weekly Edition*, June 10, 1985, 13.
12. Lou Cannon, "Big Spending-Cut Bill Studied," *Washington Post*, November 29, 1984, A8.
13. Bernard Weinraub, "Reagan Sets Tour of Nation to Seek Economic Victory," *New York Times*, January 25, 1985, 43.
14. Bernard Weinraub, "Reagan Calls for 'Spirit of Cooperation' on Budget and Taxes," *New York Times*, February 10, 1985, 32. On Democratic suspicions of Reagan's motives see Hedrick Smith, "O'Neill Reflects Democratic Strategy on Budget Cuts and Tax Revisions," *New York Times*, December 6, 1984, B20; and Margaret Shapiro, "O'Neill's New Honeymoon with Reagan," *Washington Post National Weekly Edition*, February 11, 1985, 12.
15. Bernard Weinraub, "In His 2nd Term, He Is Reagan the Liberated," *New York Times*, March 11, 1985, 10.
16. David E. Rosenbaum, "Reagan Approves Primary Elements of Tax Overhaul," *New York Times*, May 16, 1985, 1.
17. Robert W. Merry and David Shribman, "G.O.P. Hopes Tax Bill Will Help It Become Majority Party Again," *Wall Street Journal*, May 23, 1985. See also Rosenbaum, "Reagan Approves Primary Elements of Tax Overhaul," 14. Instances such as those reported here continued into summer. See, for example, Jonathan Fuerbringer, "Key Issues Impede Compromise on Cutting Deficit," *New York Times*, June 23, 1985, 22.
18. These figures are reported in Richard E. Cohen, *Changing Course in Washington* (New York: Macmillan, 1994), 180.
19. The account of this meeting comes from Bob Woodward, *The Agenda* (New York: Simon and Schuster, 1994).

2

How Washington Has Changed

The incompatibility of bargaining and going public presents some pressing theoretical questions. Why should presidents come to favor a strategy of leadership that appears so incompatible with the principles of pluralist theory? Why, if other Washington elites legitimately and correctly represent the interests of their clients and constituents, would anything be gained by going over their heads? The answers to these questions are complex, reflecting changes in the capital and in presidents. In this chapter we consider the changes within Washington, the locale of presidential activity. In chapter 3 we examine changes in the kinds of politicians who occupy the White House and Congress.

Some would account for the rise of going public by resorting to the imperative of technology. Certainly, advances in transportation and communications have been indispensable to this process, but they have not been sufficient in themselves to alter political relations in such a contradictory way. And, as we shall see in chapter 5, advancing technology can work in reverse, rendering the president's ability to communicate with the public more difficult.

There are more fundamental reasons for the discrepancy between theory and current practice. Politics in Washington may no longer be as tractable to bargaining as it once was. Presidents prefer to go public because the strategy offers a better prospect of success than it did in the past. Perhaps the most consequential development in the modern era is the regularity of divided party control of government. Every president since Jimmy Carter has at some time had to deal with a Congress in which the opposition party controlled one or both chambers. On such occasions, each side frequently finds political advantage in frustrating the other and playing a blame game. Posturing in preparation for the next election takes precedence over bargaining and passing new policy.

Moreover, beginning in the 1970s close observers of American politics detected a pervasive decoupling of traditional allegiances. The most prominent of these trends saw voters abandoning their political party affiliations. From the 1960s to the 1980s the proportion of survey respondents who classified themselves as Independent (or some other noncommittal category) grew from 24 to 41 percent; twenty-five years later, despite a resurgent partisanship among both voters and politicians on a number of dimensions, this basic, defining fact has not changed. Entering the 2006 midterm election period, most surveys show Independent to be the single most popular choice when respondents are asked their party identification.[1] And voters continue to split their ballots, if not quite at the record rates of the 1980s, still to a degree unknown in the 1950s and 1960s.* Consequently, political relations among politicians in Washington remain loose and individualistic. In part ballot splitting reflects the dramatic growth of incumbency advantage, especially in House elections, during the 1980s. From 1976 until 1992 at least 90 percent of these incumbents who sought reelection won both their primary and general elections. Some years the figure reached a 98 percent success rate. If this success better insulated these politicians from party and institutional leaders, it served paradoxically to make many of them more sensitive to public opinion from their constituencies. After all, they were winning, in their view, by dint of heroic effort to respond to their constituents.[2]

As politicians in Washington became more sensitive (and perhaps responsive) to public pressure, presidents learned that mobilizing these pressures worked. For exposition I classify the earlier era up to the 1970s as "institutionalized pluralism" and the latter era as "individualized pluralism." Since the 1994 midterm congressional elections, when an ideologically infused resurgent Republican Party surprisingly took over control of the House of Representatives and the Senate for the first time in a generation, politics in Washington has in one important respect shifted away from those relations described by individualized pluralism. Specifically, a series of vigorous Republican Party leaders in Congress have restored a level of discipline and policy coherence unseen since the 1960s. Nonetheless, given the recentness and limited scope of this development and continuing, unabated expectations of presidential leadership via public relations, I have retained this bifurcated classification of the modern evolution of Washington politics from predominantly private elite transactions to the mobilization of interested publics. We will consider how recently strengthened partisanship in Congress may temper presidents' incentives to go public.

INSTITUTIONALIZED PLURALISM:
The Bargaining Community

With the publication of *Politics, Economics, and Welfare* in 1953 Robert A. Dahl and Charles E. Lindblom helped establish a framework for the study of American politics that would guide scholars for the next generation. They

---

* During the 1990s, the American National Election Surveys found 30 percent of respondent voters reporting that they had split their ballot between the presidential and House candidates. This compares to 18 percent in 2004 and the 1960s and 14 percent during the 1950s. The author wishes to thank Martin B. Wattenberg for supplying these figures in a personal communication, March 10, 2006.

described the practice of politics in such a way as to make the appearance of a bargaining president inevitable:

> The politician is, above all, the man whose career depends upon the successful negotiation of bargains. To win office he must negotiate electoral alliances. To satisfy his electoral alliance he must negotiate alliances with other legislators and with administrators, for his control depends upon negotiation. Most of his time is consumed in bargaining. This is the skill he cultivates; it is the skill that distinguishes the master-politician from the political failure.[3]

For what structure of politics is bargaining ideally suited? It is one in which political elites, and for the most part only elites, matter. Limiting politics to Washington impacts both discretion and stability. Politics needs to be structured this way so that elites retain the flexibility to bargain and the certainty that once an accord is reached it will not be undone. The citizenry's interests are not ignored, however. The citizenry has limited and occasional avenues of participation—through periodic elections and membership in mediating associations such as unions, trade and professional associations, voluntary societies, and churches. Partitioned geographically, citizens participate vicariously through their elected representatives; partitioned functionally, they participate through interest groups and the agencies for whom they are clients.

In this pluralistic system each politician must be reckoned with not only according to the strength of his or her constituency but also according to the institutional resources provided by his or her office. Through intensive constitutionalism, the Framers sought to mitigate the plebiscitary tendency of democracy by giving officeholders legitimacy apart from their representative role. They succeeded and bestowed on Washington what has evolved into the pronounced institutional character of its politics.

In the absence of some overriding criterion, such as party fidelity, authority within institutions is generally distributed by seniority. Everywhere, senior partners matter more than junior partners, and transients for whom Washington is a way station to some private career count for little. These, in Hugh Heclo's words, are "the low credit risk in a high credit market."[4]

From time to time some politicians will graduate to new roles as seniority rules are triggered to fill vacancies at the top. Others will try to rise to higher office by expanding their electoral constituency. Some of these, inevitably, will be defeated, along with others who merely seek reelection. And many of those forced off the career ladder will elect to leave Washington altogether.

Elections may be commended by democratic theory, but from the local vantage of a bargaining society they mostly pose disruptions. By generating turnover, they raise uncertainty for bargaining. A politician at risk in the next election will have greater interest in receiving credit than in extending it. But, recognizing his precarious existence, his potential trading partners may see themselves giving something for nothing. This leaves, of course, little common ground for transacting business.

Beyond this, campaigns and elections are unwanted distractions from the real business of politicians in Washington. Under the pressure of reelection, some community members may be tempted to hector, to make excessive demands of unaccommodating bargaining partners, or to behave in other ways that make future negotiation and compromise more difficult.

The same disruptive tendencies are true of public opinion more generally. To function smoothly, a bargaining society must insulate itself against short-term swings in popular sentiment. Appreciating this, the Constitution's Framers minimized the influence of the citizenry through staggered elections, which would require that "public passions" be sustained for a long time before they could influence the policies of each branch of government. And by differentiating constituencies into states and delegating to these subdivisions specific constitutional prerogatives, they sought to give minorities a sufficient toehold to resist short-lived majorities.

A Washington ideally suited for bargaining should therefore be a stable and somewhat insular community if the circumscribed avenues of mutual adjustment through negotiation are to work effectively. But this setting works against the president, who may be viewed as an interloper. The system also needs to be so configured to accommodate the local political economy. Negotiation occurs within a market where dissimilar goods and services are bartered. Identifying mutually attractive exchanges takes time, and once a transaction is initiated it may not be consummated immediately. Indebtedness is commonplace; unspecified IOUs may not be called in for years.

I call this system "institutionalized pluralism" for several reasons. First, political exchange occurs within a dense institutional milieu that allocates resources among actors and identifies the relevant bargaining partners. Second, a stable bargaining society may be expected to institutionalize informal rules of the marketplace that regulate behavior and reduce uncertainty. Perhaps the most sacred commandment is "Honor one's commitments." Variants are tailored to each role. For the lobbyist it means never lie by knowingly giving legislators incorrect information on which they may base a vote or seek to persuade others. For the correspondent it means never publish material provided off the record or directly attribute background information to the source. Playing it straight with one's colleagues does not require that a participant reveal sincere preferences at the bargaining table, but it does demand that once a bargain is agreed to, the politician strives to fulfill his or her part of it.

Another commandment is "Don't use force," for the simple reason that force usually does not work. Dahl and Lindblom noted, "The politician does not often give orders. He can rarely employ unilateral controls. Even as a chief executive or a cabinet officer he soon discovers that his control depends upon his skill in bargaining." [5] Even if politicians or bureaucrats enjoy hierarchical superiority over another or in some other way could unilaterally preempt another's choice, they should hesitate to use this advantage. That force begets counter-force is a law of political physics. Politicians may be able to avoid compensation one day, but they cannot ensure themselves against retribution the next.

Besides, collectively, a politician's peers in Washington have efficient ways of judging and punishing individuals who violate trust or fail to honor the standards of mutual accommodation. Each politician carries a reputation, a continuously updated record of all the qualities that are relevant to others as they contemplate doing business with him or her. Senator A may double-cross Senator B, but in doing so, he or she may be sure that some community members are watching and that still others will soon learn about it. Depending upon the seriousness of the violation, concerted sanctions might be applied. Collective enforcement of community norms will generally be unnecessary, however. Other actors' pursuit of simple self-interest will suffice. The violator will naturally suffer ostracism proportionate to his or her transgression. What other senators, for instance, would cheerfully work with Senator A? If they were willing to deal with Senator A at all, they would require compensation to cover the added risks Senator A represents. Prudently, they would insist that Senator A first perform his or her end of the bargain.

Another venerable understanding that enjoys less cachet today but was once rigorously adhered to allowed senators and representatives when back home to rail against Congress, the other party, and its leadership as much as they felt necessary to satisfy constituents; but in Washington, such displays were deemed inappropriate. Having been exposed only to public rhetoric before arriving in Washington as a freshman member of the House of Representatives in the 1950s, Rep. Clem Miller marveled at the "cocoon of good feeling" that enveloped Congress.[6]

Reciprocity is so vital to a bargaining society that it is deeply ingrained in the normative order. Writing about the Senate of the mid-1950s, Donald R. Matthews observed, "It is not an exaggeration to say that reciprocity is a way of life in the Senate." As a senator's administrative assistant told him, "My boss . . . will—if it doesn't mean anything to him—do a favor for any other Senator. It doesn't matter *who* he is. It's not a matter of friendship, it's just a matter of I won't be an S.O.B. if you won't be one."[7]

Trust and fellow feeling will at times give rise to more focused and ambitious reciprocity arrangements. Whether because of shared goals, complementary resources, or both, two politicians may come to recognize the mutual gain possible through a continuing relationship. The bargain may never be explicitly stated, much less negotiated, and no ledger of indebtedness kept. Instead, a simple understanding to work together exists until one party decides the relationship is too costly and ends it.

Bargains in the form of relationships occur most naturally among proximate participants who share interests—for instance, members of a political party or a congressional committee, or between an agency head and the lobbyist of a clientele group the agency serves. The time-honored practice of "cue giving" between pairs of like-minded members of Congress during floor voting is a minor instance of this form of bargaining.

Protocoalitions

The president is doubtless the bargaining community's most prominent member. But even the consummate bargainer in this high office can participate in only a small fraction of the transactions that must occur daily in Washington to form governing coalitions. Exchange is thus a necessary and ubiquitous activity of Washington elites. It does not, however, proceed randomly.

Institutionalized pluralism promotes a two-tiered process of coalition building. The higher-level, presidential coalition can be distinguished by its greater size, the diversity of its membership, the specificity of its goals, and its fragility. Presidential coalitions are typically temporary associations, forming and dissolving around a single issue or bill. Arrived at in an ad hoc fashion, they rarely survive the resolution of the issue in question.

The building of lower-level coalitions, or protocoalitions, follows predictable lines by adhering to a couple of political principles. First, it spans the constitutionally mandated policy course from enactment to implementation. Because institutional barriers confine communication, exchange proceeds more easily and commonly within rather than between organizations. Well-known examples of protocoalitions are Senate Majority Leader Lyndon Johnson's Democratic "troops"; Rep. Wilbur Mills's Ways and Means Committee, which never divided into subcommittees; the Justice Department's civil rights lawyers under Richard Nixon; even Dwight Eisenhower's military-industrial complex, if there was such a thing.

Second, those building protocoalitions seek out bargaining partners with mutual needs and complementary resources. The proverbial "iron triangles" among agencies, clienteles, and congressional committees are so called because they follow the policy course, spanning institutional boundaries as they do so and incorporating dissimilar yet compatible partners. These dense networks of political exchange form the subcommunities of institutionalized pluralism.

Many protocoalitions may be ad hoc and short lived, but those that matter most tend to be constructed more coherently and durably. They arise not from some fleeting issue but from kindred interests or the continuing need of ideologically or institutionally proximate participants to work together. For example, the agency heads in the Department of Agriculture, the subcommittee members of the House and Senate Agriculture Committees, and the Washington representatives of farm groups must cooperate if they are to satisfy the interests of their common client—America's farmers. Rarely are these entities self-sufficient. Iron triangles notwithstanding, a protocoalition typically must join with others if its bill is to be passed or its policy implemented effectively. Leaders of protocoalitions arise if for no other reason than to conduct these external relations.

Activities and transactions among these groups may be far more consequential for the president's own success than any business he might conduct
with them directly. Limits on time, energy, and resources may prevent presidents from intruding even when they recognize the damage others' transactions may have on their own designs. More often than not, presidents must
look on as interested bystanders. These protocoalitions define presidents'
options; they may require particular combinations of coalition partners; they
may even dictate the substance of exchange. Once the protocoalition pacts are
concluded, they come to the president as givens from which he will try to stitch
together a larger, more expansive coalition that will traverse the constitutionally required path—one easily ambushed by numerous veto players—in order
to successfully make new public policy.

The President's Place in Institutionalized Pluralism

Constructing coalitions across the broad institutional landscape of Congress,
the bureaucracy, interest groups, courts, and state governments requires a
politician who possesses a panoramic view and commands the resources necessary to engage the disparate, parochial interests of Washington's political
elites. Only the president enjoys such vantage and resources. Traditional presidential scholarship leaves little doubt as to how they should be employed.
Nowhere has Dahl and Lindblom's framework of the bargaining society been
more forcefully employed than in Richard E. Neustadt's classic *Presidential
Power,* published in 1960. Neustadt observes:

> Status and authority yield bargaining advantages. But in a govern-
> ment of "separated institutions sharing powers," they yield them to all
> sides. With the array of vantage points at his disposal, a President may
> be far more persuasive than his logic or his charm could make him.
> But outcomes are not guaranteed by his advantages. There remain the
> counter pressures those whom he would influence can bring to bear
> on him from vantage points at their disposal. Command has limited
> utility; persuasion becomes give-and-take. . . .
>   The President's advantages are checked by the advantages of oth-
> ers. Continuing relationships will pull in both directions. These are
> relationships of mutual dependence. A President depends upon the
> men he would persuade; he has to reckon with his need or fear of
> them. They too will possess status, or authority, or both, else they
> would be of little use to him. Their vantage points confront his own;
> their power tempers his.*

---

* Richard E. Neustadt, *Presidential Power,* 28–29. Copyright 1980. Reprinted by permission of John
Wiley and Sons, Inc. Compare with Dahl and Lindblom's earlier observation: "The President possesses more hierarchical controls than any other single figure in the government; indeed, he is often
described somewhat romantically and certainly ambiguously as the most powerful democratic

Bargaining is thus the essence of presidential leadership, and pluralist theory explicitly rejects unilateral forms of influence as usually insufficient and ultimately costly. The ideal president is one who seizes the center of the Washington bazaar and actively barters with fellow politicians to build winning coalitions. He must do so, according to this theory, or he will forfeit any claim to leadership.

A president has the potential for symbiosis. Protocoalitions provide him with economy: he need not engage every coalition partner; talking to their leaders will do. In return the president provides protocoalitions with much-needed coordination. Although there are no guarantees of success, institutionalized pluralism clearly offers the virtuoso bargainer in the White House an opportunity for real leadership.

For years critics complained that autocratic committee chairs, indifferent party leaders, and the conservative coalitions of both Republicans and Southern Democrats prevented Democratic presidents from achieving their ambitious policy goals. Yet institutionalized pluralism requires the president to keep company with these "obstacles" if he is to succeed. Leaders of lower-level coalitions may extract a steep price for cooperation, and at times they may defeat him outright. As difficult as a Lyndon Johnson in the Senate, a Wilbur Mills in the House, a Wilbur Cohen at Social Security, or a J. Edgar Hoover at the FBI might have been when he got his back up, each was indispensable as a trading partner. The reason is not difficult to see. Consider what these politicians had to offer: a majority leader who could strike a deal with the president on compromise legislation and then return to the chamber floor and deliver the critical votes necessary for its passage; a committee chair who spoke so authoritatively that his committee's markup sessions were spent detailing the language of an agreement reached earlier; or an agency head who, once persuaded, effectively redirected his organization's activities. Presidents simply have insufficient authority to command their way to success and lack the time and energy to negotiate individually with everyone whose cooperation they need.

Bargaining Techniques

Perhaps the best way to specify more concretely how presidents behave under institutionalized pluralism is to list some of the things they have traditionally done when they have run into trouble with Congress. The doors of the Oval Office would fling open and scores of representatives and senators—some reluctantly, others with shopping lists in hand—would traipse through to hear the president's case. When large blocks of votes needed to be shifted, White House aides readied compromise positions with an eye toward giving the pres-

---

executive in the world. Yet like everyone else in the American policy process, the President must bargain constantly—with Congressional leaders, individual Congressmen, his department heads, bureau chiefs, and leaders of nongovernmental organizations" (Dahl and Lindblom, *Politics, Economics, and Welfare*, 333).

ident the margin of victory at the least expense. As the vote date neared and the requisite number of converts shrank, fence sitters would be singled out for special treatment. Outstanding IOUs would be called in and fresh ones tendered as the president courted ambivalent legislators with promises of goods and services for their constituencies.

These and many of the other tactics traditionally part of the presidential repertoire are essentially private transactions among elite negotiators. Beyond understanding the character of the game, the president must also sense the needs of the potential partners in the coalition and discover the most cost-effective exchange. What constitutes the "right stuff" for bargaining presidents has been a frequent subject of rich description. Douglass Cater's offering is typical:

> A President has to have an acute awareness of the resistances that exist
> to any step he takes. The elements of his essential knowledge can be
> picayune: that he must communicate with a certain committee chair-
> man in the mornings because he is too drunk by afternoon—any after-
> noon—to be coherent; that a certain bureaucrat is so buttressed by
> interest-group support that he can regularly defy the occupant of the
> White House, Democrat or Republican; that a certain issue has grown
> so mired in lobbyist intrigue that it is irredeemable. If he is to be any
> good, a President must have a mental catalogue of the movers and
> shakers in the Washington community, their habits and habitats. He
> needs to know the crotchets of M. De Gaulle of France, Mr. Meany of
> AFL-CIO, Mr. Reston of the *New York Times,* and many, many others.[8]

Subtlety and fine-tuning in bargaining are vital to conserve resources in such situations. The president's bargaining chits are limited, but demand for their expenditure is insatiable. No president understood the requirements of institutionalized pluralism better than Franklin Roosevelt. Occasionally there were lapses, but usually the congruence between the actions expected and Roosevelt's practice was remarkable—so much so that at times the model of the bargaining president appears to be little more than a generalization of Roosevelt's style. In his actions alone, every aspect of bargaining can be illustrated. I shall resist the temptation to add to the already voluminous Roosevelt hagiography, but not before considering an example of the paragon at work. In a memo dated September 16, 1941, Roosevelt instructs his aide Marvin McIntyre in the art of grooming members of Congress:

> I have been disturbed about things I am hearing very frequently about
> "the Hill." You have probably heard the same. A large number of
> Senators and Congressmen, who should be and usually are our
> friends, have been saying entirely too frequently that they get no
> cooperation from the White House; that no one in the White House
> will talk to them unless we want their votes. A new refrain is that the
> only way to get attention from the Administration is to vote against it
> a few times.

I do not think there is too much basis for these complaints. As you well know, a large portion of the favors they ask for we cannot give them. But I do think we should create a medium for them to register their complaints—and I want you to do that job.

I certainly do not mean that you should be a liaison man with the Hill. . . . But you should be the man in the White House whom Senators and Congressmen can talk to. It does not matter so much that they don't get what they want. If they can tell their colleagues and friends "I told Marvin McIntyre at the White House so and so" that will be a psychological advantage. If they can also say "Marvin McIntyre told me so and so," they will soon have a feeling their advice is being listened to.

I think the way to get this started is to do it in a very casual manner. If you could start telephoning two or three of your Congressional friends a day just to ask how they are and what they know, word will soon get around that Marvin McIntyre will listen to them. In a few weeks or so, the casual phone calls will soon develop into an ironclad system. [Emphasis in original.]*

The moral of Roosevelt's instruction to his aide was that the president's success rests upon satisfying others' needs.

PUBLIC OPINION AND INSTITUTIONALIZED PLURALISM

Public pressure has little place in the community I have described. To be effective it would generally need either to emanate from a dominant economic interest of the constituency or client, such as the tobacco industry in North Carolina, or to be an otherwise pervasive and strongly held value, such as anti–gun control sentiments among hunters in Montana. Presumably, representatives who know their districts, or agency heads or lobbyists who understand their clients, will represent the values of the constituency, thereby making grassroots expression redundant. Writing about the Senate of the 1940s and 1950s, William S. White asserted, "Constituent pressure . . . is rarely the *cause* of any Senator's

---

* Franklin Delano Roosevelt Library, Hyde Park, New York; PSF: McIntyre, 1–4. The memo continued:

In this connection, there is something else I wish you would do. Up to now Jim Rowe [Justice Department official and Roosevelt confidant] has been clearing all nominations with the Democratic National Committee and on the Hill. For your very private information, there is too much friction between the Committee and the Senators on patronage. I want you to handle the Treasury and Justice nominations with Flynn and the Senators. I think I shall let Jim Rowe continue to handle the independent agencies. After you have cleared these nominations for a while, perhaps you can be a mollifying influence and bring the Committee and the Senators more into harmony. Let Jim Rowe know about this so he can shift over his arrangements with the Committee, Treasury and Justice to you.

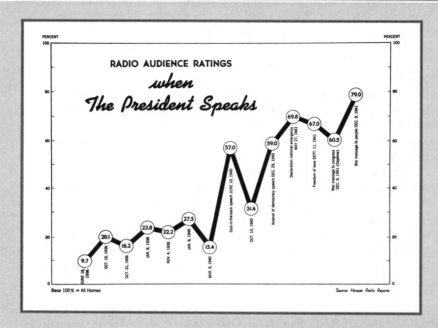

FDR Radio Audience Ratings

RADIO AUDIENCE RATINGS
when
The President Speaks

Base 100% = All Homes

Source: Hooper Radio Reports

This chart, found in President Roosevelt's office files, depicts the early development of mass audiences in presidential communications.

Source: Franklin Delano Roosevelt Library, Hyde Park, New York.

action." White recalled a conversation with Sen. Theodore Francis Green of Rhode Island, who was at the time receiving hate mail from some of his state's McCarthyites. Pointing to "shoals of postcards," White asked, " 'What about all these, Senator?' 'Old disgusting little things, aren't they?' [Green] said in a bored fastidious drawl, using the very end of his fingernail to flick his communications into the wastebasket. That closed the subject with him." [9]

Of interest group tactics during the same period, David Truman observed, "Skillful interest groups ... make limited use of letters, telegrams, and petitions." He cited comments in a trade association publication that one or two personal contacts were "of far greater value than a hundred letters or telegrams from persons unknown to the legislator." [10]

Given such conditions, a president who goes public would only undercut the abilities of other Washington elites to act as representatives—and these are peo-

ple with whom he must deal. Moreover, to the degree that the community is insulated, the strategy would not work. In denying elites their place at the bargaining
table, the mobilization of public opinion becomes little more than an abrasion.
One can see this in a 1944 survey of members of Congress that found them by
and large resentful of the Roosevelt administration's occasional use of public
opinion polls to buttress its case before Congress. One midwesterner responded,
"A poll is supposed to represent the people; the Congressman represents them; he
should know what the people think." He added, "Polls are in contradiction to representative government." Others interviewed concurred that polls were injurious.* Mobilizing public opinion might succeed occasionally, but in a setting of
institutionalized pluralism, where reciprocity is normative and memory long, its
regular use as a strategic device can sow only ill will and ultimately reap failure.

Public Opinion and Bargaining Presidents

Not all the tactics and resources available to bargaining presidents are private.
Among Washington's political elites, the president is, after all, the only one chosen by the national electorate. Even some nineteenth-century presidents—the
manufactured products of political machines who delivered their State of the
Union messages to Congress via courier—found occasions between elections
to solicit popular support.

Going public is sufficiently well precedented that statements of the pluralist theory of presidential leadership must take it into account. According to this
view, however, if public pressure is to be applied, it must be insinuated into the
bargaining process. Timely leaks of information—as age-old as they appear
modern—have long made the president's bargaining posture more defensible
to those outside Washington and hence more formidable to those inside. Trial
balloons floated by presidents or their associates have also been a favorite technique to test the political winds before embarking on a new policy course.
More direct public pressure has at times taken the form of personal overtures
to sympathetic constituencies and organizations to voice their grievances to
their representatives who would deny the president's policies. But in pluralist
theory each of these public tactics is appropriate for the bargaining president
only to the degree that it helps clarify the stakes and heighten others' appreciation of the need to bargain with him.

Consistent with the dictates of institutionalized pluralism, bargaining presidents of an earlier era rarely relied upon public strategies. With some, this

---

* Martin Kriesberg, "What Congressmen and Administrators Think of the Polls," *Public Opinion
Quarterly* 9 (fall 1945): 333–337. Concluding from this and other sources, historian Richard Jensen
states: "The threat [of polls] was a short-circuiting of the representative form of government. It was
one thing for Roosevelt, in his capacity as party leader and candidate, to appeal for support. It was
quite another to use the agencies of government to mold public opinion and thereby to force
Congress to relinquish its authority to set policy" (Richard Jensen, "Public Opinion Polls: Early
Problems of Method and Philosophy," Paper delivered at the Oxford Conference on History and
Theory of the Social Sciences, Oxford, England, July 23, 1977, 14.)

TABLE 2-1 **Presidential Survey of Public Opinion on Reallocation of Jobs under the Works Progress Administration, 1936**

States	Actual curtailment until Dec. 15, 1936[1] (%)	Possible further reductions for Jan., Feb., Mar. 1937[1] (%)	Reaction of workers	Reaction of public	Reaction of press
Ala.	0	5	none	none	none
Ariz.	13	20	none	none	none
Ark.	8	0	none	favorable	favorable
Calif.	1	0	unfavorable	none	none
Colo.	20	14	unfavorable	none	favorable
Conn.	8	0	unfavorable	favorable	favorable
Fla.	2.25	10.6	none	favorable	none
Ga.	6.4	5	unfavorable	favorable	favorable
Idaho	0	0	unfavorable	none	favorable
Ill.	0	0	unfavorable	none	none
Ind.	5	0	unfavorable	unfavorable	none
Iowa	6	0	unfavorable	unfavorable	unfavorable
Kan.	10	0	unfavorable	unfavorable	unfavorable
Ky.	0	0	none	none	none
La.	7	0	none	none	none
Maine	0	0	favorable	favorable	favorable
Md.	8	0	unfavorable	none	none
Mass.	0	7	unfavorable	favorable	favorable
Mich.	9	0	unfavorable	favorable	favorable
Minn.	7	0	unfavorable	50-50	favorable
Miss.	9.04	6.9	unfavorable	favorable	favorable
Mo.	3	0	none	none	none
Mont.	20	0	unfavorable	unfavorable	unfavorable
Neb.	10	0	unfavorable	unfavorable	unfavorable
Nev.	0	0	none	none	none
N.H.	0	0	unfavorable	unfavorable	unfavorable

(continued on next page)

appears in their skepticism toward public opinion surveys. Harry Truman stated flatly, "I never paid any attention to the polls myself," arguing that they "did not represent facts but mere speculation." [11] Franklin Roosevelt, a president with a stronger public mandate to draw upon, showed more interest in surveys. Before scientific surveys were available, Roosevelt's staff monitored public opinion as best it could in other ways. The White House mail was continuously tallied, and the editorial stances of the nation's newspapers were routinely reported to Roosevelt in summary form.[12] Sometimes Roosevelt more actively sought out such information, as in late 1936 when he asked each state director of the National Emergency Council to assess public opinion toward an announced reallocation of jobs under the Works Progress Administration. The results of this canvass are displayed in Table 2-1. That the directors' reading of public opinion strongly correlated with the editorial positions of local papers is evidence of the poor state of knowledge about public opinion in the presurvey era.

TABLE 2-1   **Presidential Survey of Public Opinion on Reallocation of Jobs under the Works Progress Administration, 1936 (Continued)**

States	Actual curtailment until Dec. 15, 1936[1] (%)	Possible further reductions for Jan., Feb., Mar. 1937[1] (%)	Reaction of workers	Reaction of public	Reaction of press
N.J.	4	0	unfavorable	favorable	favorable
N.M.	7.9	9.4	none	none	none
N.Y.	5.5	0	unfavorable	50-50	50-50
N.C.	0	12	none	favorable	favorable
N.D.	0	0	unfavorable	unfavorable	unfavorable
Ohio	8	0	unfavorable	none	none
Okla.	0	0	unfavorable	none	none
Ore.	0	0	none	none	none
Pa.	10	0	unfavorable	unfavorable	unfavorable
R.I.	5.4	0	unfavorable	favorable	favorable
S.C.	3	4	unfavorable	unfavorable	unfavorable
S.D.	49.5	0	unfavorable	unfavorable	unfavorable
Tenn.	13	0	unfavorable	none	none
Texas	1.9	2.8	unfavorable	favorable	favorable
Utah	10.3	0	unfavorable	none	none
Vt.	15	0	unfavorable	none	none
Va.	0	10	none	none	none
Wash.	0	0	none	none	none
W.Va.	1	7	none	none	none
Wis.	0	10	none	none	none
Wyo.	0	0	unfavorable	none	none

[1]Based on employment as of September 1, 1936.

Source: Franklin D. Roosevelt Personal Collection, National Emergency Council box, Franklin Delano Roosevelt Library, Hyde Park, New York.

After polling came into vogue, the Roosevelt administration occasionally commissioned official surveys. Except at elections, the president was usually more concerned with the views of specific publics who might be adversely affected by his policies than with any summary of national opinion.* According to Richard W. Steele:

He saw public attitudes not as a mandate for initiatives generated outside the White House, but as potential obstacles to courses he had

---

* A case in point occurred in 1943 when farm organizations announced their opposition to the president's farm subsidy program. The White House responded by commissioning private surveys on farmers' views of his agricultural policies. On finding that by and large farmers had no idea what his policies were, Roosevelt used the results to refute farm group leaders' claims that their constituents opposed his program. Richard W. Steele, "The Pulse of the People: Franklin D. Roosevelt and the Gauging of American Public Opinion," *Journal of Contemporary History* 9 (October 1975): 210–212.

already decided upon. Since the President's interest in the public's views stemmed largely from his concern for preserving or strengthening Administration power, the information he sought was issue oriented, and especially attuned to the attitudes of those Americans whose opinions were most intense, and usually most negative, toward a given policy. Thus midwesterners came in for special attention in regard to their attitudes toward intervention; mothers, and women in general, concerning draft extension; farmers in regard to farm policy; Poles and Catholics in regard to relations with Russia, and so forth. This also helps explain Roosevelt's strong interest in the generally hostile views of the press and the business community. *The opposition of these publics could encourage obstructionism in Congress. . . . If the President could get by these formidable groups without generating excessive criticism, he had a good chance of success. . . .* Roosevelt's conception of the public's role tended to focus his attention on the opinions of the powerful and hostile. [Emphasis added.][13]

President Roosevelt occasionally went public to improve his position in Washington. Before World War II he delivered radio "fireside chats" directing public attention to his legislative agenda. Only once, however, did he succumb to the temptation to exhort the citizenry to pressure Congress. Using the advanced ages of current Supreme Court members as an excuse, Roosevelt tried in 1937 to increase their number by six. This instance, the "Court-packing" proposal of 1937, ended in fiasco.* Compared with today's presidents, Roosevelt enlisted public strategies sparingly. His interest in public opinion was motivated by a need to anticipate and, when possible, to neutralize the representatives of interested publics who might oppose his programs. In this way, his game remained in Washington.

Nowhere is the value of public opinion to a bargaining president more systematically explored than in Neustadt's treatise on presidential power. On the importance of public prestige, he writes:

The Washingtonians who watch a President . . . have to think about his standing with the public outside of Washington. They have to gauge his popular prestige. Because they think about it, public standing is a source of influence for him, another factor bearing upon their willingness to give him what he wants.

It works on power just as reputation does through the mechanism of anticipated reactions . . . they anticipate reactions from the public. Most members of the Washington community depend upon

---

* Befitting the lapse, the Court-packing case is one of the few instances in which FDR failed to sound out congressional leadership before announcing his plan at a press conference. There are many good accounts of this event. One that does a good job conveying the surprise and consternation of Roosevelt's usual supporters at his "high-handed" tactics is Joseph Alsop and Turner Catledge, *The 168 Days* (New York: Doubleday and Co., 1938).

outsiders to support them or their interests. The dependence may be as direct as votes, or it may be as indirect as passive toleration. Dependent men must take account of popular reaction to *their* actions. What their publics may think of them becomes a factor, therefore, in deciding how to deal with the desires of a President. His prestige enters into that decision; their publics are part of his. Their view from inside Washington of how outsiders view him thus affects their influence with them.[14]

Elsewhere Neustadt argues that presidents must husband their prestige just as they would their reputation and bargaining chits. Still, politics remains the exclusive domain of Washingtonians. Public opinion never does more than passively color the bargaining context. Within this intentionally confined role for public opinion, Neustadt concedes only that strong popular support purchases the president some leeway in his dealings with other elites.

Moreover, he does not consider that the president might abandon negotiation (or even threaten to) and take his case directly to the American people. But if Washington politicians are so dependent on public opinion and so sensitive to a popular president's standing, why should they not be all the more accommodating when the president summons public opinion to his side, especially when failure to do so could identify them as possible adversaries? If a politician's next election allows the president's prestige to be insinuated into the bargaining society, why do they not also open the community to the president's active solicitation of popular support?

Neustadt offers two reasons. First, as a substitute for bargaining, going public amounts to little more than the application of force and necessarily violates the interdependence and reciprocity that make bargaining possible. It assumes a status akin to "command"—Neustadt's term for the unilateral application of authority—which he argues is costly and usually indicates an earlier failure to achieve one's goal through persuasion.*

There is a second and more fundamental reason. The public in the world of institutionalized pluralism normally pays little attention to what politicians do or say. Only when events and conditions press upon the nation and the welfare of citizens does the president win an audience.[15] Presidents stand or fall on their performance in providing satisfactory conditions for the ordinary citizen. Neustadt explains, "What a president should be is something most men see by light of what is happening to *them*. Their notions of the part a president should play, their satisfaction with the way he plays it, are affected by their private hopes and fears. Behind their judgments of performance lie the consequences in their lives. What threatens his prestige is their frustration."[16] Whatever slant the press may take, bad news

---

* Neustadt's use of the word "command" to mean the unilateral use of authority to alter others' behavior without compensation has entered the presidential literature as the chief alternative to bargaining as a mode of influence.

will mirror objectively unfavorable conditions and events—that is, poor performance. Stacked against paychecks and prices, a "bad press" and criticism from other politicians are inconsequential. So the argument goes. Maligned presidents may respond to the rhetoric of others, but they are just making noise as far as public opinion is concerned. Their performance is all that really matters.

With this in mind, Neustadt speculated that press revelations that Eisenhower's chief of staff, Sherman Adams, had improperly accepted gifts from an individual who transacted business with the government probably caused the White House more consternation than it should have.[17] President Eisenhower's approval rating remained stable, as stable as national conditions were at the time. His popularity surged temporarily with the peace in Korea and briefly dipped below 50 percent during the recession of late 1957. Much the same kind of story can be told for every president's public standing. President Johnson's popularity declined steeply as U.S. casualties in Vietnam mounted; by 1968—less than four years after his landslide victory—he withdrew his bid for reelection. Nixon's and Carter's approval ratings tracked inflation; Ronald Reagan's popularity fell sharply in 1982 as unemployment skyrocketed. The cushion of support Desert Storm, the first war with Iraq, gave George H. W. Bush in early 1991 did not prevent his popularity rating from dropping below 50 percent later in the year as the recession deepened. Despite repeated charges of scandal and impeachment, Clinton's popularity remained as buoyant as the economy. The terrorist attacks of 2001 and back-to-back military deployments within the next eighteen months temporarily tamped the downward pressures on George W. Bush's approval rating. Shortly after his reelection in 2004, with more than 2,500 American soldiers' deaths and many thousands more of civilian Iraqis, Bush's job performance rating began a steady decline. These are the kinds of experiences conventionally enlisted to explain past presidents' declining popular support.[18] They make eminent sense. If such experiences are *all* that matter, however, presidents' self-promotion through intensive public relations would make no sense at all. In sum, Washington's insulation from short-term swings in public opinion is thus complemented by the country's inattention to elite relations.

The public's reliance upon experience rather than news about Washington politics is consonant with the kind of political setting for which a bargaining president is ideally suited. It discounts public relations from the White House. Indeed, it shields the bargaining society from intensive public posturing by any of its members. In the following, extraordinary exchange during one of President Eisenhower's news conferences in the fall of 1953, consider the chances of such an incident remaining off the evening news in today's Washington. Meeting with the regular assemblage of White House correspondents shortly after his attorney general, Herbert Brownell, accused former president Harry Truman of having harbored a known "communist spy" during his administration, President Eisenhower found himself quickly dogged with pointed questions about Brownell's statement.[19] Following his customary practice of handling conflict, President Eisenhower obfuscated and temporized. When challenged by a reporter's rhetorical question about whether the Eisenhower administration was, with these accusations, embracing McCarthyism, the president, stunned and flustered by the questioner's directness, replied that he would "take the verdict of the body on that." From the available accounts, it appears that at this point the president lost control of the conference. He stood watching, dumbfounded, as *New York Times* reporters Anthony H. Leviero and James Reston canvassed fellow correspondents. The verdict went against Eisenhower. That such an incident occurred is less remarkable than the fact that it was never reported as news. Were such a thing to happen today, how many minutes would expire before some news-hounding blogger posted it on a Web site? The real question concerns why none of the professional correspondents reported it as news in 1953. Veteran correspondent James Deakin explained in his memoirs:*

> Very little of the atmosphere of Eisenhower's confrontations with reporters found its way into their stories. There was an occasional hint that the proceedings had been raucous, but overall the news accounts were bland. What had been a knock-down-drag-out at the press conference emerged in the news stories as a waltz-me-around-again-Willie. The press conferences were essentially in-house encounters between the president and the reporters. The news, in the Eisenhower era, was objective. The flavor was lacking. So the public was not aroused. It slept easy.[20]

The short answer is that here as within Congress, members of a bargaining society abide by a commonly understood set of norms, which in this instance dictated that reporters not create situations that embarrass the president. Had there been a public eagerly awaiting such stories, chances are that one of the correspondents would have broken ranks. The political relations between presidents and those professionals who report their activities offer a rich and revealing history we shall take up in chapter 4.

Two Early Cases of Going Public

With Washington insulated from public pressure and the public largely inattentive, going public was normally not a viable option. Hence, presidents rarely

---

* A sample of newspaper reports on these press conferences confirms Deakin's recollection: James Reston, "Patriotism Backed," *New York Times*, November 12, 1953, 1; Robert W. Richards, "Velde to Press Quiz of Truman on Spies," *San Diego Union*, November 12, 1953. Some reporters complained that their criticisms of Eisenhower were being muted by Republican editors and publishers. A year later, TRB (Richard Strout) offered the following instances of insufficient questioning of administration policies: "The Administration's security risk 'numbers game'; the phony unleashing of Chiang Kai-shek; the President's personal order directing the Atomic Energy Commission to write the Dixon-Yates contract" (TRB, "Washington Wire," *New Republic*, December 27, 1954, 2).

enlisted it. Dramatic, even heroic, instances of going public have tended historically to occur against a backdrop of prior failure. Consider briefly what are perhaps the two outstanding twentieth-century instances when presidents have gone public to pressure Congress.

The first is Woodrow Wilson's attempt to force Senate ratification of his version of the League of Nations treaty. Unwilling to accept any of the reservations to the treaty being promulgated by Republican Majority Leader Henry Cabot Lodge and a Foreign Relations Committee stacked with "irreconcilables and strong reservationists," President Wilson decided as "a last resort" to abandon Washington and take his case to the American public.[21] His travel schedule would have been grueling even for a healthy man, which Wilson was not. The trip began on September 3, 1919, and ended with his stroke on October 3. During the month he logged in over eight thousand miles, made thirty-seven speeches, and endured countless hand-shaking gatherings. For all of his "resolve to overpower his opposition," his effort won him no new support in Washington, and by most accounts it stiffened opposition.[22] Going public broke Wilson politically as well as physically.

A second instance, though it too began in adversity, yielded a far different outcome. The Truman Doctrine speech is widely credited not only with securing President Truman his emergency aid legislation for Greece and Turkey but also with laying the groundwork for the more comprehensive Marshall Plan that shortly followed. In this instance the public appeal rested not on a prior failure of bargaining but on its remote chance of success before an isolationist, Republican-dominated Congress. Seeking counsel from Republican Senate leader Arthur Vandenberg, Truman reportedly was advised that he would first have to "scare hell out of the country" if he hoped to persuade Congress to pass his emergency aid program.*

Describing the new world order as comprising the forces of freedom on one side and of totalitarianism on the other, the statement President Truman delivered to the joint session of Congress on March 12, 1947, was plainly hortatory.† Congress responded with an enthusiastic standing ovation. Although

---

* David S. McLellan and John W. Reuss, "Foreign and Military Policies," in *The Truman Period as a Research Field,* ed. Richard S. Kirkendall (Columbia: University of Missouri Press, 1967), 55–57. Curiously, this widely cited quotation is absent from Vandenberg's memoirs. It is ironic that Neustadt treats the Truman Doctrine speech, which was perhaps the most successful use of public opinion in the postwar era to gain the president leverage vis-á-vis other political elites in Washington, as a prime example of pluralist exchange. He notes that Truman and others rallied the public to the subsequent Marshall Plan, but this was necessarily preceded, he argues, by elite exchange. Neustadt, *Presidential Power,* 36–40.

† Truman in his memoirs vividly describes his rewriting of the "half hearted" draft from the State Department: "The key sentence, for instance, read, 'I believe that it should be the policy of the United States. . . .' I took my pencil, scratched out 'should' and wrote in 'must'. . . . I wanted no hedging in this speech. This was America's answer to the surge of expansion of Communist tyranny. It had to be clear and free of hesitation or double talk" (Truman, *Memoirs,* vol. 2, 105–109). For further discussion of the writing of the Truman Doctrine speech, see chapter 7.

the ripples of elite and public opinion that followed over the next several weeks were less than uniformly supportive, it soon became clear that most of the public and Congress were lining up behind the president's program. By early summer Truman's proposals for Greece and Turkey had become U.S. policy, and the more comprehensive Marshall Plan was headed toward enactment.

These two instances of going public differ in a way that helps to explain their dissimilar results. President Wilson sought through public pressure to force the Senate to accept his version of the League. His form of going public has become a familiar modern activity for which there are few historical examples. President Truman's effort was less confrontational: only after conferring with congressional leaders and being warned to take a strong public stance did he begin to draft his address. President Truman and the members of Congress who counseled him perhaps foresaw potential opposition in the country that could be preempted only by an appeal that would generate a more favorable climate of public opinion. The speech identified no individuals or blocs of politicians in Washington as opponents. In strategic terms Truman's act of going public was part of a larger bargain in which he agreed to try to make this internationalist posture more palatable to the country and to shoulder responsibility for any adverse reactions in return for support from members of Congress who were rarely his allies. Wilson failed miserably; Truman succeeded brilliantly. Both men's standing in history has been heavily influenced by these performances in going public.

These instances, however much they differ, do share an important feature. In both cases negotiation alone had or would have failed. Historically, public strategies were employed after other avenues proved insufficient.

The reciprocity of exchange and the complementarity of tasks between presidents and protocoalitions—especially when the latter equitably represents the interests of the nation—render institutionalized pluralism the look of a finely regulated clock. The synchronization of such a system of cogs and escapements would gratify those Newtonian mechanics whom we call our Founding Fathers. Of course, the American political system has never really achieved such clockwork performance. At best the model of institutionalized pluralism offers a rough approximation of reality, making recognizable and explaining some of its less obvious features. According to most students of American politics and not a few politicians, however, it illuminates even less about American politics today than at any time during the past half century. A consensus is emerging that at both the protocoalitional and presidential levels, leadership based on reciprocity and negotiation is in increasingly short supply.

INDIVIDUALIZED PLURALISM: The Modern Washington Community

If institutionalized pluralism depicts a society whose members are bound together by calculated fealty to a network of protocoalitions and a dense normative system for which bargaining is the prescribed behavior, for what kind of political community should going public be an appropriate strategy? It is one constituted of independent members who have fewer and weaker group or institutional loyalties. These politicians are, by comparison, less interested in sacrificing short-run, private career goals for the longer-term benefits of their party's success or good relations with bargaining partners. Social pluralism and institutional decentralization guarantee that exchange will remain a ubiquitous activity, but these more individualistic traders will rarely subscribe to the kinds of commitments and tacit understandings that allow bargains to assume the form of relationships. Instead, these politicians will generally prefer immediate, explicit, and tangible exchanges, for which an important currency is campaign contributions. This in itself offers evidence of the extent to which politics in the country has intruded on relationships in Washington.

A protocoalition's success in securing its members' collective interest is a function of its internal integration. When members agree on goals (or at least are prepared to subordinate their private interests), when they adhere to reciprocity agreements and endure personal apprenticeship, and when they invest in their party and institutional leaders the authority and flexibility to negotiate with other leaders, the protocoalition achieves the internal coherence that makes it both a formidable and yet an attractive trading partner to others in Washington. Conversely, protocoalitions containing members who are less willing to cede discretion to leaders will find themselves less able to engage in coalitional activities necessary to achieve their shared collective goals.

Weak protocoalitions reinforce the propensity of members toward independence. Unsustained by collective rewards, members must resort to their own devices to secure their political fortunes. Unfettered by the commitments strong protocoalitions require, members are free to pursue private career goals. Because it is both burden and freedom, self-reliance creates uncertainty, which prompts many elected officeholders to assume a continuous campaign footing. They spend proportionately more time cultivating clients and constituents than they do cementing relations with their Washington colleagues. Governing and campaigning lose their distinctiveness. This is manifest in innumerable ways, from the ongoing polling and intensive communications activities of the White House to the same, smaller-scale activities in a freshman representative's office. Pervasive free agency makes for a more erratic community—one less well regulated by standing commitments or internal mechanisms of exchange and less shock resistant to short-term perturbations of public opinion.

How might so different a system of political relations come to replace institutionalized pluralism? One can think of many possible reasons, any of them potentially sufficient and all probably true, which ensuing chapters will analyze as the appropriate data are introduced. For now, I will simply state the possible causes for the rise of individualized pluralism. First, the growth of the modern welfare state has increased the size and number of organized constituencies having a stake in national policy. Second, modern communications and transportation have brought the details of Washington politics into America's living rooms to a much greater extent than in the pretelevision era or even in the 1960s and 1970s. Accelerating the trend, personal computers have introduced a lightning fast news dissemination technology. Over-the-shoulder inspection and second-guessing by constituents and clients can easily upset the transactions of politicians trying to assemble competing interests into a collective action. For example, the Bush administration discreetly endorsed a Dubai company's purchase of terminal rights at several major American cargo ports. Within days a political blog had posted the information, and over the coming weeks coverage of the story by the national news media was so extensive and prominent that that public opinion surveys began recording public opinion about the agreement (respondents opposed by 2 to 1).[23]

Third, the most manifest evidence of the decay of institutionalized pluralism could initially be seen in the decline of political parties both among voters and Washingtonians. As growing numbers of voters split their ballots, divided government in Washington became the norm. More congressional candidates concealed their party labels in their campaign advertising, and once elected, many ignored their party leaders' appeals for votes and other sacrifices for the party's collective good. This decline seriously weakened affinity relations among political leaders that in the past had made exchange easier and occasionally unnecessary.

Over the past decade or so, political parties have exhibited remarkable resurgence both in the country and in Washington. Democratic and Republican voters and politicians appear more polarized today in their political views than at any time in the past several decades. This raises the question, might forces be in motion that could eventually restore some semblance of institutionalized pluralism? It is too early to offer a definitive assessment. Southern whites have finally made the long trek into the Republican Party that began in the 1964 presidential election. Their realignment converted formerly conservative Democratic seats into more consistent Republican conservative seats, rendering clearer ideological divisions between political parties in Washington.[24] With their members in closer agreement, party leaders—at least House Republican leaders—speak more authoritatively when they represent their members' views in discussions at the White House and with their counterparts in the Senate. Another result is that both parties' congressional members are more likely to express similar views. This allows voters to better understand their appeals and to form a more valid and reliable image of the parties' policy preferences.

Yet rekindled partisanship has not so much fixed voters' preferences as left presidents with little opportunity to sway opinion. The share of voters who identify with one of the major political parties remains at historic lows. Seventy-four percent of respondents on average identified with one of the parties during the 1950s and 1960s. This figure shrank to 64 percent in the 1980s, and in the 2004 National Election Survey, it stood at 60 percent.* Voters still display willingness to split their ballots, and nearly as many survey respondents say they prefer divided party control of government as those preferring one (presumably, their) party in full control. From all indicators, politicians remain wary of relying on party labels in their campaigns.

Each of these forces—expansion of the number of interested constituencies, new communication technologies, and more fluid partisan loyalties—created opportunities and pressures for Washington's elected politicians to become more independent. How precisely this new setting affected strategic behavior differed from one office to the next, but the expansion of federal services, the ability to send—as well as the probability of receiving—messages to and from targeted constituencies, and the fading of party feeling thoroughly altered the way Washington politicians viewed their and others' political options.[25] Nowhere should such self-awareness be more acute than in the White House.

For presidents seeking to construct broad-based coalitions, the implications of individualized pluralism are profound. From their vantage point, the leveled political topography offered fewer clues about where precisely a president's efforts at coalition building should begin. Instead of a subcommunity of leaders with solid reputations and convertible credits, presidents found themselves surrounded by a larger number of weaker leaders who titularly presided over shaky protocoalitions. It was not that these people were uninterested in trading and unable to deliver their end of the bargain. The problem was that in the absence of local hierarchies where a few members authoritatively represent many others, presidents quickly discovered they needed to trade with many more participants, even though they were unsure as they did so which would or even could deliver on their promises. It is an unmanageable prospect, one that guarantees overload and multiplies the chances of failure. For Neustadt's bargaining president it poses a conundrum without solution.

A different kind of president, one inclined to go public, will find, however, frequent opportunities for leadership among rampant free-agency and emaciated protocoalitions. The sensitivity of self-reliant politicians to public opinion is their vulnerability and the key to his influence. By campaigning around the country, the president can create uncertainty for them while offering refuge in their support for his policies. By giving up bargaining with individuals and instead working with politicians' preferences *en masse*, a president may achieve comparative economy.

---

* Professor Martin P. Wattenberg kindly supplied these calculations, based on National Election Study surveys. A similar result occurs when respondents are asked to rate their like/dislike of the Democratic and Republican Parties on a 10-point scale. In the 1950 election surveys only 14 percent of respondents rated both as neutral; by the 1980s the figure had more than doubled at 34 percent and in the 2004 election survey it stood at 28 percent.

From Institutionalized to Individualized Pluralism

During the 1970s and 1980s Washington shifted rapidly from institutionalized to individualized pluralism on every front from the takeover of bureaucracies by issue specialists to weakened leadership in Congress.[26] Appropriately, the causes were compound—some general, like those described above, and others specific to the institution. Articles and books on the subject, often carrying worried if not apocalyptic overtones, proliferated from think tanks and commercial presses. One is hard pressed to identify a development in Washington that someone did not credit with contributing to the decay of institutionalized pluralism. They may all be correct.

A 1981 anthology of essays by leading scholars, suggestively entitled *The New Congress*,[27] examined several such developments, showing how pervasively relations in Washington had changed. Throughout the book, the case mounted against the hegemony of institutionalized pluralism. Thomas Mann singled out the heightened career concerns of members of Congress: "The forces fueling the individualistic tone of the present-day Congress remain strong. . . . Senators and representatives are in business for themselves."* As a consequence, "they all are likely to view themselves first and foremost as individuals, not as members of a party or as part of a president's team." [28]

In another article Michael Robinson offered a reason: "Compared with the class of 1958, the class of 1978 was three times more likely to make heavy use of the congressional recording studio, three times more likely to regard the House TV system as 'very useful,' three times more likely to have relied 'a lot' on TV in the last election." From these findings Robinson concludes that "although these figures pertain to campaign style more than legislative character, one may infer that the increasingly greater reliance on the media for nomination, election, status in the Congress, and reelection is one sign of a new congressional character—one more dynamic, egocentric, immoderate, and, perhaps, intemperate." [29] In short, contemporary observers found many members of Congress themselves busily and successfully engaged in going public.

Robinson's use of the class of 1958 nicely complements Douglass Cater's earlier observations. Writing in 1959, Cater was among the first to spot this new-style member of Congress: "There has *begun to emerge* in the halls of Congress a new type of politician conditioned to the age of mass media and more keenly aware of the uses of publicity. He is not apt to be a member of . . . the 'Inner Club,' where emphasis is still put on seniority and skill in negotiation [emphasis added]." In fact, "usually he is lacking in direct influence among his

---

* On announcing his retirement from the Senate after fifty-one years in Congress, Sen. Jennings Randolph was asked what major changes in politics he had seen. Randolph responded, "There is a lack of discipline in the Senate—a deterioration every year I've been here. I just don't understand it" (Marjorie Hunter, "From Roosevelt's Outings to Reagan's Greetings," *New York Times*, October 5, 1984, B10). See also Steven V. Roberts, "Senate's New Breed Shuns Novice Role," *New York Times*, November 26, 1984, 1.

colleagues." [30] Today, no prudent member of the House fails to maintain an up-to-date Web site. The more industrious routinely feed their local television news programs "news" tapes ready for broadcast. Most members in the earlier era had office staff who informally performed the role of the member's press secretary if and when the need arose. In many offices today this function is called "media relations" and is performed by an entourage of specialists.

Roger Davidson began his chapter in *The New Congress* by noting that the new, less cooperative, and certainly less submissive member of Congress, described above, has created "persistent pressures . . . to expand the number of available workgroups and the overall number of seats and leadership posts." He then catalogued the proliferation of subcommittees and assignments, the growth of informal working groups, and the multiplication of staffs and budgets. Leadership posts were so numerous in the 96th Congress, Davidson pointed out, that "all but two Democratic senators and nearly half of all Democratic representatives chaired a committee or subcommittee." [31] Only a quarter of the Democratic members held these positions in the mid-1950s. Davidson noted that to accommodate the diffusion of power, additional institutional innovations, such as the practice of referring bills to several committees rather than only to one, have occurred to give more subcommittees an opportunity to get their hands on the president's program.

Institutional Arrangements in Congress

Within Congress, new organizational forms emerged to serve members' particular interests directly and to undermine the function of the legislative party and members' commitment to them. Two that give ample expression to the centrifugal forces at work are congressional caucuses and political action committees (PACs). Both potentially compete with the legislative parties for influence. Each redirects members' attention and loyalties away from the collective interests of party and national welfare to the narrower interests of particular constituencies. They deserve our detailed consideration not so much because they dominate legislation as because they reveal the centrifugal forces spawned by individualized pluralism present in the modern Congress contending with traditional authority for influence.

Caucuses. Today's venerable Democratic Study Group (DSG) was founded in 1959 by a cadre of liberal northern House Democrats who were frustrated with the dominance of southern conservatives in the chamber's leadership positions. By offering an alternative legislative program and by providing a mechanism for bloc voting that in turn leveraged liberals' negotiating positions with the leadership, the DSG was credited with moving the Democratic Party's legislative agenda in a liberal direction.[32] Its success provided inspiration and a blueprint for the informal organization of dozens of other caucuses during the 1970s and 1980s.

With several hundred voluntary associations to choose from, members typically affiliate with a half dozen or so of these organizations. Most of the caucuses created before 1971 concentrated on broad issues of national policy; those formed since then have assumed a decidedly parochial cast. According to some scholars, these caucuses provide many of the same services as their counterpart interest groups with whom they cooperate closely.[33] The Congressional Arts Caucus reveals how narrow these would-be protocoalitions can be. Its single goal in 1983 was passage of the National Heritage Resources Act, which would have made it possible for artists and authors to deduct from their taxes the full market value of any of their works they donate to charitable organizations. (The legislation failed.)[34] Apparently, no interest or issue is too esoteric to deserve organizational embodiment.

Even were they so inclined, these organizations, founded upon affinity of interest among the various actors who must agree in order for a policy to be adopted, are ill suited to negotiate agreement among competing interests. Whatever bargains a caucus may make will count for little unless its members are well placed on the relevant committees. To the degree the Arts Caucus, for instance, fails to include the members of the House Ways and Means and Senate Finance Committees, it is deficient. Moreover, to the degree it includes members not on these committees, it is inefficient. Whatever their standing as functioning coalitions, committees remain the vital juncture of the legislative process.

Caucuses are also deficient as protocoalitions because they are casual, voluntary associations that lack the rewards or sanctions necessary to induce members to adhere to collective goals. Even when a consensus on policy and tactics emerges and the caucus negotiates as a bloc with other leaders or with the president, its effectiveness remains limited. Everyone recognizes that each member of the caucus retains independent judgment about the relative merits of whatever group stances its leaders are able to muster, and therefore, the consensus could unravel at any moment.

When the Republican majority assumed control of the House of Representatives in 1994 the new House Speaker, Newt Gingrich, immediately began removing resources provided to the larger caucuses by the chamber and individual members. No longer would the DSG, the Black Caucus, and several other caucuses be assigned space in the House office buildings; neither could members detail their office staffs to work for the caucuses. Instead of starving these entities into some emaciated, weaker role, legislators successfully found new financial support among the interest groups whose concerns their caucus promotes. The Sportsmen's Caucus received a nearly $1 million donation from the nonprofit, tax-exempt Sportsmen's Foundation, which in turn had received its funds from gun manufacturers and the National Rifle Association. Arguably, the reforms intended to weaken caucuses succeeded only in making them more beholden to narrow constituencies and special interests.[35]

Political Action Committees. The rapid increase in the number of congressional caucuses has been more than matched by the rise of political action committees. In the sixteen elections from 1974 through 2004, the number of PACs grew from 608 to 4,184. During this period their contributions to House and Senate races increased from $12 million to $310 million.[36]

Before the passage of the Federal Election Campaign Act in 1971, private groups participated openly in political campaigns at great risk. Some, such as unions and professional associations (the American Medical Association, for example), had flexed their financial muscle from time to time, but others, including corporations, had shied away from overt participation for fear of running afoul of ambiguous election laws. The campaign finance reforms that began in 1971 have changed all that. All organizations, and particularly corporations, now have clear guidelines for participating in congressional elections.

The first PACs registered with the Federal Election Commission (FEC) were largely the traditional organized contributors, principally the unions. With each subsequent election, however, more and more businesses have joined.* Many, if not most, corporate donations go to incumbents and are motivated more by defensive consideration than by any aspiration to alter the ideological disposition of Congress. A smaller share, but still a large amount, of PAC money goes to influence members, if not elections. Challengers and vulnerable incumbents are frequently invited to disclose their preferences on issues of concern to the PAC, and here is where the parochial character of this money leaves its greatest imprint. The assertion by Rep. David Obey, D-Wis., that "ten thousand dollars may come against you from one group because of a single vote" is supported by the experiences of many members of Congress.[37]

Contrary to the unflattering stereotype of the unctuous lobbyist, representatives of interest groups have traditionally spurned the unrefined tactics portrayed in Obey's remark. When some occasionally succumbed to the temptation to lubricate the legislative process with financial contributions, they were often caught and punished. One of the most frequently recounted instances occurred in 1956 when President Eisenhower, citing the natural gas industry's heavy-handed use of campaign funds, vetoed a gas deregulation bill that he was on record as favoring.[38] Memory was long, and such instances did not need to be repeated frequently. The opposite message was conveyed in 1982 when, after spreading nearly one million dollars among three hundred candidates, the National Automobile Dealers Association easily won a congressional veto of the Federal Trade Commission's proposed "full disclosure" regulation for used cars.†

---

* The rapid growth in participation of political action has not been limited to corporations and trade associations. The two PACs reporting the heaviest spending in the 2003–2004 election cycle—MoveOn.org and EMILY's List at $30 million and $26 million, respectively—promoted mostly liberal and Democratic candidates.

† Defending the Senate's action, Sen. Larry Pressler inadvertently made the critic's point: "We got 69 votes, and we might have been able to top out at 80. With that many votes I don't think you can attribute it to campaign contributions alone" (Albert R. Hunt, "Special-Interest Money Increasingly Influences What Congress Enacts," *Wall Street Journal,* July 26, 1982, 13).

Under institutionalized pluralism the *modus operandi* of lobbyists was quiet diplomacy. "Never lie" and "don't threaten" were their operational codes. Quiet diplomacy has not disappeared, but it increasingly gives way to more direct, public strategies of influence. These include inspiring pressure from the constituency as well as targeting the group's PAC contributions.

One of the last groups to catch on to the opportunities of individualized pluralism was the national Chamber of Commerce. For years the chamber was one of the more staid, even stolid, inside players on Capitol Hill. After watching its legislative success rate drop with each successive Congress it adopted an aggressive public relations strategy. Today, the chamber has its own public affairs television network, called BizNet, which produces weekly programs. Fed from Washington to cable and independent broadcast stations around the country, these programs do not hesitate to advise viewers of what they need to do to protect their interests in Congress.*

One late 1970s survey of 175 lobbying groups found that while the great majority said they were doing more of almost all kinds of lobbying activity, the greatest increases have occurred in the realm of going public. Of the twenty-seven classes of lobbying identified in the study, "talking with people from the press and media" scored the greatest gains. A close second were reported increases in "mounting grass roots campaigns" and "inspiring letter-writing or telegram campaigns." [39] Environmentalists, anti–gun control organizations, Mothers Against Drunk Driving, and the health care industry have all won quick victories with grassroots strategies of influence. Today's campaigns extend well beyond encouraging members to write their legislators. Rather, they include sizable advertising budgets targeting print and television media in Washington and in those media markets throughout the country that contain persuadable members of Congress—i.e., those facing a tough reelection fight. By one count, during the 107th Congress (2001–2002) 167 corporations, trade associations, and other interests spent $105 million in issue advertising in Washington alone. [40]

Judged against the requirements of institutionalized pluralism, political action committees and caucuses are functionally primitive entities. Serving only to articulate generally narrow positions on issues, these organizations are neither designed for nor interested in brokering the diverse interests brought into play by policy proposals. With their narrower interests, PACs inherently compete with legislative parties and presidents and threaten to "balkanize the political process." [41]

---

* In addition to contributing heavily to probusiness (almost exclusively Republican) candidates, the chamber has sought to coordinate the political donations of smaller business PACs. In 1982 it produced a closed-circuit show called "See How They Run," which reviewed 50 key races for 150 PAC managers around the country. Much of the information reported here on the Chamber of Commerce comes from the program titled "Congress and the Media" from the series *Congress: We the People*, PBS network, 1984. See also "Running with the PACs," *Time*, October 25, 1982, 20–26.

To counteract their influence and, indeed, harness their resources for the benefit of their congressional party, Republican leaders in 1995 formed the "K Street Project," named after the addresses of the biggest lobbies in Washington. Essentially, these leaders informed the major interest groups whose policy concerns normally caused them to align with Republicans—particularly, business groups and trade associations—that their continued access to Congress would be harmed if they hired Democrats as lobbyists and contributed to Democratic candidates. Over the next decade FEC reports were monitored to check on and enforce these guidelines, and groups that hired Democrats were threatened with legislative ostracism.[42]

GOING PUBLIC AND INDIVIDUALIZED PLURALISM

The present-day susceptibility of relations within Washington to public opinion manifests itself in a variety of ways. The influence of single-issue constituencies has been abetted by the discovery that by defeating one targeted incumbent a clear message will be sent to others. Issues also blow into Washington more quickly and in less-filtered form. During the 97th Congress, for example, President Reagan's supply-side program, with its unprecedented deficits, was being enacted while a majority in each house appeared ready to endorse a constitutional amendment requiring a balanced budget. And off to the side, a large bipartisan huddle was forming to carry forward the recently arrived "flat tax" reform package.

In a 1981 appraisal of coalition politics within Congress during the previous thirty years, Barbara Sinclair made the same connection between internal organization and the effect of external forces: "Instead of a policy process dominated by powerful, conservative committee chairmen, one in which crucial decisions were made in secret and thus were relatively insulated from public influence, we now see a process characterized by extreme individualism, one in which open, public decision making often hinders compromise." * When asked by a reporter about changes in Congress, Reagan lobbyist Kenneth Duberstein echoed this conclusion: "It's not been like Lyndon Johnson's time, being able to work with 15 or 20 Congressmen and Senators to get something done. For most issues you have to lobby all 435 Congressmen and almost all 100 Senators." [43] As a result, "how Congress performs its legislative role," continued Sinclair, "depends much more upon the character of the environmental forces impinging upon its members than upon its internal organization." [44]

---

* Barbara Sinclair, "Coping with Uncertainty: Building Coalitions in the House and the Senate," in *The New Congress*, ed. Mann and Ornstein, 220. At the 1976 convention of the American Society for Public Administration, Dean Rusk observed, "In the 1950s and 1960s we handled sensitive foreign affairs policy questions with the Congress by dealing with the 'whales'—Rayburn, Vinson, men like that. They could make commitments. Now it is as if we were dealing with 535 minnows in a bucket" (from a statement to the plenary session, Panel of Former Cabinet Officers, National Convention of the American Society for Public Administration, Washington, D.C., April 1976).

The Calculus of Those Who Deal with the President

Those Washingtonians who conduct business with the president observe his behavior carefully. Their judgment about his leadership guides them in their dealings with him. Traditionally, the professional president watchers have asked themselves the following questions: What are his priorities? How much does he care whether he wins or loses on a particular issue? How will he weigh his options? Is he capable of winning?

Each person will answer these questions about the president's will and skill somewhat differently, of course, depending upon his or her institutional vantage. The chief lobbyist for the United Auto Workers, a network White House correspondent, and the mayor of New York City may size up the president differently depending upon what they need from him. Nonetheless, they arrive at their judgments about the president in similar ways. Each observes the same behavior, inspects the same personal qualities, evaluates the views of the same recognized opinion leaders—columnists and commentators, among others—and tests his or her own tentative opinions with those of fellow community members. Local opinion leaders promote a general agreement among Washingtonians in their assessments of the president. Their agreement is his reputation.[45]

A president with a strong reputation does better in his dealings largely because others expect fewer concessions from him. Accordingly, he finds them more compliant; an orderly marketplace prevails. Saddled with a weak reputation, conversely, a president must work harder. Because others expect him to be less effective, they press him harder in expectation of greater gain. Comity at the bargaining table may give way to contention as other politicians form unreasonable expectations of gain. Through such expectations, the president's reputation regulates community relations in ways that either facilitate or impede his success. In a world of institutionalized pluralism, bargaining presidents seldom actively traded upon their prestige, leaving it to influence Washington political elites only through their anticipation of the electorate's behavior. As a consequence, prestige remained largely irrelevant to other politicians' assessments of the president.* Once presidents began going public and interjecting prestige directly into their relations with fellow politicians, and once these politicians found their resistance to this pressure diminished because of their own altered circumstances, the president's ability to marshal public opinion soon became an important ingredient of his reputation. New questions were added to traditional ones: Does the president feel strongly enough about an issue to go public? Will he follow through on his threats to do so? Does his standing in the country run so deep that it will likely be converted into mail to members of Congress, or is it so shallow that it will expire as he attempts to use it?

---

* Neustadt observed that President Truman's television appeal for tighter price controls in 1951 had little visible effect on how Washington politicians viewed the issue. This is the only mention of a president going public in the original eight chapters of the book. Neustadt, *Presidential Power*, 45.

In today's Washington, the answers to these questions contribute to the president's reputation. Consequently, his prestige and reputation have lost much of their separateness. The community's estimates of Carter and Reagan rose and fell with the polls. Through reputation, prestige has begun to play a larger role in regulating the president's day-to-day transactions with other community members. Grappling with the unclear causes of Carter's failure in Washington, Neustadt arrived at the same conclusion:

> A President's capacity to draw and stir a television audience seems every bit as interesting to current Washingtonians as his ability to wield his formal powers. This interest is his opportunity. While national party organizations fall away, while congressional party discipline relaxes, while interest groups proliferate and issue networks rise, a President who wishes to compete for leadership in framing policy and shaping coalitions has to make the most he can out of his popular connection. Anticipating home reactions, Washingtonians . . . are vulnerable to any breeze from home that presidential words and sights can stir. If he is deemed effective on the tube they will anticipate. That is the essence of professional reputation.[46]

The record supports Neustadt's speculation. In late 1978 and early 1979, with his monthly approval rating dropping to less than 50 percent, President Carter complained that it was difficult to gain Congress's attention for his legislative proposals. As one congressional liaison official stated, "When you go up to the Hill and the latest polls show Carter isn't doing well, then there isn't much reason for a member to go along with him." [47] A member of Congress concurred: "The relationship between the President and Congress is partly the result of how well the President is doing politically. Congress is better behaved when he does well. . . . Right now, it's almost as if Congress is paying no attention to him." [48]

The President's Calculus

The limited goods and services available for barter to the bargaining president would be quickly exhausted in a leaderless setting where every coalition partner must be dealt with individually. When politicians are more subject to environmental forces, however, other avenues of presidential influence open up. No politician within Washington is better positioned than the president to go outside the community and draw popular support. With members more sensitive to influences beyond Washington, the president's hand in mobilizing public opinion has been strengthened. For the new Congress—indeed, for the new Washington generally—going public may at times be the most effective course available.

Under these circumstances, the president's prestige becomes his political capital. It is something to be spent when the coffers are full, to be conserved when they are low, and to be replenished when they are empty. Early in 1997, when asked by campaign-weary news reporters why President Clinton maintained such a heavy travel schedule after his election victory, press secretary Michael D. McCurry lectured them on modern political science: "Campaigns are about framing a choice for the American people. . . .When you are responsible for governing you have to use the same tools of public persuasion to advance your program, to build public support for the direction you are attempting to lead." [49]

If public relations are to be productive the message must be tailored to a correctly targeted audience. For this, presidents require accurate, precisely measured readings of public opinion. Modern presidents must be attentive to the polls, but they need not crave the affection of the public. Their relationship with it may be purely instrumental. However gratifying public approval may be, popular support is a resource the expenditure of which must be coolly calculated. As another Clinton aide explained, "Clinton has come to believe that if he keeps his approval ratings up and sells his message as he did during the campaign, there will be greater acceptability for his program. . . . The idea is that you have to sell it as if in a campaign." [50]

Bargaining presidents require the sage advice of politicians familiar with the bargaining game; presidents who go public need pollsters. Compare the relish with which President Nixon reportedly approached the polls with the disdain Truman expressed. "Nixon had all kinds of polls all the time," recalled one of his consultants. "He sometimes had a couple of pollsters doing the same kind of survey at the same time. He really studied them. He wanted to find the thing that would give him an advantage." [51] The confidant went on to observe that the president wanted poll data "on just about anything and everything" throughout his administration.

Indicative of current fashion, presidents from Carter through Bush have all had in-house pollsters taking continuous—weekly, even daily—readings of public opinion.[52] When George H. W. Bush reportedly spent $216,000 of Republican National Committee (RNC) money on in-house polling in one year, many Washington politicians probably viewed it as an excessive indulgence, reflecting the RNC's largesse more than any practical need for data. But this figure soon looked modest after Clinton spent nearly ten times that amount in 1993, when he averaged three or four polls and an equal number of focus groups each month.[53]

Pollsters vigilantly monitor the pulse of opinion to warn of slippage and to identify opportunities for gain. Before recommending a policy course, they assess its costs in public support. Sometimes, as was the case with Clinton's pollsters, they go so far as to ask the public whether the president should bargain with congressional leaders or challenge them by mobilizing public opinion.* These advisers' regular and frequently unsolicited denials that they affected policy belie their self-effacement.

---

* In 1993 Clinton's chief pollster, Stanley Greenberg, added such a question to one of his national surveys. It is of no surprise that a sizable majority favored cooperation with Congress. Bob Woodward, *The Agenda* (New York: Simon and Schuster, 1994), 268–269.

How Not to Orchestrate a "Spontaneous" Event

Addressing a large crowd at Fargo, North Dakota, President George W. Bush delivered his standard speech and then took questions from the audience to converse with "ordinary" Americans. Yet, as the following exchange reveals, this was hardly a spontaneous event.

The President: All right, Tricia Traynor, welcome.
Mrs. Traynor: Welcome.
The President: Thank you. You are married? For how long?
Mrs. Traynor: Three months—almost three months. My husband, Dan—
The President: Where is he?
Mrs. Traynor: He is over to the right, waving his hand.
The President: There he is. Fine-looking man. That a boy, Dan. (Applause). The interesting thing about Tricia is she is a—
Mrs. Traynor: Major in the Air Force Reserve.
The President: There you go. (Applause). Have you been overseas yet?
Mrs. Traynor: Yes. I was in the Middle East for six months in 2003, for Operation Iraqi Freedom.

To see how the strategic prescriptions of going public differ from those of bargaining, consider the hypothetical case of a president requiring additional votes if he is to prevail in Congress. If a large number of votes is needed, the most obvious and direct course is to go on prime-time television to solicit the

The President: Good. Thanks for serving. (Applause). Your nation is grateful. . . . (Applause). So tell me what's on your mind about Social Security. You're young.

Mrs. Traynor: We're in our '30's.

The President: Yes, you fall in the category of those who should be worried about whether or not Congress and the President has got the will to act.

Mrs. Traynor: We'd like to make sure that the money we are investing in Social Security now will be there 30 years from now, 40 years from now.

The President: Right . . . let me ask you something. So you've heard about personal retirement accounts. Give me—just tell the folks here what you thought when you heard it.

Mrs. Traynor: Mr. President, it gives us hope that somebody is willing to address the issue. It's too easy to just push it down the road and it's better to prevent the crisis before the crisis takes place.

The President: Thank you. (Applause.) . . . You probably think I hired her, or something. (Laughter.) Did you talk to my mother this morning? (Laughter.) Thanks. Look, here's the thing. The threshold question is whether there's a problem that needs to be solved. And if there is, then who can come up with solutions that work. Once people say, well, there is a problem, what are you going to do about it? That's what the Major just said. And so, Major, personal accounts, any feel for that at all?

Mrs. Traynor: The thrift savings plans were opened up to the military just a couple years ago.

The President: You're in one?

Mrs. Traynor: I am in one. I participate. What it is, is it's a safe investment, and it allows me to take a portion of the income I'm earning and put it away to save it for the future. And I'm happy with that, and I like the idea of sharing that with the American public, and not just limiting it to federal employees.

The President: Federal employees. See, she's in a thrift savings plan very similar—in other words, we're not inventing something new. What's new is that it would be associated with a retirement through Social Security. It's not new. It's already being used . . . you could start with $1,000, and over time it grows. And as interest compounds, Tricia and her husband would have a nice nest egg to complement that which would be coming out of Social Security. Is that the way you see it?

Mrs. Traynor: Yes.

The President: That's the way it's going to be. If only we can get Congress to vote it in.

Source: George C. Edwards III, *Governing By Campaigning* (New York: Pearson, Longman, 2007), 227–231.

public's active support. Employed at the right moment by a popular president, the effect may be dramatic. This tactic, however, has considerable costs and risks. A real debit of lost public support may occur when a president takes a forthright position. There is also the possibility that the public will not

TABLE 2-2 **The Emergence of the President as Chief Fund-raiser**

Time Frame	Clinton 2000		Bush 2002		Bush 2006[1]	
	Number of trips	$ (000's)	Number of trips	$ (000's)	Number of trips	$ (000's)
Preceding Year	90	$55,856	6	$48,050	15	$62,100
Election Year						
January–March	39	20,179	14	13,870	11	32,525
April–June	54	51,369	18	83,680	16	55,505
July–September	55	24,466	27	30,125	6	5,300[1]
October–December	50	13,825	9	9,000		
Total	293	165,694	74	184,725	48	155,430[1]

[1]Figures for 2006 cover events through July 31.

Source: Mark Knoller of CBS Radio News kindly supplied these estimates.

respond, which damages the president's future credibility. Given this, a president understandably finds the *threat* to go public frequently more attractive than the *act*. To the degree that such a threat is credible, the anticipated responses of some representatives and senators may suffice to achieve victory.

A more focused application of influence via public relations becomes available as an election nears. Fence-sitting representatives and senators may be plied with promises of reelection support. This may be done privately and selectively, or it may be tendered openly to all who may vote on the president's program. Presidential support can be much more substantial than endorsement. Presidents at least as far back as 1938, when Franklin Roosevelt failed to purge anti–New Deal Democrats in the midterm elections, have at times actively sought to improve their own fortunes in the next Congress by influencing the current election. During the 1970 midterm congressional election campaigns, President Nixon raced around the country "in a white heat," trying desperately to secure a Republican Congress that would not convene for another generation.[54] In the 1999–2000 election cycle outgoing President Clinton pushed the modern president's efforts to serve his party's candidates to what would seem to be an individual's physical limits. By one count he participated in 295 congressional fund-raising events garnering more than $160 million for his party's candidates (see Table 2-2). Were it not for the tragic events of 9/11 and the subsequent invasion of Afghanistan, President Bush might have matched his predecessor. After getting off to a slow start in the next election cycle, the president made up ground rapidly. By the 2002 election he had attended seventy-four fund-raisers, an impressive number except when compared to Clinton, but he garnered significantly more money for Republican congressional candidates than had his Democratic counterpart. By August 2006, President Bush appeared on track to easily eclipse his own record.[55]

The variety of methods for generating publicity notwithstanding, going public offers fewer and simpler stratagems than does its pluralist alternative. At the heart of the latter lies bargaining, which must involve choice: choice among alternative coalitions, choice of specific partners, and choice of the goods and services to be bartered. Above all, it requires empathy, the ability of one politician to discern what his or her counterpart minimally needs in return for cooperation. The number, variety, and subtlety of choices place great demands upon strategic calculation, so much so that pluralist leadership must be understood as an art. In Neustadt's schema, the president's success ultimately reduces to intuition an ability to sense "right choices." [56]

Going public also requires choice, and it leaves ample room for the play of talent. If anyone doubts it, consider the obviously staged town meetings that President Bush's advance team assembled during his "sixty cities in sixty days" promotion of Social Security reform (see box, "How Not to Orchestrate a 'Spontaneous' Event"). Public relations is a less obscure matter than bargaining with fellow politicians, every one of them a professional bent on extracting as much from the president while surrendering as little as possible. Going public promises a more straightforward presidency than its pluralist counterpart—its options fewer, its strategy simpler, and consequently, its practitioner's actions both more predictable and easily observed.

NOTES

1. An excellent source for monitoring these trends is www.pollingreport.com.
2. Gary C. Jacobson, *The Politics of Congressional Elections*, 5th ed. (New York: Longman, 2001), 21–34.
3. Robert A. Dahl and Charles E. Lindblom, *Politics, Economics, and Welfare* (New York: Harper and Row, 1953), 333.
4. Hugh Heclo, *The Government of Strangers* (Washington, D.C.: Brookings Institution, 1977), 194.
5. Dahl and Lindblom, *Politics, Economics, and Welfare*, 333.
6. Clem Miller, *Member of the House* (New York: Charles Scribner's Sons, 1962), 93.
7. Donald R. Matthews, *U.S. Senators and Their World* (Chapel Hill: University of North Carolina Press, 1960), 100–101.
8. Douglass Cater, *Power in Washington* (New York: Vintage, 1964), 75.
9. William S. White, *The Citadel* (New York: Harper and Brothers, 1956), 135–153.
10. David B. Truman, *The Governmental Process* (New York: Alfred A. Knopf, 1951), 391.
11. Harry S. Truman, *Memoirs by Harry S Truman: Years of Trial and Hope*, vol. 2 (Garden City, N.Y.: Doubleday and Co., 1956; reprint, New York: New American Library, 1965), 207–208.
12. Leila A. Sussman, "FDR and the White House Mail," *Public Opinion Quarterly* 20 (spring 1956): 5–15.

13. Steele, "The Pulse of the People," 125. Newton N. Minow, John Bartlow Martin, and Lee M. Mitchell present Franklin Roosevelt as more actively mobilizing national opinion than argued by Steele. See their *Presidential Television* (New York: Basic Books, 1973), 29–32.

14. Richard E. Neustadt, *Presidential Power* (New York: John Wiley and Sons, 1980), 64–65.

15. Ibid., 74–75.

16. Ibid., 70.

17. Ibid., 22.

18. Lest the reader believe that I am chastising scholars for their work on the subject, I offer as an example of this literature my "Explaining Presidential Popularity," *American Political Science Review* 72 (June 1978): 506–522.

19. This case study draws heavily from an account by James Deakin, *Straight Stuff; The Reporters, The White House and The Truth* (New York: Morrow, 1984), 159–162.

20. Ibid., 161.

21. Alexander L. George and Juliette L. George, *Woodrow Wilson and Colonel House* (New York: J. Day Co., 1956), 290–292.

22. John Morton Blum, *Woodrow Wilson and the Politics of Morality* (Boston: Little, Brown, 1956), 189–191.

23. Carl Hulse, "A Rebellion in the GOP," *New York Times,* March 9, 2006; Jonathan Wiseman, "House Agrees to Vote on Ports," *Washington Post,* March 8, 2006.

24. Gary C. Jacobson, *A Divider, Not a Unifier* (New York: Pearson Education, 2007): 19–45.

25. See on each of these points, respectively, Morris P. Fiorina, *Congress: Keystone of the Washington Establishment* (New Haven: Yale University Press, 1977); Austin Ranney, *Channels of Power* (Washington, D.C.: American Enterprise Institute, 1983); and Martin P. Wattenberg, *The Decline of American Political Parties, 1952–1992* (Cambridge: Harvard University Press, 1994).

26. For similar treatment of the bureaucracy, see Hugh Heclo, "Issue Networks and the Executive Establishment," in *The New American Political System,* ed. Anthony King (Washington, D.C.: American Enterprise Institute, 1978), 87–124; and Nelson W. Polsby, *Consequences of Party Reform* (New York: Oxford University Press, 1983), 90–104.

27. Thomas E. Mann and Norman J. Ornstein, eds., *The New Congress* (Washington, D.C.: American Enterprise Institute, 1981). See also Eric L. Davis, "Legislative Reform and the Decline of Presidential Influence on Capitol Hill," *British Journal of Political Science* 9 (October 1979): 465–479; and Bruce I. Oppenheimer, "Policy Effects of U.S. House Reform: Decentralization and the Capacity to Resolve Energy Issues," *Legislative Studies Quarterly* 5 (February 1980): 5–30.

28. Thomas E. Mann, "Elections and Change in Congress," in *The New Congress,* ed. Mann and Ornstein, 53; Alan Ehrenhalt, "In the Senate of the '80s, Team Spirit Has Given Way to the Rule of Individuals," *Congressional Quarterly Weekly Report,* September 4, 1982, 2175–2182.

29. Michael Robinson, "Three Faces of Congressional Media," in *The New Congress,* ed. Mann and Ornstein, 93. For confirmation of Robinson's reference, see Julia Malone, "Party 'Whips' Lose Their Snap to TV and Voters Back Home," *Christian Science Monitor,* June 27, 1984, 16; and Bob Michel, "Politics in the Age of Television," *Washington Post,* June 4, 1984, 27.

30. Douglass Cater, *The Fourth Branch of Government* (Boston: Houghton Mifflin, 1959), 65.

31. Roger Davidson, "Subcommittee Government: New Channels for Policy Making," in *The New Congress,* ed. Mann and Ornstein, 109.

32. For the early history of the Democratic Study Group, see Mark F. Ferber, "The Formation of the Democratic Study Group," in *Congressional Behavior,* ed. Nelson W. Polsby (New York: Random House, 1971), 249–269. Dennis Farney reports on the DSG's efforts to overcome its complacency in "Democratic Study Unit in Ferment," *Wall Street Journal,* April 25, 1984, 54.

33. Susan Webb Hammond, *Congressional Caucuses in National Policy Making* (Baltimore: Johns Hopkins University Press, 1998).

34. Michael Kinsley, "The Art of Deduction: Writer's Loophole," *Wall Street Journal*, March 11, 1983, 21.

35. Alan K. Ota, "Caucuses—Bring New Muscle to Legislative Battlefield," *CQ Weekly Report*, September 27, 2003, 2334.

36. Gary C. Jacobson, *The Politics of Congressional Elections*, 4th ed. (New York: Longman, 1997), 56; Harold W. Stanley and Richard G. Niemi, *Vital Statistics on American Politics*, Washington, D.C.: CQ Press, 2006, 103.

37. Quoted in J. David Gopoian, "What Makes PACs Tick? An Analysis of the Allocation Patterns of Economic Interest Groups," *American Journal of Political Science* 28 (May 1984): 259–281.

38. For an account of this incident, see White, *The Citadel*, 144–146.

39. Kay Lehman Schlozman and John T. Tierney, "More of the Same: Washington Press Group Activity in a Decade of Change," *Journal of Politics* 45 (May 1983): 351–377.

40. Erica Falk, "Legislative Issue Advertising in the 107th Congress," Annenberg Public Policy Center, Washington. D.C. (July 2003), 12.

41. According to Stuart Eizenstat, Carter's domestic affairs adviser, "PACs balkanize the political process." Walter Isaacson, "Running with the PACs," *Time Magazine*, October 25, 1982, 21.

42. Barbara Sinclair, *Party Wars*, (Norman: Oklahoma University Press, 2006), 309–316.

43. Steven R. Weisman, "No. 1, the President Is Very Result Oriented," *New York Times*, November 12, 1983, 10.

44. Barbara Sinclair, "Coping with Uncertainty: Building Coalitions in the House and Senate," in *The New Congress*, 220.

45. This discussion of reputation follows closely that of Neustadt in *Presidential Power*, chap. 4.

46. Neustadt, *Presidential Power*, 238.

47. Cited in Gary C. Jacobson, *The Politics of Congressional Elections*, 4th ed. (New York: Longman, 1997), 193–194.

48. Statement by Rep. Richard B. Cheney cited in Charles O. Jones, "Congress and the Presidency," in *The New Congress*, eds. Thomas E. Mann and Norman J. Ornstein (Washington, D.C.: American Enterprise Institute, 1981), 241.

49. Alison Mitchell, "Clinton Seems to Keep Running Though the Race Is Run and Won," *New York Times*, February 12, 1997, A1, A12.

50. Ibid., A12.

51. Cited in George C. Edwards III, *The Public Presidency* (New York: St. Martin's Press, 1983), 14.

52. B. Drummond Ayres Jr., "G.O.P. Keeps Tabs on Nation's Mood," *New York Times*, November 16, 1981, 20.

53. These figures are cited in George C. Edwards III, "Frustration and Folly: Bill Clinton and the Public Presidency," in *The Clinton Presidency: First Appraisals*, eds. Colin Campbell and Bert A. Rockman (Chatham, N.J.: Chatham House, 1996), 234.

54. Rowland Evans and Robert Novak, *Nixon in the White House: The Frustration of Power*, (New York: Random House, 1971).

55. Samuel Kernell and Gary C. Jacobsen, *The Logic of American Politics*, 3rd ed. (Washington, D.C.: CQ Press, 2006), 500. The author thanks White House correspondent Mark Knoller for access to his logs of presidential fund-raising. The figures are estimates based on conversations with the president's and party committees' events staffs.

56. Neustadt, *Presidential Power*, especially chap. 8.

3

How the Politicians Entering Washington Have Changed: Outsiders and Divided Government

The 1950s textbook description, "The president proposes and Congress disposes," refers to the complementary division of labor between the two branches. Today, the student could fairly misconstrue "disposes" to mean "dead on arrival."

At some point all presidents find themselves at loggerheads with Congress. After all, disagreement is precisely what the Framers had in mind when they designed the executive and the legislative branches. One need look no further than the Constitution's "separation of powers" provisions to understand the basis for policy disagreement between these institutions. The Framers placed Congress and the president in formal opposition to each other by giving each the wherewithal to block the actions of the other. The president enjoys a veto with a difficult override provision, while Congress controls appropriations. The Framers also sought to separate the political views of these institutions' occupants by having their members elected from different-sized constituencies at different times and for different term lengths.*

Yet there was a time known as institutionalized pluralism (see chapter 2) when political parties spanned the institutional gulf between president and Congress. These politicians generally agreed on what the government needed to do and how to go about doing it. Presidential candidates were typically recruited from the mainstream of their party, mostly comprised of Washington-based politicians. As a result, their ideological positions on issues generally accorded well with their fellow partisans in Congress. Moreover, during this era of institutionalized pluralism, unified party control of the legislative and executive branches was the norm. Not only did presidents generally transact business with like-minded fellow partisans in Congress, they had a stake in working cooperatively since political fortunes were bound together in the next election.

Needless to say, things have changed. Modern politics in Washington has trended away from cooperation based on kindred partisanship. Since the early 1970s control of presidential nominations has shifted from party leaders to

---

* And until a constitutional amendment took Senate elections away from the state legislatures and made these offices popularly elected, occupants of the House, Senate and presidency were all recruited and retained through different electoral mechanisms.

states' voters in presidential primaries. The reformed nomination system sends presidents to Washington who may have weak ties to core constituent groups within their parties. It also promotes politicians to the White House with little experience in Washington but a lot in campaigning. These presidents tend to come to Washington as "outsiders," with different priorities and leadership styles. And more often than not they confront a Congress controlled by the opposition party. Disagreement inheres in the setting and frequently erupts in public conflict as each side attempts to persuade voters in the next election of the reasonableness of its position and the imprudence of the opposition's. As bargaining becomes less manageable and feasible, "outsider" presidents readily abandon negotiation in favor of going public.

PRESIDENTIAL SELECTION REFORMS: Outsiders in the White House

Campaigning and governing have always tended to draw upon the same conceptions of politics. Studying the former helps one comprehend the latter. In the nineteenth century, presidential candidates resulted from negotiations among political machines that came together at conventions to identify an acceptable candidate for whom their state organizations could work. Acceptability had something to do with electability and a lot to do with the perceived fairness of the candidate in distributing patronage to their locale. Frequently, aspiring politicians with established national reputations were ruled out because of their inevitable association with party organizations in one region of the country. This explains why conventions were commonly deadlocked, and unknowns, or "dark horses," occasionally emerged with the nomination. In office these presidents were typically weak, which suited the needs of the state party organizations: they wanted someone at the patronage levers who would follow established protocol in distributing the federal largesse.

Twentieth-century bargaining presidents have been activists who were expected to build coalitions in government and to lead their party to victory, rather than simply head the ticket. Just as in governing, these presidents succeeded as candidates by stitching together the disparate elements of their party. With state delegations to the convention handpicked by party leaders and bound to them by unit rules, aspiring presidential candidates sought the support of those who were, in the words of Thomas B. Reed, turn-of-the-century Speaker of the House and nemesis to reformers, "guided by the base desire to win." [1] Writing in 1968, Nelson W. Polsby and Aaron B. Wildavsky described this process of presidential nomination:

> Decision-making at conventions is ordinarily coordinated by a
> process of bargaining among party leaders. Each leader represents a
> state party or faction within a state which is independently organized
> and not subject to control by outsiders. . . . In order to mobilize

enough nationwide support to elect a President, party leaders from a large number of constituencies must be satisfied with the nominee.[2]

During the middle decades of the twentieth century, presidential candidates mostly came from a class of politicians with established political careers—careers increasingly located in Washington, particularly in the Senate. Reflecting the rise of the national government in public life at home and abroad during the early post–World War II era, the Senate replaced the states' governors as the chief source of presidential timber. Senators enjoyed resources that few other officeholders can match. Unlike their House colleagues, who are forced to specialize by their districts' narrower concerns and their chamber's greater number, senators find that their varied committee responsibilities and the relaxed floor procedures permit them to be reputable and vocal dilettantes on any number of domestic and foreign issues that arise from day to day.* The Senate serves as a megaphone with which its members champion policies before a national constituency. Moreover, the Senate is a school for the pluralist arts. When elected to the White House, Lyndon Johnson and John Kennedy—but not Richard Nixon, who served in the Senate only briefly before entering the isolation booth of the vice presidency—were familiar with, if not expert in, the requirements of a bargaining president.[3] Leadership through bargaining was the leitmotif of their era.

In the last decade of the twentieth century, these political arrangements gave way to those in which coalition building proceeds less through mediating organizations and elite negotiation and more through the direct mobilization of national constituencies. No aspect of the presidency has escaped this transformation. It encompasses how candidates seek their party's nomination, how they campaign in the general election, and which kinds of candidates enjoy a competitive edge at both enterprises. Specifically, modern presidential candidates are more likely to take an outsider route to the White House both geographically and dispositionally. The modal president today is a current or former governor who won nomination and election by running against Washington.

How the Reforms Changed Presidential Nominations

Until the 1972 Democratic convention adopted the proposed reforms of the McGovern-Fraser Commission, the convention system of nominating candidates had remained largely untouched during the twentieth century. Since then, reforming the presidential selection procedures has become a quadrennial political exercise as candidates have begun their campaigns by seeking to

---

* This hard fact of life for House members caused veteran and venerable representative Morris Udall of Arizona to report a dream he had, shortly after ending his brief and uneventful run for the Democratic nomination among a crowded field of Democratic senators: "I dreamed that the presidential election was to be decided by secret ballot in the U.S. Senate. When they counted the ballots, every senator had one vote." (Personal interview with Morris Udall videotaped in 1974.)

alter the rules under which they would compete for the nomination. The rules of the game have become an important part of the game itself.

The cumulative effect of these reforms has been to transfer the nomination of the party's candidate from party leaders at the convention to the mass electorate in state primary elections and caucuses. One telltale indicator of this change can be found in the number of delegates who come to the convention already bound to a particular candidate. In 1960, committed delegates constituted 20 percent of all Democratic delegates and 35 percent of all Republican delegates. By 1980 these figures had grown to 71 and 69 percent, respectively.[4] (Since 1984 the Democratic Party has sought to give the convention some flexibility in nominating the candidates by creating a class of nonpledged superdelegates, comprised of elected officeholders.[5] These changes reflect several specific reforms. Although the number of primaries was on the rise before the 1972 reforms they increased sharply after state parties were required to open delegate selection procedures. From 1960 to 2004, the number of states holding primaries more than doubled to thirty-eight. Other reforms beefed up the primaries as the arena in which the nomination took place. Under the new rules, primary voters would choose candidates rather than anonymous slates of delegates, and delegates selected in primaries would be bound to their declared candidate at least for the first ballot at the convention. Finally, the winner-take-all primary was replaced with some form of proportional distribution of delegates based on the candidates' shares of the popular vote. This has inspired obscure candidates to enter early primary campaigns they have no chance of winning. They claim some measure of success by running better than expected and thereby winning some pledged delegates.[6]

In addition to these primary reforms, other reforms were also at work dismantling the convention system. State parties that did not opt for a primary were required to open their caucuses to all party members and to democratize delegate selection procedures. No longer could a state's delegation be selected well before election season, nor could it be led into the convention bound by a unit rule to some state party leader. As a result, delegates began showing up at the convention having little familiarity with, much less loyalty to, state party leaders. Instead, they gave their allegiance to a particular candidate or cause they wanted the convention to embrace.[7]

Among the chief losers under these reforms were the representatives of core constituency groups—most notably union leaders within the Democratic Party who found their influence dwindling piecemeal with reform. Their position further deteriorated with the enactment of new campaign finance laws that gave federal matching money to candidates for the nomination who could raise $5,000 in small contributions from each of twenty or more states and who agreed to abide by ceilings on campaign spending. This loosened the dependence of all candidates on the parties' core constituent groups for organizational and financial support.[8] More to the point, candidates who had little hope of

FIGURE 3-1a   **Campaign Lengths of Candidates
for Parties' Presidential Nomination (Pre-reform)**

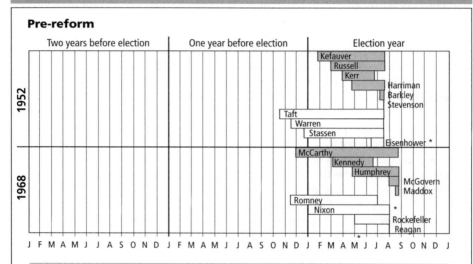

Sources: For 1952, Michael G. Hagen and William G. Mayer, "The Modern Politics of Presidential Selection," in William G. Mayer, ed., *In Pursuit of the White House 2000* (New York: Chatham House, 2000), 22–23. For other years, Harold W. Stanley and Richard G. Niemi, *Vital Statistics on American Politics, 2005–2006* (Washington, D.C.: CQ Press, 2006), 67–68.

Note: Beginning of campaigns is date of formal announcement. Asterisk designates the party's nominee. Shaded bars identify Democratic candidates, clear bars Republican.

winning endorsement from these groups could, nonetheless, raise and spend as much money as necessary to compete in the primaries.

Added together, these reforms ended any semblance of the nominating convention as a forum where the leaders of the party's constituencies came together to select the party's standard-bearer from the ranks of Washington-based politicians. Figure 3-1 reveals the extent to which the reforms substituted for a "deliberative" nominating convention as a multiphased popularity contest with low entrance barriers. After reforms many more candidates began showing up, few of whom would have stood a chance under the old convention arrangements. That some of these long-distance runners have won their party's nomination and the presidency and that others did well enough to ruin the chances of more conventionally styled candidates contribute independently to modern presidential leadership. Our presidents are, after all, the products of the system that selects them.

During the prereform era, the parties would occasionally find irresistible a candidate like Dwight Eisenhower, whose fame and reputation rested on a nonpolitical career. More often, however, candidates were drawn from the mainstream of the party and frequently from among well-positioned members

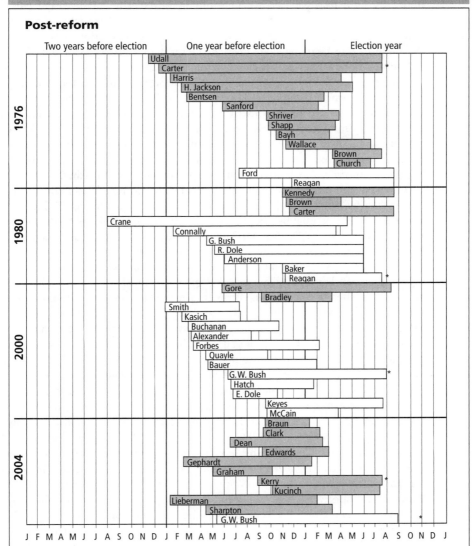

FIGURE 3-1b　**Campaign Lengths of Candidates for Parties' Presidential Nomination (Post-reform)**

Sources: For 1952, Michael G. Hagen and William G. Mayer, "The Modern Politics of Presidential Selection," in William G. Mayer, ed., *In Pursuit of the White House 2000* (New York: Chatham House, 2000), 22–23. For other years, Harold W. Stanley and Richard G. Niemi, *Vital Statistics on American Politics, 2005–2006* (Washington, D.C.: CQ Press, 2006), 67–68.

Note: Beginning of campaigns is date of formal announcement. Asterisk designates the party's nominee. Shaded bars identify Democratic candidates, clear bars Republican.

of the Washington political community. Others, "outsiders" even if technically Washington residents, did not stand a chance. Having established national visibility in conducting televised hearings into organized crime in the early 1950s, Democratic senator Estes Kefauver won virtually every presidential primary he entered in 1952. Yet largely because of a suspect reputation among the Washington elite, he managed to move no closer than his party's vice-presidential nomination.[9] Kefauver was clearly a man ahead of his time.

By the time Jimmy Carter and Ronald Reagan came to Washington, outsiders were no longer being shunted aside. Back-to-back, these two men were the first in memory to assume the Oval Office without any experience in Washington. Jimmy Carter's statement in his memoirs, "We came to Washington as outsiders . . . we left as outsiders," signifies how thoroughly the selection reforms have altered presidential recruitment.[10] Not even General Eisenhower had such impeccable credentials for boasting his nonpolitical rearing.

A candidate achieves his outsider status less by his non-Washington residency than by his standing within the party or governmental establishment. What precisely this establishment means is left to the candidate to define. It may be as specific as Eugene McCarthy's Lyndon Johnson or as general as Reagan's "bumbling bureaucrats" and "spendthrift politicians" who occupy the "puzzle palaces on the Potomac." For a Democrat to succeed as a credible outsider, organized labor must be included in the establishment. Generally, the strategy plays better when one is competing against a front-runner who occupies a credible "insider's" position. In 1972 George McGovern took apart Sen. Edmund Muskie in the early primaries and Sen. Hubert Humphrey in the later ones. Both appeared to have labor's support. In 1984 Gary Hart could not have campaigned nearly so well on the ambiguous platform of "new ideas" and being "less beholden" if his adversary, Sen. Walter Mondale, had not been so conspicuously "more beholden" to the "old ideas" of the Democratic establishment.

The 1992 campaign for the Democratic nomination followed much the same script. Of the five candidates who competed in the first state primary in New Hampshire, only two then held public office in Washington. And two of the candidates—Paul Tsongas and Jerry Brown—had not held public office in years. Over the next six weeks, two Washington-based politicians and a former senator dropped out of the race. Neither of the finalists—Bill Clinton or Jerry Brown—was tainted with having previously held public office in Washington.

More recently, another class of presidential candidates who enjoy even stronger credentials as outsiders has begun entertaining presidential aspirations. Individuals who have never held public office but who possess the requisite resources—ample television exposure, political action committees, and either a private fortune or a lucrative fund-raising list—have become serious contenders for this pinnacle office of the political career structure. When television evangelist Pat Robertson declared his presidential candidacy in 1987, his announcement was greeted in Washington not with derision but with an invitation to speak at the National Press Club. Four years later, another never-elected television personality, Patrick Buchanan, undertook the apparently quixotic task of winning the Republican Party's nomination away from its sitting president. That he turned in a surprisingly strong performance in the early presidential primaries strengthened the credibility and, hence, the prospects of subsequent candidates who had never been tainted by public office.

Then, in 1992, came billionaire H. Ross Perot. Virtually unknown to ordinary voters the previous year, Perot spurned both of the major political parties. Through the sheer force of massive television advertising, he propelled himself into the presidential debates and, briefly, even enjoyed "frontrunner" status over Bush and Clinton in national public opinion polls. Perot paved the way for another fabulously rich political neophyte in 1996. With an attractive "insider" foil available in the person of Senate Majority Leader Bob Dole, Steve Forbes anted in with heavy advertising and ran strongly until his deficient organization and weak appeal to southern Republican primary voters finished his candidacy. Another Republican candidate, Lamar Alexander, also sought the coveted mantle of "outsider" and normally would have gotten it. But next to Forbes this former Tennessee governor and cabinet official suspiciously resembled a political "insider," which even his signature plaid shirt could not disguise.

There is no better evidence that the reformed selection process confers advantages to outsiders than Bob Dole's decision during the 1996 primaries to resign from the Senate. In a tearful announcement he surrendered his Senate seat of twenty-seven years, opened his collar, and asked voters to regard him no longer as "senator" but simply as "citizen Dole." While Dole's action offers the most dramatic example of the liability of insider status, other Senate colleagues had previously shown the way by retiring to strengthen their bids for the presidency. In 1984 another Republican majority leader, Howard Baker, left the Senate after finding his duties had encumbered his uneventful bid for the presidential nomination in 1980.[11] For much of 1985, three years before the election, private citizen Baker could be found roaming the circuit of New Hampshire's civic lunches and coffee klatches, which quadrennially provide citizens of that state with their special form of entertainment. While Baker was laying the groundwork for another campaign, his former Senate Republican colleagues, some of whom also aspired to the presidency, were stuck in Washington grousing with their president and struggling with such unpleasant subjects as the budget deficit, import quotas, and the multiple problems of the American farmer. The same consideration prompted Colorado senator Gary Hart to forego a promising reelection race in 1986 in order to free himself to seek the Democratic Party's presidential nomination in 1988.

The presidential selection system constitutes a strategic environment that enhances certain skills and resources while penalizing others. Politicians on the sidelines go to school on the experiences of candidates in the arena. In addition to its direct effect on candidates' fortunes, the presidential selection system shapes the kinds of presidents we elect by influencing the career decisions and stylistic adaptations of future candidates.

Outsiders as Presidents

Fresh from an extended and successful stint of campaigning, an outsider will most likely enter the White House uninterested and ill prepared to play the bargaining game. As an outsider president, deciding whether to promote policies in Washington by attending to a great many transactions with other elites or by going over their heads to enlist popular support with a television appeal may be an easy choice.

Bargaining, however, is not dead. In the modern Washington characterized by individualized pluralism, presidents will continue to receive many invitations to the bargaining table. Beyond familiarity with the formal procedures and informal folkways that govern exchange even today, successful bargaining requires of the president a keen sense of the needs and preferences of those whom he seeks to influence. Bargaining may, however, surpass the capacities of the outsider president. Recognizing future bargaining partners and figuring out what a particular bargain might look like may seem trivial, but experience shows that both may escape White House occupants. When President Carter canceled nineteen water projects without consulting fellow Democrats on Capitol Hill, did he appreciate the political costs he was inflicting upon others and eventually upon himself? Given the self-congratulatory aplomb with which he announced his decision, one suspects not. Several of these projects had been long-sought goals of Sen. Russell Long and Louisiana's Democratic House delegation. Senator Long chaired the important Senate Finance Committee through which much of the White House's legislative program was destined to pass, and where in fact some of it came to rest.[12]

No less important and probably even more demanding for the outsider in the White House is awareness of an opportunity to bargain when it presents itself. At the least, the president must understand that his formal responsibilities and prerogatives are convertible in barter. In addition, he must know the customary routines of exchange that have grown up in Washington over the years to reduce the uncertainty of coalition building for all participants. Without such knowledge even an avid negotiator might quickly become overwhelmed. The inability of outsiders in the White House to recognize these routines not only constitutes lost opportunity but also may assume real political costs.

President Carter, for example, repudiated the vestigial practice of replacing the other party's federal district attorneys with local partisans recommended by the districts' Democratic members of Congress. The questionable legitimacy of such blatant partisanship muted the outcry among House and Senate Democrats, but those adversely affected by the decision no doubt recognized that they alone bore the costs of the president's unilateral action. Another political custom, seemingly costless to the president but invaluable to his party's members of Congress, has been that of allowing the local representative to claim some credit by announcing new federal programs in the district. The Carter administration, in contrast, issued periodic press releases from the White House that summarily listed new programs.[13]

I have dwelt on President Carter's shortcomings for a reason. Although other presidents have from time to time failed to enlist routine exchange systems, Carter did so more consistently and more flagrantly. Even taking into account the centrifugal forces at work in present-day Washington, the large Democratic majorities in Congress offered Carter the luxurious prospect that even uninspired, routine bargaining would reap great legislative rewards. As it was, his legislative accomplishments are generally judged to have been modest. Even his victories appeared grudgingly delivered by the Democratic congressional leaders. The explanation, of course, is his path to the White House.

One would be hard pressed to find a better illustration of the outsider's propensity for going public than the following colloquy between House Speaker Thomas P. O'Neill Jr. and President Carter during a pre-inauguration briefing in Plains, Georgia:*

> **O'Neill:** Mr. President, I want you to understand something. Some of the brightest men in America are in this Congress of the United States. Don't make the mistake of underestimating them. . . . We want to work together, but I have a feeling you are underestimating the feeling of Congress and you could have some trouble.

> **Carter:** I'll handle them just as I handled the Georgia legislature. Whenever I had problems with the Georgia legislature I took the problems to the people of Georgia.[14]

Whatever the emerging job requirements or the partisan disposition of Washington, the style of presidential leadership will largely reflect the skills and experiences of the person in office. A president who developed his political skills in the chambers and corridors of Congress will understandably find it exasperating to deliver salutations to a television camera. Similarly, the outsider whose career success is founded largely upon the stylized public presentation of self will derive greater gratification and even stimulation from traveling around the country delivering speeches and appearing on television than in following the private, daily, all-too-mysterious rituals of cultivating support from other politicians. That today's Washington elites are less responsive to such methods only adds to modern presidents' distaste for them. Whenever the advantages of the recruitment process for outsiders prove decisive, going public will enjoy favored status within the White House. By now, outsiders' accession to the White House is hardly noteworthy; nor is their record of going public. Norman Ornstein and John Fournier conclude in their assessment of President Bush's early success in 2001 that "no new president traveled to so many states so early and no new president used this explicit strategy of appeal-

---

* Two months later they were having the same dialogue but in public. Hedrick Smith reports: " 'It upsets me when they say, "we'll bring it to the people," ' the stentorian white-haired speaker declared. 'That's the biggest mistake Carter could ever make' " ("Congress and Carter: An Uneasy Adjustment," *New York Times*, February 18, 1977, B16).

ing over the heads of particular Senators in order to affect their votes in Washington." Nothing is different here; just *more* of the same.[15]

THE POLITICS OF DIVIDED GOVERNMENT

One of the most prominent political developments over the past several decades is the emergence of divided party control of Congress and the presidency. Earlier in the century, the electorate had occasionally punished the governing party at midterm by giving the opposition control of one or both legislative chambers. When it occurred in the 1946 midterm elections it had a generation of politicians consulting history books to see how such a system would work. A young senator J. W. Fullbright called on President Truman to resign and allow Republicans to participate in a kind of collective presidency until the 1948 election restored order.* But not until 1956 had a presidential candidate from one party and a congressional majority from the other been elected at the same time. Beginning with 1956, seven of the thirteen presidential elections have resulted in divided government (see Table 3-1).

When party control of Congress and the presidency is unified, leaders from both branches of government have a special incentive to resolve disagreements harmoniously and in private. Whatever their policy differences, party members negotiate with one another, recognizing that each will be judged for the party's collective performance. If the governing party's leaders were to allow internal disagreements to erupt into public discord, they would be flirting with defeat in the next election. Instead, they engage in quiet diplomacy to reach the compromises necessary to unify the party and give it an attractive record for the next campaign. In this circumstance, going public will frequently be unnecessary and, as an application of force, might well upset party harmony. Members of the governing party team in the legislative and executive branches therefore have a strong incentive to resolve their differences discreetly.

But when party control of Congress and the presidency is divided, a different dynamic arises. Instead of private conversations at the White House—FDR lunched with House and Senate Democratic leaders every Tuesday and Thursday to hash out legislative priorities and coordinate schedules—negotiations move into the public arena and typically assume the form of threats and counterthreats. Politics becomes a zero-sum game in which each side tries to gain advantage both in the current tussle over policy and in the next election. Under divided government opposing sides can gain electoral advantage by frustrating and embarrassing the other, even if this thwarts their own policy goals. During the 102nd Congress, the Democratic majority rejected President Bush's overtures for concessions on bills expanding civil rights pro-

---

* From then on, President Truman customarily addressed his former Senate colleague as Senator Halfbright.

TABLE 3-1 The Growth of Divided Government, 1928–2004

Election year	President	House of Representatives	Senate
1928	R (Hoover)	R	R
1930	R (Hoover)	D	R
1932	D (F. Roosevelt)	D	D
1934	D (F. Roosevelt)	D	D
1936	D (F. Roosevelt)	D	D
1938	D (F. Roosevelt)	D	D
1940	D (F. Roosevelt)	D	D
1942	D (F. Roosevelt)	D	D
1944	D (F. Roosevelt)	D	D
1946	D (Truman)	R	R
1948	D (Truman)	D	D
1950	D (Truman)	D	D
1952	R (Eisenhower)	R	R
1954	R (Eisenhower)	D	D
1956	R (Eisenhower)	D	D
1958	R (Eisenhower)	D	D
1960	D (Kennedy)	D	D
1962	D (Kennedy)	D	D
1964	D (Johnson)	D	D
1966	D (Johnson)	D	D
1968	R (Nixon)	D	D
1970	R (Nixon)	D	D
1972	R (Nixon)	D	D
1974	R (Ford)	D	D
1976	D (Carter)	D	D
1978	D (Carter)	D	D
1980	R (Reagan)	D	R
1982	R (Reagan)	D	R
1984	R (Reagan)	D	R
1986	R (Reagan)	D	D
1988	R (Bush)	D	D
1990	R (Bush)	D	D
1992	D (Clinton)	D	D
1994	D (Clinton)	R	R
1996	D (Clinton)	R	R
1998	D (Clinton)	R	R
2000	R (Bush)	R	D
2002	R (Bush)	R	R
2004	R (Bush)	R	R

Source: Compiled by the author.

Note: Shading indicates divided government.

tection and extending unemployment benefits, preferring instead to repeatedly send him popular legislation he had publicly vowed to veto.* In the 104th Congress, the Republican majority turned the tables on a Democratic president by repeatedly passing resolutions and legislation calling for a balanced budget in seven years and by attaching conditions to this legislation that invited a veto. Force and conflict replace cooperation, ending frequently in legislative "gridlock." [16]

Presidents generally employ going public to accomplish positive goals that require Congress to pass a bill, ratify a treaty, confirm an appointment, and the like. Divided government invites this strategy because the prospects for cooperation between the executive and the legislative branches are low; opposition legislators might agree to the president's policy but only under public pressure.

An interesting "natural" experiment, revealing the propensity of presidents to resort to public strategies under divided government, occurred in the spring of Bush's first term (2001) when Senate Republican Jim Jeffords of Vermont crossed the aisle and, in doing so, flipped majority control to the Democrats. Suddenly, the Republicans had to surrender their floor leadership posts and their committee and subcommittee chairs to their Democratic colleagues. With this the Democrats gained a degree of control over the Senate's consideration of administration policy. When Andrew Card, the president's chief of staff, was asked about this development, he downplayed its impact on the president's program. "This experience is one obviously we wish we didn't have to live through," he averred, then added that to move the education bill through the Senate "the president may have to use the bully pulpit a little more." Another adviser spurned compromise with the Senate's new leadership. Instead, they would pressure Democrats in states where the president is popular: "That's how we get Zell Miller [Georgia] and Ben Nelson [Nebraska]." [17] The president followed his aide's advice and campaigned throughout the summer, for his "No Child Left Behind" reforms, most of which Congress enacted.

Going Public as an Electoral Strategy

Conflict and confrontation may serve a party's electoral purposes even when its policy goals are the casualty. In 1985 Richard Cheney, then House Republican whip, stated: "Polarization often has very beneficial results. If everything is handled through compromise and conciliation, if there are no real issues dividing us from the Democrats, why should the country change and make us the majority?" [18] Under divided government, the desire to achieve policy goals through give-and-take at the bargaining table yields to the strategic dictates of the next election.

For some legislation, presidents sense they can score points in public opinion by vowing publicly to veto some unpopular bill in Congress. In 1996

---

* In both instances, the president eventually relented to mounting public pressure and signed essentially Democratic bills.

President Clinton threatened and then vetoed a law limiting damages in product liability suits, citing provisions that might prevent plaintiffs from recovering their medical and other costs from products juries deemed liable.[19] In the summer of 1976 President Ford went on an election-year veto binge against a busy Democratic Congress—twenty-four bills (of which twelve were overridden) in order to substantiate his claim that only he "stood between the national treasury and the Democratic Party." Here again is a president engaging in public posturing in preparation for the next election, but this time he sports the "negative," a synonym for the veto frequently used by the Constitution's Framers.

Congressional instances of baiting the president to veto popular bills, notwithstanding, the president's veto authority provides him with a powerful tool for warding off undesirable legislation from an opposition Congress.

Case 1: Truman Spurns Cooperation and Succeeds

After the 1946 midterm election in which the Republicans captured control of Congress for the first time since the 1920s, President Truman faced an outpouring of unsolicited advice from mostly Republican politicians and newspaper editorial writers urging him to cooperate with Congress. Some even championed novel institutional arrangements such as regularly scheduled "summit" meetings between the Democratic president and the Republican congressional leaders to hash out policy accords.

Observing from a distance the pressure being exerted on the uncertain president, James Rowe, a former White House assistant to Roosevelt, wrote Truman a lengthy, unsolicited memo entitled "Cooperation or Conflict?"[20] He sought to dissuade the president from agreeing to formal mechanisms of cooperation with the opposition Congress, arguing that they were just Republican schemes to ensnare the president. Truman found Rowe's argument persuasive and followed its advice in his relations with Congress.[21]

The premise of Rowe's argument was that the main business of an opposition Congress is to prepare for the next election. Investigations of administration decisions, contentious confirmation hearings, and passage of popular bills fashioned to elicit the president's veto were some of the devices available to an opposition Congress. Nowadays divided government is expected, but at the time this memo was written, the country had not experienced it for fourteen years. Democrats viewed with great alarm the prospects of an opposition Congress on the prowl. There was not much the president could do, Rowe advised, but grin and bear it.

What the president could do—and this was the thrust of Rowe's argument—was to avoid being suckered into naively negotiating with Congress. With each side maneuvering the other into a position to be exploited, summit resolution becomes a sharp game in which the president plays with several distinct disadvantages stemming from the institutional differences between the legislature and executive. First is the presidency's "extremely public nature," which "leaves no room whatever for the private give-and-take, the secrecy and anonymity of compromise, which is the essence of negotiation. . . . The presidency is rigid—when its incumbent speaks the world soon knows exactly what he said." Second, in agreeing to negotiate, "the president yields his one source of strength—the backing of public opinion for his point of view. He brings that opinion to his view only by means of public statements. But reaching agreement with [the opposition] . . . means sitting around the conference table with them and indulging in bargaining and negotiation with them. The agreements would be made public as a combined product and the people would not know which were the contributions—or the concessions—of the . . . President." Third, the president has the ability to deliver on his agreements, but congressional leaders do not or can easily claim not to. Once a compromise is reached, they can return to the bargaining table for more concessions to gain votes from members holding out. In the end, "cooperation is a one way street."

So what is the president to do? "Unlike majority presidents [in unified government] who are able to do business with their party . . . minority presidents are forced to fall back on their chief weapon—the marshaling of public opinion." Rowe identified two types of opportunity especially appropriate for going public: veto messages and press conferences. Today, in an era of jet transportation and television, these avenues of public persuasion seem rather timid and unimaginative, but they were the principal opportunities available to a president in the 1940s. He was being urged to confront the opposition Congress not because the prospects for going public were bright but rather because the opportunities for bargaining were bleak.

In his dealings with the Republican 80th Congress, President Truman followed Rowe's advice. He selectively vetoed legislation on which he could take forceful and politically attractive positions. Foremost, he refused to bow to pressure to engage in summit diplomacy. In public statements, he proposed popular social policies to Congress, daring it to reject them. And in 1948 he called the Republican Congress back into special session and presented it with popular social legislation, not in expectation of making policy but in order to create potent issues for his fall reelection campaign. Indeed, these activities laid the groundwork for his famous, come-from-behind victory, which taught future presidents—among them Bill Clinton, who learned these lessons well—how to make an opposition Congress a campaign issue.

Veto Rhetoric

In addition to publicly pressuring Congress to attend to presidents' legislative agenda or creating issues for the next election, divided government presents a third rationale for presidents to go public. When the opposition party controls Congress—especially both chambers—a common story in the routine news coverage of the White House has the president or some administration official threatening to veto a bill currently wending its way through Congress. Why do presidents bother to inform Congress of their plans and why do they do so in public? If the "threat" is merely a statement of intent, let the opposition majority spin its legislative wheels, and if and when it manages to send the legislation to the White House, then the president exercises the veto. Presidents generally need not mobilize public opinion to resist legislation except in the unusual circumstance where two-thirds of both the House and Senate appear poised to override the veto. Toward the end of his term President Eisenhower vetoed numerous Democratic bills for which he did not bother to announce publicly his plans in advance.

Although presidents have been quick to score points against a congressional opposition passing legislation principally for the benefit of its core constituencies, such opportunities are far too few to account for the heavy volume of threats reported in Figure 3-2. This figure plots the number of bills that presidents have threatened to veto since 1981.* Note that during Clinton's first Congress (103rd) he issued no threats against his only Congress in which Democrats controlled both the House and Senate. Once Republicans took control in the 1994 midterm elections, Clinton's veto rhetoric soared. Another ebb in threats occurred during the 107th through 109th Congresses of President George W. Bush, again a period of unified party control of government. The other Congresses with comparatively few threats occurred during President Reagan's first term. As we shall see in chapter 5, at that time the "Great Communicator" was busy engaging in more positive efforts at going public, trying with some success to bend a Democratic House of Representatives to his will regarding limited government. Once scandal—specifically, Irangate—took over the news and Reagan's approval ratings began falling, the president staged a retreat to protect his early legislative gains and to resist other Democratic initiatives with frequent veto threats, some of which he was obliged to make good.

A closer inspection of the details of the threats finds that the great majority involves the president couching his threat in a proposed compromise. Typically, the threat identifies those provisions that the president objects to and suggests that their removal or alteration along specified lines would lead to his signature. This looks a lot like bargaining; yet it takes place in public and is premised on unilateral action, both antithetical to the quiet diplomacy essential for successful bargaining. In fact, veto threats represent a peculiar genus of presidential rhetoric that has presidents going public to achieve what is essentially a bargaining outcome.

During divided party control of these branches, both sides prudently suspect the other of misrepresenting its views in order to obtain as favorable a political or policy result as possible. For example, when the president advises Congress that a "minimally acceptable" bill (a common phrase employed in

---

* These figures were culled from the online *CQ Weekly Report* database, except for 1981 and 1982 where paper issues were examined. Only one threat is scored per bill, unless an amendment was offered that elicited a separate veto threat. This time series is highly correlated with counts of references to veto threats in Associated Press stories and in Statements of Administration Policy listed in Samuel Kernell, ed., *Presidential Veto Threats in Statements of Administration Policy: 1985–2004,* (Washington: CQ Press, 2005).

FIGURE 3-2 **Presidential Veto Threats over Time: 1981–2006**

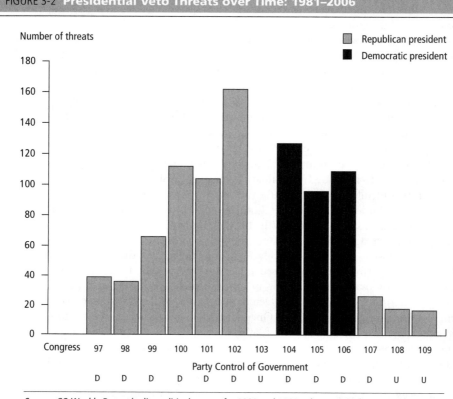

Source: *CQ Weekly Report* (online edition) except for 1981 and 1982, where original paper copies were examined. Numbers represent actual veto threats as reported in CQ's textual coverage. These figures exclude CQ's use of the term in describing its summary presidential support variable. The 2006 counts end in August.

Note: Black bars identify Democratic administrations; gray bars, Republican.
D represents divided party control of president and Congress; U, unified.

threats) must remove provisions X, Y, and Z, legislators should question whether the president really means what he says. Perhaps a bill without these provisions would actually constitute the president's "maximally attractive" policy. Legislators are bound to recognize this possibility and, reluctant to surrender any of these provisions unnecessarily, they may pass a final bill that retains all three provisions, or one that deletes one, two, or all three. In larger part this decision will rest on the credibility of the president's threat.

Here is where going public can serve bargaining in these settings. One thing presidents can do to instill credibility, thereby improving their chances of receiving more desirable legislation, is to commit themselves publicly to veto the bill containing X, Y, and Z. The more visible and categorical the rhetoric, the less wiggle room presidents would leave themselves to sign a bill that does not satisfy the conditions listed in the threat. Both presidents and legislators appreciate that if a president were to renege on such a threat, voters would punish him in the next election. Legislators observe the president's action and conclude that he can ill afford politically to sign a bill that fails to give him what he has demanded, or at least something pretty close.[22] By tying their hands to a course of action, presidents can strengthen the signals they send to Congress and improve their chances of getting bills they can sign.

This can be a dicey game for presidents, one they may generally be reluctant to play. The more public and binding the threat, the less credibility they will have in the future. Moreover, steadfastness is a virtue, but hard-headedness to reasonable alternatives is not. Presidents may find that a policy does not provide a convenient place to draw "a line in dirt" (a phrase President Reagan used in one of his threats). As we see in the following famous case study, to issue a threat and then back down can be devastating. I am referring to George H. W. Bush's disastrous "read my lips" declaration. Surely every president since has "gone to school" on this incident; they will continue to do so for a long time. In the second case study Republican leaders calculated that President Clinton was also bluffing in his threat to veto unacceptable appropriations bills and shut down the government. They were wrong. President Clinton followed through on the threat and buttressed it with national speeches and DNC-financed commercials. After a series of bruising maneuvers, President Clinton emerged with a budget more to his liking and approval ratings that put him in good position to win reelection.

Case 2: President Bush Cooperates and Fails

In the fall of 1990, as President Bush sat staring at the teleprompter, waiting to deliver only his third prime-time appeal to the American people, he may well have wondered how he landed in his predicament. With the nation facing a mounting budget deficit that was about to trigger draconian, across-the-board cuts in government services, Bush waited for his cue to announce a deficit reduction plan of increased taxes and reduced spending. Compounding his discomfort was the knowledge that the legislation he was about to unveil more closely resembled the preferences of congressional Democrats than any plan he or his fellow Republicans had put forward. The speech omitted any reference to the Republican mantra—cut capital gains taxes. It did, however, include a tax hike for wealthy, mostly Republican taxpayers. And yet here was the president about to shoulder responsibility for it with the American people.

An unpleasant irony for Bush was that he had worked hard to reach this uncomfortable moment. First, he had to sacrifice his earlier image of resoluteness in order to get budget negotiations moving. The Democrats had insisted that the president retract his 1988 campaign slogan, "Read my lips: no new taxes," before they would participate in any discussions that might result in new taxes. The president tried to minimize the political fallout by slipping the concession into a press release that buried "tax revenue increases" among a list of topics open to negotiation.

Throughout the summer of meetings, Bush had refrained from publicly criticizing the Democratic Congress, lest he drive its members away from the bargaining table. However, this necessitated surrendering his advantage on the public stage, which Rowe had advised Truman was the strongest card available to a president facing an opposition Congress.

One can therefore sympathize with Bush's predicament as he began his television address, feigning enthusiasm for the budget compromise. No wonder his appeal was brief and tepid, without impact in the country or Congress. This, his first solicitation of the public's support—"Tell your Congressmen and Senators you support this deficit reduction agreement"—did little to stem the "avalanche" of mail opposed to some feature of the legislation. The only indicator to register any movement after the speech was the further weakening of the president's job performance rating in the opinion polls.

Congressional Republicans had been largely ignored in developing the budget compromise. With little investment in the product, and fearing that, as members of the president's party, they would be tagged with responsibility for the tax increases in the upcoming congressional elections, these Republicans were the first to bolt. Many congressional Democrats strategically followed the Republicans in highly public criticism of the budget compromise. Within seventy-two hours of the president's national appeal, the package of taxes and spending that had taken all summer to hammer out collapsed.

With congressional Republicans in open revolt, President Bush was stuck with a dilemma. He could allow the provisions of the current law to kick in and automatically reduce the deficit with severe, across-the-board cuts in discretionary spending or he could return to the negotiating table to develop a package that would attract stronger Democratic support. He opted for the latter, but not without a lot of bickering within the administration that spilled over into the press. The collective consternation was brought on by the realization that the bipartisan compromise no one in the White House was enthusiastic about would become the administration's new bargaining position from which an even less attractive, more Democratic policy would be fashioned.

As soon as the new package was signed, President Bush left town to repair his relations with congressional Republicans by helping in their reelection campaigns. He conjured up the image of himself as a Reaganesque outsider—"God, I'm glad to be out of Washington"—and painted congressional Democrats, his erstwhile trading partners, as "America's biggest and most entrenched special interest." And he adopted what his aides called a "Harry Truman style" by claiming the budget had been held "ransom" by Congress, and in the future he was "absolutely going to hold the line on taxes." [23]

There was little confidence among fellow partisans, however, that the president could switch from cooperation to confrontation so easily. A "senior Republican strategist" summed up the matter this way: "They're going to sign off on the budget deal, then try to pin it on the Democrats, say George Bush didn't do it and expect the voters to believe this whole budget was an immaculate conception. . . . It's not going to be easy."

Republican congressional candidates also viewed this as a dubious strategy. A hundred or so had made campaign commercials with Bush earlier in the fall, but only a few candidates chose to air them. Many canceled the president's visit to their districts, and some of those who required his presence to raise campaign funds with the party faithful stayed in Washington on "pressing business." Sometimes matters did not improve even when the president succeeded in joining a candidate on stage. Surely the following introduction offered by a House Republican from Oklahoma was well intended: "George Bush on his worst day is a whole lot better than Michael Dukakis on his best day." The *coup de grace* came while the president was stumping in Vermont for another House Republican incumbent. Seeking maximum distance from the president, who was seated within a stone's throw, the candidate addressed the audience: "Ask yourselves, why did this President, last May, decide that the issue he had run on and won on now had to be laid on the table as a point of negotiations? We're talking about his pledge on taxes." [24]

President Truman's dealings with the Republican Congress may have been too distant to provide guidance to George H. W. Bush. But certainly, Bush's lesson was fresh in the minds of the principals who confronted each other across Pennsylvania Avenue in the fall of 1995. Bill Clinton, a Democrat, was now president. Survey evidence suggests that Clinton owed his White House residence to Bush's retraction of "read my lips" as much as anything else. Republican leaders Newt Gingrich in the House and Bob Dole in the Senate remembered Bush's fiasco more ruefully. Perhaps now that they controlled Congress they could make Clinton accommodate them the same way congressional Democrats had their president.

This case illustrates the full extent of the risks in failing to follow Truman's example. Bush stumbled into every minefield James Rowe had mapped for Truman nearly half a century earlier. Now for a more astute use of veto rhetoric, even though here too the president found himself having to back it with action.

Case 3: Bill Clinton Becomes Trumanesque

In fairness to congressional Republicans, nothing about President Clinton's performance during his first two years in office gave anyone cause to believe that he would stand up to pressure. He had demonstrated such a readiness to compromise and otherwise straddle policy choices, even his loyal staffers found themselves wondering what he stood for. [25] And in the spring of 1995, with the new Republican majorities in both houses of Congress busily enacting their Contract with America, President Clinton's standing in Washington fell to the lowest depths of his presidency. That Congress might ignore Clinton became starkly apparent when House Speaker Newt Gingrich in February gave

By Mark Streeter. Copyright 1995. Courtesy *Savannah Morning News.*

his own, nationally televised address to the nation. In mid-April Clinton scheduled a rare prime-time news conference to return to center stage. Only one network showed up, and the president was pelted with questions about whether people in Washington and across the nation were still paying attention to him. Bristling, Clinton asserted, "The president is relevant here." [26] In the fall, as the Republican budget wended its way through the final stages of congressional approval, President Clinton still had not demonstrated the validity of this statement.

By late September it was clear that the president had failed in his efforts to moderate deep cuts in social spending by slowing down the rate of reduction of the budget deficit and staving off a massive tax cut that favored wealthier constituencies. As they approached the endgame, Republican leaders believed they had a card that would trump the president's veto. By attaching the spending and revenue legislation to a debt ceiling bill that the administration needed to keep meeting payrolls and entitlements, the president would be forced to accept the whole package. If Bush had flinched at automatic cutbacks in 1991, surely Clinton would not shoulder responsibility for closing the government altogether, the Republican leaders reasoned. "I think the President will be forced to move toward us," predicted Republican John Kasich, the House

Budget Committee chair. He added, "At the end of the day he will explain why he made our program unreasonable while signing our program." [27]

Instead, President Clinton vetoed the budget and two days later went on national television to denounce its "deep and unwise cuts" and prepare the nation for a government shutdown. Deploring the draconian budget reductions, Clinton argued, "If America has to close down access to education, to a clean environment, to affordable health care, to keep our government open, then the price is too high." He added, "Yes to balancing the budget. No to the cuts." One White House aide confided to a reporter, "He's prepared to fight all winter" on this issue. Two days later, eight hundred thousand federal workers were sent home, and they would not return for six days.

News media surveys immediately detected that public opinion had swung to the president's side. When asked whether the president should have vetoed the budget, 56 percent of the respondents said yes and only 36 percent no. When the same sample was asked to assess Clinton's leadership, 49 percent agreed that he was acting as "a strong leader and standing up for what he believes in." By comparison, Republican House Speaker Newt Gingrich and Senate Majority Leader Bob Dole scored 33 and 30 percent, respectively, on this same measure. [28]

Perhaps the public's favorable response to Clinton's message can be at least partly attributed to television commercials the Democratic National Committee had begun running in late October to explain the president's stand on the budget. "It was a decision by the President that we need to have the capacity to present his position to the people," according to a Democratic Party official. The party planned to target approximately $1 million of ads a week until the end of the year to buttress the president's position.

After sparring for the greater part of a week with the president landing most of the punches, Republican leaders backed off temporarily by agreeing to appropriations to fund the government until mid-December. Negotiations resumed and the public opinion battle heated up as the Republicans launched their own commercials depicting President Clinton flip-flopping on the deficit. In retrospect, the president's public strategy brilliantly balanced the appearance of moderation with an eagerness to veto "radical" Republican bills. The Democratic National Committee chair, Donald Fowler, had publicly cautioned the White House that the strategy was "very risky" and would succeed only "if the public gets the impression Republicans are intransigent." * As if following a script, the president could be seen on television characterizing the Republican strategy as "an exercise of raw, naked power."

---

* Christopher Georges, "Balanced-Budget Talks between GOP, White House Stall after Three Days," *Wall Street Journal,* December 1995. Clinton had similarly advised Democratic lawmakers: "We have to exercise a high degree of humility. We're going to make some very complicated demands, and the American people are going to judge us on how we handle this debate." David E. Rosenbaum, "With Crisis Over, Clinton Now Seeks the High Ground," *New York Times,* November 21, 1995.

On December 16, after weeks of fruitless negotiation, the government shut down again. By mid-January both sides were negotiating again and facing the specter of a government default on its debts. A weary Speaker Gingrich came out of one long session "close to exhaustion" and conceded to a reporter that the president and his team "were tougher than I thought they would be. . . . They have less flexibility than I thought they would have. Our strategy failed." During the next couple of weeks, Republican and Democratic negotiators agreed to fund the government for the next year at reduced levels. Republican leaders backed off a seven-year balanced budget commitment and more than half of their tax cuts passed in October. Both sides accepted the principle that this disagreement would not finally conclude until the following November, when Republicans would try to elect a president to go with their Congress. Few programs were eliminated, seven-year budget targets were postponed indefinitely, and mutually acceptable savings were achieved by broadly scaling back discretionary domestic spending.

From a strict budgetary index, both sides found features in the February agreement they could point to and claim credit. From a political vantage, however, Clinton and the Democrats won a significant victory. The president reestablished his presence in Washington and recaptured the attention of the American public. Instead of sinking further in the public's opprobrium, his approval rating actually rose during this confrontation that twice closed the federal government. In an early October Gallup poll, his approval rating had stood at an anemic 46 percent; as the confrontation unfolded, Clinton's popular support unexpectedly began to rise. By mid-November it stood at 53 percent, and despite another shutdown in December, Clinton had added a point to his popular support by the time an agreement was finally hammered out. Meanwhile, Republican leaders Gingrich and Dole saw their fortunes sink over this time period. A Gallup straw poll the previous September pitting Clinton against the Republican Party's eventual nominee, Bob Dole, found the Republican leading the president by five percentage points. Six months later, as the budget confrontation ended, the president held a commanding twelve-point lead he would never relinquish. By standing up to the Republican Congress with a veto and frequent and varied appeals to the American public, Bill Clinton rescued his presidency and won reelection.

Congress and the presidency are different kinds of institutions, mostly having to do with the number of principals involved. The modern institutional presidency has a staff of thousands, but only one individual can commit the institution. This gives that person the opportunity to credibly commit to a course of action that leaders of a bicameral, decentralized Congress typically do not enjoy. They can sign on to a *quid pro quo,* but they cannot guarantee that their colleagues will execute their side of the bargain. When circumstances are aligned in such a way as to allow the legislative opposition to profit by reneging on bargains, presidents should assume that they will. The moral: during divided government prudent presidents should engage an opposition

Congress gingerly (insisting that they move first) and from a distance in full view of the public.

CONCLUSION

We have thus far considered several major developments in national politics as causes for the rise of going public as a presidential strategy: political relations in Washington that discourage quiet diplomacy; presidential selection reforms that send politicians into the White House who are more inclined and skilled at public relations; and divided party control of government, which introduces a zero-sum game that shrinks the availability of mutually acceptable policies and otherwise makes bargaining risky by rewarding reneging. Although on the surface these developments appear quite different and suggest a confluence of several separate streams of political change, they share at least one common source: the declining value of political parties to the electorate during the 1970s and 1980s. During this era voters increasingly loosened their identification with the Democratic and Republican Parties; Independent became a more popular self-classification than either party. The strength of party loyalty weakened even among those who continued to identify themselves as Democrat or Republican. More were willing to defect to an opposition candidate, particularly if he or she was the incumbent. Increasing numbers split their votes between party candidates for Congress and the presidency.

This attitude filtered into Washington. Politicians could no longer depend on their contribution to the party's collective performance to assure their personal success in the next election. Instead, they had to cultivate their voters with personal services and intensive campaign advertising.[29] Many plausible explanations have been advanced for the rise of divided government, for which full consideration would lead us far afield.[30] However, the simple fact is that divided government in Washington involves voters splitting their ballots and choosing candidates from both parties. Hence, the rise of both divided party control of government and going public can be located in weakening party loyalties.

With voters' choices up for grabs, mobilization has been of less importance. State party organizations consequently have had less to offer and a weaker claim for control of party affairs. Since the 1940s the parties' national committees had been steadily weakening, and in the late 1960s the nominating convention was reformed to strip state organizations of the control they once had. Delegates were to be selected in primaries or highly public and open caucuses, and at the convention the majority of a state delegation could no longer control all of its delegates. Among those who benefited from the parties' decline, of course, were those self-styled outsiders who would never have received their party's endorsement.

Some of these trends have begun to reverse: since the mid-1990s marginally more voters identify with one of the political parties, although

Independent remains a highly popular choice. And identifiers are somewhat less likely to split their ballots. Whether these countertrends will continue and if so, whether they will alter the strategic calculus of presidents, remains unclear. Certainly, we have already reported numerous cases of Clinton and Bush enthusiastically engaging public relations; more evidence of this will be presented throughout the remainder of the book. And we shall be attentive to the possibility that with going public now a fixture in presidential leadership, other politicians in Washington have come to expect it and even insist that presidents follow this course.

In the next chapter we continue to explore the historical transformation of Washington from a community of institutionalized pluralism to one of individualized pluralism with respect to one special relationship—that between the president and the press. The evolution of this relationship, containing all the elements of old and new Washington, is special in that it plays a pivotal role in the development of going public as an alternative style of presidential leadership.

NOTES

1. William A. Robinson, *Thomas B. Reed, Parliamentarian* (New York: Dodd, Mead, 1930), 100–101.
2. Nelson W. Polsby and Aaron B. Wildavsky, *Presidential Elections,* 2nd ed. (New York: Charles Scribner's Sons, 1968), 80–81.
3. For a discussion of the Senate's special role in spawning presidential candidates and, in the process, incubating new policy issues, see Nelson W. Polsby, *Political Innovation in America* (New Haven: Yale University Press, 1984).
4. Nelson W. Polsby, *Consequences of Party Reform,* (New York: Oxford University Press, 1983), 64.
5. At the 2000 Democratic convention 18 percent of delegates served as super delegates. Nelson W. Polsby and Aaron B. Wildavsky, *Presidential Elections,* (Lanham, Md.: Rowman and Littlefield, 2004), 131–132.
6. Polsby describes the reforms and convincingly argues their effects on the kinds of presidents elected in *Consequences of Party Reform.*
7. William Cavala, "Changing the Rules Changes the Game: Party Reform and the 1972 California Delegation to the Democratic National Convention," *American Political Science Review* 68 (March 1974): 27–42.
8. Richard B. Cheney, "The Law's Impact on Presidential and Congressional Election Campaigns," in *Parties, Interest Groups, and Campaign Finance Laws,* ed. Michael J. Malbin (Washington, D.C.: American Enterprise Institute, 1980), 238–248. On growing PAC participation in presidential elections, see Sara Fritz, "Changing Rules in Game of Politics Shaping Races," *Los Angeles Times,* December 22, 1983, 1.
9. Joseph Bruce Gorman, *Kefauver: A Political Biography* (New York: Oxford University Press, 1971), 80–106. For an account of the rise of Kefauver as an overnight television personality, see G. D. Wiebe, "Responses to the Televised Kefauver Hearings," *Public Opinion Quarterly* 16 (summer 1952): 179–200.
10. Jimmy Carter, *Keeping the Faith* (New York: Bantam Books, 1982). For a more detailed treatment of the rise of outsiders, see Samuel Kernell, "Campaigning, Governing, and the

Contemporary Presidency," in *The New Direction in American Politics,* eds. John E. Chubb and Paul E. Peterson (Washington, D.C.: Brookings Institution, 1985), 117–141.

11. Martin Tolchin, "Baker Reported Planning to Quit Senate After '84," *New York Times,* January 11, 1983, Al.

12. Haynes Johnson, *The Absence of Power* (New York: Viking, 1980), 159–161.

13. Ibid., 166–167.

14. Ibid., 22.

15. Norman Ornstein and John Fortier, "Relations with Congress," *PS: Political Science and Politics* 35:1 (2002): 47–50.

16. David W. Brady and Craig Volden, *Revolving Gridlock,* 2nd ed. (Boulder, Colo.: Westview, 2006).

17. Dana Milbank and Amy Goldstein, "Campaign v. Senate Democrats Planned," *Washington Post,* May 26, 2001.

18. Walter J. Oleszek, "The Context of Congressional Policy Making," in *Divided Democracy,* ed. James A. Thurber (Washington, D.C.: CQ Press, 1991), 99.

19. "Presidential Veto Message: Product Liability—Bill Rejected Over Consumer, State Issue," *CQ Weekly,* May 4, 1996, 1253.

20. James H. Rowe, Oral History Interview, 1969 and 1970, Harry S. Truman Library, Appendix.

21. "Oral History of the Truman White House," 1980, Harry S. Truman Library.

22. Daniel E. Ingberman and Dennis A. Yao, "Presidential Commitment and the Veto," *American Journal of Political Science* 35 (May 1991): 351–389.

23. David E. Rosenbaum, "In Appeal for Support for Budget, President Calls Plan Best for Now," *New York Times,* October 3, 1990, A1.

24. Michael Oreskes, "Advantage: Democrats," *New York Times,* October 29, 1990, A14; Maureen Dowd, "From President to Politician: Bush Attacks the Democrats," *New York Times,* October 30, 1990, A13.

25. Bob Woodward, *The Agenda* (New York: Simon & Schuster, 1994).

26. Robert Brownstein, "Washington Outlook, Clinton's Political Recovery Will Be Fleeting Unless He Sticks to Course," *Los Angeles Times,* December 4, 1995.

27. Robin Toner, "Budget Battle Has Come Down to a Game of Chicken," *New York Times,* November 12, 1995.

28. Dennis Farney, "Clinton Seems to Have Emerged in Good Shape from the Blame Game Over the Budget Impasse," *Wall Street Journal,* November 21, 1995.

29. Morris P. Fiorina, *Divided Government,* 2nd ed. (Boston: Allyn and Bacon, 1996).

30. For a careful inspection of the alternative causes, see Gary C. Jacobson, *The Electoral Origins of Divided Government: Competition in U.S. House Elections, 1946–1988,* (Boulder, Colo.: Westview, 1990).

The President and the Press

O n May 18, 1937, with some two hundred reporters packed around the president's desk in the Oval Office, Franklin Roosevelt opened his normal Tuesday press conference by saying,

> Off the record, wholly off the record. I wanted to tell you a story that I think you ought to know because it does affect the press of the country. . . . As you know, I have always encouraged, and am entirely in favor of, absolute freedom for all news writers. That should be and will continue to be the general rule in Washington.[1]

He then pulled out the latest pink sheet (the color signifying "not for publication") from the McClure Syndicate to approximately 270 member newspapers, and began to read:

> Unchecked. A New York specialist high in the medical field is authority for the following, which is given in the strictest confidence to editors: Toward the end of last month Mr. Roosevelt was found in a coma at his desk. Medical examination disclosed the neck rash which is typical of certain disturbing symptoms. Immediate treatment of the most skilled kind was indicated, with complete privacy and detachment from official duties. Hence the trip to southern waters, with no newspapermen on board and a naval convoy which cannot be penetrated.
>
> The unusual activities of Vice President Garner are believed to be in connection with the current situation and its possible developments. "Checking has been impossible." [2]

Then Roosevelt read another pink-sheet item that reported on a conversation at a private New York dinner party in which an official of American Cyanamid called the president "a paranoiac in the White House"; he declared that "a couple of well placed bullets would be the best thing for the country, and that he would buy a bottle of champagne as quick as he could get it to celebrate the news." In the ensuing conversation with reporters, the president revealed that the editor responsible for the stories was Richard Waldo. Waldo, who is better remembered for having originated the Good Housekeeping Seal of Approval, was not a Washingtonian and clearly must have felt he had little to lose by taking on the president.[3] After about fifteen minutes, Roosevelt closed the discussion by reminding the reporters, "It is all off the record; all strictly in the family and nothing else."[4]

Institutionalized pluralism requires continuous face-to-face negotiations among partisan participants and inculcates strong norms of propriety. Cordial relations are functional. This incident reveals, however, that politics in this former era—especially when outsiders were involved—could be just as virulent as anything the egoism of individualized pluralism can produce. As startling as the episode must have been to the men and women gathered around the president's desk, it is, nonetheless, indicative of the FDR system of presidential-press relations, examined later in this chapter. It also shows how the normative order of the day dealt with deviant behavior.

Consider first that Roosevelt made his remarks "in confidence" to the regular assemblage of the Tuesday press conference. No effort was made to recruit sympathetic reporters. Nor did he have to resort to any hidden-hand strategies; the standard dictum "off the record" sufficed. Yet if Roosevelt did not wish his remarks to become news, why did he tell newspaper reporters? Two motives are possible. First, it is apparent on careful reading of his statement that FDR sought retribution against McClure's editor—not at his own hands, but at those of the Washington press corps. When asked, he did not hesitate to reveal the culprit's name. Roosevelt's fellow community members did not let him down.

Organically integrated societies commonly banish those guilty of serious violations of community norms, and Washington was no exception. The White House correspondents could not run Waldo out of town, but they could strip him of standing. Some tried to have him expelled from the National Press Club. When brought before the club's board of governors to answer charges, Waldo threatened to sue everyone present. According to one account, "The board members naturally hesitated." Although no formal action was taken, Waldo left the club.[5] The confidentiality of the president's remarks kept the story off the pages of the nation's newspapers and successfully summoned forth community sanctions.

A second, probably less immediate reason for giving this off-the-record information to reporters may have been to elicit the press corps' sympathy. Setting White House correspondents against this New York editor strengthened Roosevelt's ties with them and loosened theirs with distant editors. With most of the nation's newspapers and chains on record opposing his election in 1932 and again in 1936, Roosevelt made a special effort to generate good will among the working press in Washington. He largely succeeded. In consequence, Roosevelt enjoyed a more productive relationship with the press corps, over a longer time, than any president before or since.*

---

* Roosevelt's relations with the press were not twelve years of uninterrupted bliss, however. Both the president and the press at times felt abused by the other. On one occasion, for example, the president went so far as to award an absent reporter the iron cross for a derogatory story on the newly formed Women's Army Corps.

THE BARGAINING PRESIDENT AND THE PRESS

As traditionally conceived, presidential leadership flows through quiet diplomacy and is generally ill served by public pressure on bargaining partners. Why, then, should favorable press relations have been important to Roosevelt? The reason is that news contributes to pluralist leadership and affects the way elite relations are conducted. Close ties to the working press were, in fact, more highly valued in Roosevelt's time than they are today.

The universal "law of anticipated reactions" dictates that politicians in Washington will pay attention to their publics in deciding what stance to take with the president. Before scientific surveys were widely available, a politician's mail and the newspapers of the constituency substituted for public opinion. A favorable press may have only fostered an illusion of support, but frequently it sufficed. Also, prominent journalists serve as important opinion leaders in establishing the president's reputation. In Roosevelt's time the appraisals of Arthur Krock, David Lawrence, Walter Lippmann, and others were given close scrutiny by Washingtonians; others who would later take on this responsibility include David Broder, Joseph Kraft, James Reston, and Richard Strout.

The bargaining president can use press coverage in a variety of ways to improve his position. By making an issue newsworthy, he can force other negotiators to deal with it.* The president may selectively release information that enhances his position and diminishes that of his bargaining partner. By assuming a firm public posture on an issue, he can stake out a negotiating stance that everyone recognizes cannot be easily abandoned. The president can float a trial balloon from which he may identify coalition partners and test potential avenues of compromise. Many of these activities have precedents reaching far back into the nineteenth century. Unlike purely public strategies of leadership, none requires a communications infrastructure that gives the president instant access to millions of citizens, and all are directed toward the bargaining table.

To appreciate why pluralist arts are sometimes publicly practiced, one must understand the rationale of the constitutional structure and how news serves the presidency. Montesquieu's proposition that unchecked power is inherently corrupt preoccupied the Founding Fathers as they deliberated a new constitutional order. Reasoning that in a democracy tyranny requires collusion, they dispersed governmental authority wherever possible. The result was, and is, autonomous institutions with formal relations among them. On reading the Constitution, the capital's planner, Pierre L'Enfant, concluded, "No

---

* It has been suggested that Roosevelt used his press conferences at times to complement his public strategies. Graham J. White notes that initiatives announced during Roosevelt's fireside chats were followed by background briefings for the press to sustain public interest and to prepare the ground for a formal message to Congress. See *FDR and the Press* (Chicago: University of Chicago Press, 1979), 20–22. Wilfred E. Binkley argues against the perception that all Roosevelt had to do was "glance toward a microphone" and a "congressional delegation would surrender." Instead, he credits much of Roosevelt's early success with Congress to the way he worked the Washington press corps. See *President and Congress,* 3rd ed. (New York: Vintage, 1962), 305.

message to nor from the President is to be made without a sort of decorum." Accordingly, there was little reason to place the Capitol and the White House on the same hill.[6]

Despite continuous interaction today, the institutional distance created between Congress and the presidency two hundred years ago has not been greatly shortened. Even as informal, face-to-face negotiation occurs, it is commonly preceded and facilitated by the preparatory public activities institutional distance encourages. As Douglass Cater has noted, "Unofficial communication between the executive and legislative branches of government—and within each branch—goes on regularly through the press, well in advance of official communications." [7] Woodrow Wilson was surely correct when, as president, he observed, "News is the atmosphere of politics." [8] This is why a devout bargainer like Franklin Roosevelt would be so attentive to the Washington press corps.

The conspicuous deficiency of professional good will between modern presidents and the Washington press has prompted some historians and journalists whose careers spanned the administrations of Franklin Roosevelt and Richard Nixon to reexamine the "secret" of Roosevelt's success. These chroniclers give the Great Depression and the New Deal much of the credit.[9] Never before during peacetime, they have written, had the country looked so intently to Washington to solve its problems.

For reporters, the rise of Washington as the center of the nation's politics meant that Washington bylines suddenly commanded front-page space. For the president, the times posed unprecedented responsibilities and opportunities. Roosevelt sought the cooperation of more elites than any president since Lincoln. Beyond Capitol Hill, old-line agencies had to be made compliant, if not enthusiastic, about implementing the many New Deal programs. Interest groups had to be attracted to the programs. In a few instances, such as the formation of the Tennessee Valley Authority, altogether new constituencies had to be mobilized.[10] The federal courts—from those in the districts to the Supreme Court—had to be converted from the sanctity of the Constitution's contract clause that threatened to paralyze much of the administration's interventionist economic program.[11] Because the president needed to enlist so many persons dispersed throughout government, Washington correspondents could play a major role in helping Roosevelt sell the New Deal.

The urgency of the times explains what brought the presidency and the Washington press together, but it fails to account fully for the productive relationship that ensued. The rest of the explanation lies in the convergence of interests between a newly professional press corps and the presidency. The kind of relationship revealed in the news conference of May 18, 1937, served the emerging needs of both the president and the press.

From the late nineteenth century to Franklin Roosevelt's inauguration, Washington correspondents evolved from an amorphous collection of visiting editors, reporters on temporary assignment, and disguised job seekers to a stable community of professional journalists.* This professional development held consequences for a president seeking influence. Where Roosevelt excelled—and where his predecessors distinctly did not—was in recognizing correspondents' *professional* stake in a particular kind of news conveyed in a particular way. From his first day in office, Roosevelt understood this—better, one can add, than some of the correspondents' editors, who could not fathom why their reporters were toeing Roosevelt's line rather than that of their home paper.

To appreciate how the mutual interests of the president and the press formed a basis for reciprocity, one needs to understand the modern evolution of the Washington press corps. Because the institutional development of Congress has been well plotted in the political science literature,[12] it in large measure informs one's conception of the workings of institutionalized pluralism. What is largely unknown is that the development of the press corps since the late nineteenth century—a far less well-documented story—follows a parallel course and similarly contributes to the transformation of Washington into a community of institutional actors.

This is also an ideal arena for examining the refinement of bargaining leadership because presidential exchange with the press appears thoroughly, though subtly, rooted in the institutional needs of each participant. When a president cuts a quick deal with the head of a powerful committee, one is afforded only a brief and superficial glimpse of the bargaining arts. Anyone anywhere can horse trade. By contrast, the workings of tacit, ongoing reciprocity agreements described below show how pluralist leadership is embedded in the institutional milieu.

Finally, this historical survey introduces key elements in the breakdown of institutionalized pluralism. Better than any other pairing in Washington, the modern evolution of presidential-press relations describes the recent transformation of the Washington community and the rise of presidents who routinely go public.

EMERGENCE OF THE WASHINGTON PRESS AS AN INSTITUTION

Early Professionalization

Shortly after Henry Adams arrived in Washington in 1868 to pursue a career in journalism, he followed the established protocol of paying respects to the president. Adams's visit to the White House was uneventful, but that it happened at all reveals a lot about the size and pace of the Washington community in the late 1860s. "In four-and-twenty hours," reported Adams, a young man "could know everybody; in two days, everybody knew him." [13]

---

* In 1918 the editors of *The Nation* used the obituary of a prominent correspondent as occasion to criticize this practice of political jobbing. "The pernicious habit of appointing Washington correspondents to political office has also had a good deal to do with the loss of prestige of the correspondents' corps" ("Washington Correspondents," *The Nation*, November 30, 1918, 638).

President Andrew Johnson could take an informal approach to press relations because there were fewer correspondents in those days and they were not
so interested in him. Whereas about four-fifths of modern reporting of
Congress and the presidency is devoted to the latter, the opposite pattern was
the case throughout most of the nineteenth century. A study of Washington
reporting in the newspapers of one midwestern city found closer scrutiny of
congressional committees than of the presidency.[14] To discern the origins of the
Washington press corps, one must therefore look to Capitol Hill.

The press corps had gained official recognition during the late 1850s when
control over credentials to the House and Senate press galleries was turned
over to a committee of correspondents, and registered journalists began to be
listed in each year's official *Congressional Directory*. In 1868, fifty-eight
reporters were so listed. By Adams's death in 1918, the number had more than
quadrupled.

Growth contributed to the professionalization of the Washington press
corps, but as long as growth was accompanied by high turnover, the
Washington assignment remained little more than a revolving door. Above all,
professionalization required a stable membership. Though it is impossible to
state definitively what increased stability and promoted professionalization at
the turn of the century, biographical sketches and circumstantial evidence contained in gallery listings suggest several influences. One is that the number of
papers that pulled out of the press gallery declined sharply after the turn of the
century.* Also, one suspects that veteran correspondents were valued for their
personal contacts with officials. These contacts increasingly became a resource
that gave Washington correspondents an advantage over their would-be
replacements.†

By the early 1900s, reporters viewed Washington as a choice assignment.
Many correspondents were sent to Washington after years of service on local
and state political beats, often returning home to positions as their paper's
managing editor. The Washington assignment had become an important step
in career advancement.[15] The status of the Washington correspondent must
have been secure by the 1920s when press chronicler Silas Bent remarked,

---

* Before 1880 well over half of the papers represented by correspondents listed in the *Congressional
Directory* closed their Washington offices within two years. Less than 10 percent did so in 1930.

† By the 1930s when Franklin Roosevelt arrived on the scene, government contacts had become a
critical underpinning of the correspondent's professional stature. Raymond P. Brandt noted:

> The good Washington reporter has news sources which he does not discuss by name, even
> with his own colleagues. They are the key men in the various departments who can be
> called on by telephone or met at lunch or on the golf course. They are the officials who give
> the real "off the record" information. They know the existence of a little known public
> document, or what their chief is about to do. They are the men who stay on in Washington
> regardless of whether the Democrats or Republicans are in power. Their cultivation is a
> matter of years. They must know their trust will not be betrayed.

"The Washington Correspondent," *Journalism Quarterly* 13 (June 1936): 176.

TABLE 4-1 **Turnover among Washington Correspondents, Selected Years, 1864–1932**

	1864–1866	1876–1878	1890–1892	1900–1902	1914–1916	1930–1932
Turnover (%)						
Departing	75	52	37	34	34	22
New[1]	70	59	36	34	35	26
Distribution of all correspondents, by clients (%)[2]						
Single paper	100	85	66	62	51	48
Syndicate	0	0	15	9	14	30
Multiple papers	0	15	19	29	35	22
Total number of correspondents	51	132	151	159	200	351
Percent leaving over two-year period, by client						
Single paper	75	56	41	40	44	22
Syndicate	—	—	26	29	38	25
Multiple papers	—	30	31	22	17	18

[1] New additions in gallery listings from first to second year.
[2] Calculated for first year of pair.

Source: Congressional Directory for each year indicated.

"The corps of correspondents there represents the very flower of the American press." [16]

Another, more significant development that stabilized careers was the practice of writing for more than one paper. Begun as early as the 1870s, this custom resulted in consistently lower turnover rates for correspondents. Turnover declined sharply from the close of the Civil War to the election of Franklin Roosevelt (see Table 4-1). In 1864–1866, when all reporters worked for only one paper, 75 percent of the correspondents left Washington before the next session of Congress convened. By 1876, 15 percent of the gallery reporters listed in the *Congressional Directory* associated themselves with two or more papers, and turnover was down to 52 percent. By 1914, 35 percent of the listed reporters had multiple clients, and turnover was 34 percent. Turnover rates for correspondents between Congresses had been reduced to 22 percent by the early 1930s.

The trend toward working for multiple papers probably had a greater effect on career stability and professionalization than the numbers alone suggest. Many of the papers constituting multiple clients for a reporter came from smaller communities far from Washington and were only marginally interested in Washington coverage beyond that available from the wire services. Without being able to share the expenses of a correspondent with other papers, they probably would not have long maintained a Washington bureau. Also, multiple papers were a form of diversification through which reporters were able to reduce uncertainty. The more papers reporters could sign on, the less dependence they felt upon any one of them. Newspapers became, then, a market for correspondents, and the relationship changed from employer to client.*

Diversification and the establishment of client relationships fostered professionalism and set it on a course that would in time shape presidential-press relations. One conspicuous consequence was the posture of journalists toward politicians. In the past, when newspapers were as much party organs as business enterprises, correspondents served the party in the news they wrote. Absolute fidelity to the editorial position of the home paper was a prerequisite to the assignment. Client relationships, however, required flexibility on the part of reporters. While they perhaps had to be willing to color reports with whatever slant a paper's editor wanted, correspondents could ill afford to be too partisan lest they lose their appeal to other current and potential clients. Too close an association with a particular party line reduced correspondents' marketability. The more neutral the stance reporters could maintain, the better their market position.

In the 1920s Washington correspondents began writing about themselves—a self-absorption characteristic of blossoming professionalism. These articles and books are revealing in depicting correspondents largely shorn of personal partisanship. If they, as a class, held their subjects in any special regard, it was most likely one of cynicism. In 1927 Silas Bent wrote:

> Newspaper men are seldom men of strong convictions; their work seems somehow to militate against that. It is nothing unusual to see a Washington correspondent shift without the slightest jar from a newspaper of one political complexion to another of the opposite camp. . . . [H]ad it happened during the last century [it] would have provoked, almost certainly, cries of turncoat.[17]

---

* The trend toward multiple paper clients appears in Table 4-1 to have been arrested by the early 1930s. Although increased numbers of correspondents were writing simultaneously for two or more papers, they constituted a smaller share of the press corps. Two trends—one demographic, the other political—were at work. First, as America's cities continued to grow, more papers developed the circulation necessary to underwrite individual representatives in Washington. According to one study, the critical city size for Washington coverage during this era was fifty thousand to one hundred thousand. The number of cities in this population range increased sharply from the 1910 to the 1930 census. Second, with the nation's attention shifting to Washington in the late 1920s, more urban papers in all population classes began supplementing wire service news with individual coverage. Hence, over time the need for multiple clients to ensure job stability declined as well. On both points, see Malcolm M. Willey and Stuart A. Rice, *Communication Agencies and Social Life* (New York: McGraw-Hill, 1933), 168–170.

All professions strive to legitimize practice with creed, and the Washington press corps was no exception. At the same time that increasing numbers of Washington correspondents were working for multiple clients, growing syndicates, or neutral wire services, the concept of objective reporting came into vogue. The job of Washington correspondents, J. Frederick Essary explained in 1928, "demands of them scrupulous fairness and as near literal accuracy as may be possible, within human limitations, in the matter which is daily spread before their millions of readers." [18] Walter Lippmann was an early exponent of this "progressive" creed. In 1960 he served again as a bellwether for a new doctrine when he addressed the National Press Club and called for reporters to abandon mindless objectivity in favor of interpretation. From the 1920s through the 1950s, however, objective journalism reigned as the dominant ideology of the profession.[19]

Other trappings of professionalism, such as collegiality and collusive efforts to control the work environment, were also much in evidence during this era. There are many examples of the former, including the practice of "blacksheeting": reporters would informally divide up coverage of Washington events and share the carbon copies of their articles for others to rewrite for their home papers.[20] The formal expression of professional collegiality was the formation of professional societies, such as the Gridiron Club, the Press Gallery Correspondents Association, the National Press Club, and the White House Correspondents Association.

Creed, collegiality, and the recognition of collective goals all helped distinguish Washington correspondents as a separate and resourceful entity in the Washington community. Professional trappings would soon begin to alter the relations of these correspondents with the president.

Early Presidential-Press Relations

The nineteenth-century progenitor of the presidential press conference was the private interview, offered first by President Andrew Johnson (1865–1869) to selected reporters. Sensing that the public was reading published interviews more closely than his speeches, Johnson made it a practice during his impeachment trial to rebuke charges from Congress by summoning a sympathetic correspondent to the White House. Most of Johnson's nineteenth-century successors submitted to an occasional private interview.[21]

President William McKinley (1897–1901) attended to press relations more conscientiously than most of his predecessors. During important White House meetings reporters were frequently permitted to wait in an anteroom for interviews with the president's visitors. McKinley's staff also routinely gave reporters the president's speaking schedule and advance copies of his addresses. Personally, however, McKinley remained aloof, and any direct contact with the press was left largely to chance. Ida M. Tarbell described White House coverage during the McKinley years:

> It is in "Newspaper Row," as the east side of the great portico is called, that the White House press correspondents flourish most vigorously.

Here they gather by the score on exciting days and . . . watch for
opportunities to waylay important officials as they come and go.
Nobody can get in or out of the Executive Mansion without their
seeing him, and it is here most of the interviews, particularly with
Cabinet officers, are held. . . .

It is part of the unwritten law of the White House that newspaper men
shall never approach the President as he passes to and fro near their alcove
or crosses the portico to his carriage, unless he himself stops and talks to
them. This he occasionally does.[22] McKinley left ample room for innovation
in this realm to his successor—the man who called the presidency "the bully
pulpit."

Theodore Roosevelt (1901–1909) was probably the first president to
appreciate the value of public opinion in leading Washington. Certainly, he was
the first to cultivate close ties with Washington correspondents and consequently was the first important transitional figure in presidential-press relations. In his age, before "direct communication" via radio and television, public relations and press relations were operationally largely the same. Roosevelt
succeeded with the former because he was able to dictate such favorable terms
with the latter.

According to David S. Barry, a prominent correspondent of the era and a
Roosevelt favorite, the difference between Theodore Roosevelt and all the presidents who preceded him was that he read papers' treatment of the news more
than their editorials. Roosevelt "knew the value and potent influence of a news
paragraph written as he wanted it written and disseminated through the prop-
er channels."[23]

On his first day in office, Roosevelt summoned several representatives of
the wire services and enunciated a set of ground rules that would give the press
unprecedented access to the White House but leave him with a large measure
of control over what was printed. The president insisted that, above all, information given in confidence must remain confidential. "If you ever hint where
you got [the story]," Roosevelt warned, "I'll say you are a damn liar."[24] Anyone
who broke this rule would be banned from the White House and denied access
to legitimate news. Historian George Juergens described how Roosevelt maintained this hierarchical relation with the press.

He divided newsmen into distinct groups of insiders and outsiders,
and was unforgiving in banishing those he felt, justifiably or not, had
betrayed him. The fact that he could get away with such high-handed-
ness goes far to explain why he received the favorable coverage he did.
It did a journalist's career no good to be on the outside, not to know
what was going on. The reporter had every reason to play along if that
was the price for being informed. Of course the coercion only worked
because of the unequal relationship between Roosevelt and a not yet
fully mature press corps. Reporters in a later era, conscious of their

own prerogatives, would not have tolerated a president telling them who could have access to the news and on what terms. But this was a different game played by different rules.[25]

Theodore Roosevelt's approach to press relations may have greatly increased accessibility to the White House, but it also posed serious problems for the rapidly professionalizing correspondents. By retaining control over which stories could be reported and how, the president preempted journalistic discretion, a prerogative Congress had surrendered by the mid-nineteenth century. Looking back on Roosevelt's administration a decade later, Washington correspondents found intolerable his division of the White House press into "insiders and outsiders." [26] This practice created uncertainty, obviously for the outsiders because they were missing the stories, but also for the insiders because they could so easily be demoted to the ranks of the outcasts. Among professionals whose careers depended upon their access to political news, this could, of course, be devastating, which is precisely why the stringent rules were seldom violated.

Finally, Roosevelt, who sported a strict and complex ethical code, excoriated reporters who wrote for papers that held distinctly different editorial positions. As far as he was concerned, these men had "sold their ethics." It could be cause for banishment.[27] Roosevelt may have been a fan of the news business, as his biographers attest, but his attitude reveals a fundamental lack of appreciation for the emerging professional requirements of the Washington correspondent. This stance appears all the more arbitrary (and hence revealing), since it served no apparent strategic purpose.

Roosevelt could dictate the rules because, as Juergens noted, he was working with a still poorly professionalized press. Washington correspondents had neither a strong sense of their rights nor any means for enforcing them. During the next two decades, both of these deficiencies would be corrected.

The other important transitional figure in the development of presidential-press relations was Woodrow Wilson (1913–1921).[28] Like Roosevelt, a Progressive facing a conservative Washington, he also recognized the value of public opinion and sedulously set out to establish favorable relations with the press. In this case, the talent was missing, and instead of substantive reciprocity, the result was procedural reform.

Wilson extended to the press most of the prerogatives that Roosevelt had held back. Continuing Roosevelt's practice of frequent meetings, he opened them to all correspondents. The response, he discovered somewhat to his chagrin, was overwhelming. At one of his early conferences more than two hundred reporters—many of whom had never participated in a presidential interview—packed themselves into the Oval Office. This and his other meetings with the press proved to be unhappy affairs. Wilson considered reporters dullards, and they sensed his condescension. After two years of discomfort for all involved, Wilson quietly abandoned the weekly gatherings.

However unsatisfying for either party, those regular, open conferences yielded another significant advancement for the press corps. Roosevelt's small entourage of insiders, or "fair haired boys" as they would later be remembered, posed no problem for his rules of confidentiality, but Wilson's news conferences opened the door to violations. In 1913 a significant breach occurred. After Wilson had given his views "off the record" on current conditions in Mexico, the story appeared the next day on the front pages of several newspapers.[29] Recognizing the threat this incident posed to the future of the open conference, a group of reporters from the most respected papers and wire services met informally with the president's secretary, Joseph Tumulty, to rectify the situation. Out of their meeting came an agreement whereby the White House press corps would assume full responsibility for policing the president's news conference. Shortly thereafter, the White House Correspondents Association was formed with the mandate to establish standards of professional behavior and to regulate attendance at the conferences. Assuming collective responsibility, the profession gained control over its members and superseded White House regulation.

The next three presidents—Harding, Coolidge, and Hoover—experienced difficulties in the press relations they inherited from Roosevelt and Wilson. Each began well enough with a friendly announcement of frequent and open conferences. Within a few months, however, the press relations of each fell on hard times. Warren G. Harding (1921–1923) even caused some correspondents to voice concern over his incompetence with the freewheeling press conference format. When he finally made the anticipated egregious misstatement, which necessitated a White House retraction and a State Department disclaimer, Harding's aides decided the informal press conference was too risky. Subsequently, they insisted that all questions be written and submitted in advance. The correspondents complied, although privately many complained. With follow-up questions disallowed, spontaneity was lost, and the conferences became dull. Many reporters quit attending.

Calvin Coolidge (1923–1929) kept the written questions and added new stringencies. Correspondent Willis Sharp laid out the Coolidge ground rules:

> The correspondents may not say that they saw the President. They may not quote the President. They may not say that an official spokesman said what the President said. The information or views he gives out are supposed to be presented to the public without any indication of official responsibility. The correspondents are supposed to present these views as if they had dropped from heaven, and are wholly unprotected when, as has happened, Mr. Coolidge finds it expedient to repudiate them. As a climax the correspondents are forbidden to mention that a question asked at the conferences was ignored.[30]

He went on to report "murmuring among the correspondents," who especially disliked the requirement that the president could not be directly quoted without permission. This rule had been in place since President Wilson's conferences, but no president hid behind the "White House spokesman" as frequently as Coolidge. Again, the White House press complied, but in magazine articles some correspondents began to ridicule the practice. "The White House spokesman" became "the Presidential Larynx" and "the Figure of Speech."[31] For the first time, the press began to impose costs on an unaccommodating president.

By the time Herbert Hoover (1929–1933) was inaugurated, the complaints of the press about Coolidge's rules were widely known and shared by other Washington elites who had to transact business with him.[32] So when Hoover announced at his first press conference that he would liberalize the attribution rules and consult with the White House Correspondents Association on ways to improve the news conference, his remarks evoked jubilation from the press. Their glee was short-lived, however. None of the reforms were instituted, none of the promised consultations held.

Instead, Hoover managed to strain press relations further when he failed to acknowledge the great majority of questions submitted by the press and began favoring sympathetic journalists with choice stories. Twenty-five years earlier Theodore Roosevelt had gotten away with this practice, but by this time the correspondents had a clear sense of their collective interests. They retaliated. Hoover's favorites were dubbed the "White House Pen Men's Association." According to James E. Pollard, "Other [than the favored] correspondents were affronted and they not only refrained from writing favorably about Mr. Hoover but were impelled to write things that hurt him."[33] Singling out the president's favorite insider, one journalist sniped, "If Hoover is defeated, a large share of his unpopularity can be attributed to Mark Sullivan."[34] Theodore Roosevelt and Woodrow Wilson were transitional figures in advancing presidential-press relations; Harding, Coolidge, and Hoover proved to be demonstration cases of the implications for a president's options of the developing professionalism of the press.

Early Competition and Collective Interests

As the market between papers and correspondents emerged, reporters competed tacitly with one another for choice stories. Correspondents' growing independence from home editors increased their dependence on news sources—presidents included. Competition creates losers as well as winners, however, and unconstrained competition could be hazardous for budding careers.

The collective interests of the Washington press corps favored open news conferences over private presidential interviews. The reason was simple. Open news conferences gave no reporter undue advantage over another or permitted a president to divide and conquer. Within the first three decades of the century, the long-term, collective interests of the group achieved precedence over the short-term, competitive desires of its individual members, a mark of professionalization. In describing the professional needs of modern journalists,

Anthony Smith explained how, once established, standardized outlets for news are perpetuated:

> The tensions within the newsgathering process help to accentuate the dependence upon recognized channels and therefore the power of those channels over the shaping of news itself. Competition between reporters of different newspapers working at the same beat will ensure that they will not want to miss press conferences, announcements, or social functions at which principal makers of news or providers of information may be present. Competition will make them dissatisfied with the shared channels but will tend to entrench those channels in their importance.[35]

Accordingly, during Wilson's administration senior correspondents rushed in to protect open news conference when it appeared that a breach of confidentiality might end then; it also explains why Hoover was publicly derided when he showed favoritism in giving stories to correspondents. Moreover, as reporters invested heavily in the press conference format, they chafed under Harding's "written questions" rule and complained repeatedly of Coolidge's refusal to allow attribution. These professionals had a vested, collective interest in the integrity of the open press conference. The press conference became sacrosanct, not because it satisfied the competitive urges of journalists but precisely because it denied them.

As the Washington press corps solved the collective action problem and evolved into a corporate entity, its members attained standing within the Washington community that few could have hoped to achieve acting alone. Writing about this era in 1937, Leo Rosten observed, "Their help is sought by persons and organizations trying to publicize an issue; their displeasure is avoided. They are aware by virtue of the deference paid to them and the importance attached to their dispatches, that they are factors of political consequence." [36]

THE FDR SYSTEM: Hard News, Openly Conveyed

This chapter opened with a press conference that took place in 1937, early in the second term of President Franklin Roosevelt's administration (1933–1945). By most estimates the honeymoon between the president and the press corps had long ended. Still, it was evident that the mutual respect and professional intimacy begun at Roosevelt's first press conference four years earlier remained firm. Years later, near the end of his presidency, reporters would still attribute their continuing amity to the relationship he spawned in 1933.[37] By the mid-1950s, they were writing about it nostalgically.

When Roosevelt began his first news conference in 1933, he, like Wilson twenty years earlier, was met by a throng of more than two hundred reporters anxiously awaiting word as to how he planned to conduct business. Roosevelt began by announcing that he was dispensing with written questions. He then identified four classes of information that would be presented in these "delightful family conferences": (1) occasional direct quotations permitted only through written authorization from the White House; (2) press conference comments attributed to the president "without direct quotations"; (3) background information to be used in stories without a reference to the White House; and (4) "off the record" remarks not to be repeated to absent reporters. To administer the policy of authorized direct quotations and other relations with the press, Roosevelt appointed the White House office's first press secretary, Stephen Early.

When the conference ended, the correspondents applauded, the first time ever according to some veterans.[38] One seasoned reporter called it "the most amazing performance the White House has ever seen. The press barely restrained its whoopees . . . the reportorial affection for the president is unprecedented. He has definitely captivated an unusually cynical battalion of correspondents."[39] *Editor and Publisher,* the semiofficial scribe and gossip of the profession, was unrestrained:

> Mr. Roosevelt is a great hit among newspapermen at Washington. I rubbed my ears and opened my eyes when I heard hard-boiled veterans, men who had lived through so many administrations and been so disillusioned that there are calluses in their brain, talk glibly about the merits of the White House incumbent. If Mr. Roosevelt fails the craft, by any false word or deed, he will break a hundred hearts that have not actually palpitated for any political figure in many a year.[40]

That first day Roosevelt gave them what they had sought for more than a decade: assurance of hard news, openly conveyed. The president had made his pact with the Washington press corps.

Roosevelt strengthened the press conference in other ways. He met with the press frequently and routinely; only rarely did he depart from his biweekly, Tuesday–Friday schedule. By the time of his death in April 1945, Roosevelt had invited correspondents into the Oval Office on 998 occasions. Equally important to White House reporters, he used these conferences as occasions to make significant announcements. Reporters came expecting hard news. "He never sent reporters away empty-handed . . . [they] are all for a man who can give them several laughs and a couple of top-head dispatches in a twenty minute visit."[41] The White House correspondents not only appreciated the choice stories he saved for these gatherings, they also praised his "timing" and packaging in ways that enhanced an item's newsworthiness.[42] Frequently over the years, Roosevelt would go so far as to suggest how a story should be written, and rarely did the press find this spoon-feeding unpalatable.

For a talented pluralist president like Roosevelt, these delightful family conferences offered ample opportunity to employ his considerable interpersonal skills. The president was usually a model of cordiality. Even his harshest critics in the press corps freely conceded that they were treated fairly at these conferences.[43] Whenever Roosevelt complained about a particular article, he would frequently blame the paper's editor, whom he tactfully asserted must have put the correspondent up to it.[44] This technique reduced tension and gave the reporter a convenient way of dissociating himself from his paper's editorial stance.

Even the editors who occasionally traveled to Washington to observe these conferences and see "what had gotten into" the reporters were defenseless against the president's charm. Writing on an incident that took place shortly before Roosevelt's death, Walter Davenport described how one group of editors responded to the Roosevelt treatment:

> Now they [the editors] had come to Washington to be the guests of their reporters at one of America's own peculiar institutions—a Presidential press conference. They were just that—visitors. Outside, they might shout until windows broke but here they were bound by rule and precedent to be silent. Only an accredited correspondent may ask questions or make comment. . . . They stood closely grouped, tight-lipped, skeptical, narrow-eyed, as though alerted against the widely advertised charm. That is, at first. Gradually they softened, relaxed. At one of the President's early sallies . . . they grinned. Before it was over, the grin had become a chuckle.
>
> Then came that sudden "Thank you, Mr. President," after a lull, and their Washington correspondents took them by the arms and presented them to Mr. Roosevelt. . . . He shook their hands with tremendous vigor—this Tired Old Man. He thanked them for their gladly given support of the bond drive. He rejoiced to hear they were feeling well and he told them that, given time (laughter), he'd make good reporters of their Washington men (laughter).
>
> Presently they were plodding across the White House park toward Pennsylvania Avenue. For a few moments they were silent. Then one of them observed that he'd be damned. Another said that in his opinion the President was a wonder. The third said that, anyway, Mr. Harold Ickes [FDR's secretary of interior and outspoken press critic] was an old fool. And then with one accord, they began tearing Mr. Ickes apart.[45]

Roosevelt also strengthened the press conference by relying upon it almost exclusively. With but one exception, he did not give private interviews. That exception is significant, however, because it reveals the entrenched character of the normative system prevailing in the palmy days of institutionalized pluralism. On February 27, 1937, the *New York Times* published a private interview with Roosevelt by Arthur Krock, perhaps Washington's most carefully read columnist. According to Krock's account of the incident, the next press conference was an angry one. The reporters accused Roosevelt of favoritism, which he had made all the more unacceptable by extending to a bureau chief rather than to a member of the working press. J. Frederick Essary, by then a senior Washington correspondent, asked the president pointedly whether he planned to repeat such favoritism. Roosevelt promptly confessed his blame. "My head is on the block. Steve's [press secretary Early] head is on the block. I promise to never do it again." [46] During the next eight years he kept his word.

Elevating the press conference to a place of primacy, Roosevelt offered the Washington press corps all that its profession required in its relations with the White House. As the Krock incident shows, however, this arrangement was not without cost. It ceded to the press corps control over the relationship to a degree that no president had done in the past or would do in the future. A few years later when Harry Truman was similarly cross-examined at a news conference about an exclusive interview, again with Krock, he retorted, "I'll give interviews to anybody I damn please." [47]

That the profession got its hard news, openly conveyed, is apparent. To appreciate what Roosevelt gained in return, one must largely trust the compliments of correspondents and the testimonials of disgruntled conservative editors. What they indicate is that Roosevelt succeeded in splitting off Washington correspondents from the editorial stance of their papers.

Evidence of this phenomenon is readily available in the election preferences of these two groups in 1936. In the spring of that year, Leo Rosten conducted an informal survey of Washington correspondents to determine their preferences. Of the eighty-four he questioned, fifty-four named Roosevelt as their first choice. Tying for second with eight votes each were Republican pre-convention front-runners Arthur Vandenberg and Alfred Landon. Altogether the Republican candidates had the support of 31 percent of the correspondents against Roosevelt's 65 percent. [48] By contrast, during the fall campaign 61 percent of the nation's major newspapers endorsed Republican opponent Landon. [49] Throughout his twelve years in office Franklin Roosevelt lived with a hostile newspaper industry and a friendly press corps.

Transition from the FDR System

The popular thesis that FDR's sympathetic treatment was a result of the times was presented earlier in this chapter. The Great Depression and the New Deal created a moment in history when the natural inclination of the government to retain information and of the press to extract it gave way to reciprocity. As never before, the president and the press needed each other to accomplish their respective tasks. Daniel Boorstin observed that Roosevelt's frequent conferences "bred intimacy, informality, and a set of institutionalized procedures; before long the spirit of those press conferences became on both sides much like that of any other responsible deliberative body." [50]

The professional development of the Washington correspondent and the press practices Roosevelt established suggest, however, that systemic forces, unlike the crash of 1929, were also at work. Franklin Roosevelt succeeded with the press in the same way he succeeded with other Washingtonians. He

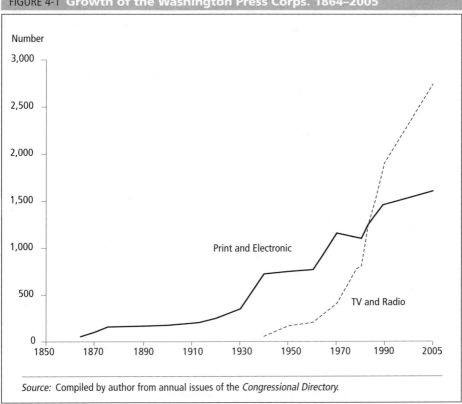

FIGURE 4-1 **Growth of the Washington Press Corps. 1864–2005**

Number

Source: Compiled by author from annual issues of the *Congressional Directory.*

founded a stable exchange relationship on the mutual professional needs of the participants.[51]

Given that the FDR system was rooted in the professional development of the Washington press, it seems ironic that these arrangements turned out to be fragile. Deterioration set in shortly after his departure not simply because Roosevelt's successors did not have his political acumen; the press conference declined because the needs of the participants changed. In different ways, advances in communications and transportation undermined the value of the FDR system for both the president and the press.

Radio, television, and air travel introduced the opportunity for presidents to engage in frequent, direct communication with the American public. No longer were they dependent upon the Washington press corps to convey their views to Washington and to the country. Going public would become a routine matter.

For the new breed of broadcast journalists who, as shown in Figure 4-1, grew rapidly in number and share of the press corps from 1940 on, Roosevelt's intimate family conferences held little attraction. As technology transformed the "press" into the "media," the press corps lost its corporate identity. "Hard news, openly conveyed" connoted something entirely different to broadcast journalists.

PRESS RELATIONS UNDER TRUMAN AND EISENHOWER

For Harry S. Truman (1945–1953) and Dwight D. Eisenhower (1953–1961), their styles and the needs of the press continued to shape presidential-press relations. Despite the manifold personal differences between Truman and Eisenhower, relations with the press retained a measure of continuity during the sixteen years after Roosevelt largely because of the professional correspondents' attachment to the FDR system.

When Truman came into office he promptly announced that he would continue FDR's ground rules. Although Eisenhower during the transition period considered dropping scheduled press conferences altogether, he, too, ultimately made few changes in the Roosevelt format. Truman's directness and occasional irascibility at times reduced the news conference to verbal sparring matches; Eisenhower's famous syntactical convolutions left reporters scratching their heads and conferring among themselves after a conference to determine what the president had said. Under both presidents, news conferences displayed the structure if not the substance of the Roosevelt press conference. Moreover, neither Truman nor Eisenhower regularly went beyond the news conference to woo reporters with private interviews or with other practices that would become commonplace in the 1960s.

What these presidents did do during their combined sixteen-year tenure was to take small steps, more as concessions to the broadcast industry than as political strategies, that would make the dismantling of the FDR system under John Kennedy appear to be little more than the next step in an incremental progression. Midway through his second term, Truman permitted radio broadcasts of recorded excerpts of his news conferences. This meant that the president would normally be speaking for the record.[52] Transcription had begun earlier as a convenience to the press, but now with his comments being heard nationally, it was of little consequence when he permitted the press to publish a paraphrased transcript of his remarks. In 1950, with international events bringing the press to the president's door in greater numbers, the conference was moved from the Oval Office to a larger room in the State Department, then across the street from the White House. Added to the fact that Truman reduced the number of meetings from two to one a week, many reporters unhappily came to feel that the press conference had become a more formal affair. To them it lacked the spontaneity, and ultimately the newsworthiness, of the Roosevelt news conference with which it was invariably compared.

Eisenhower further eroded the intimacy of press conferences by holding them less frequently—only twice a month on average (see Table 4-2)—and by

TABLE 4-2 **Average Number of Solo and Joint Press Conferences per Month, 1929–2006**

President	Type of Press Conference	
	Solo	Joint
Hoover (1929–1933)	5.6	0
F. Roosevelt (1933–1945)	6.7	0.2
Truman (1945–1953)	3.3	0.1
Eisenhower (1953–1961)	2.0	0
Kennedy (1961–1963)	1.9	0
L. Johnson (1963–1969)	1.9	0.3
Nixon (1969–1974)	0.6	0
Ford (1974–1977)	1.3	0
Carter (1977–1981)	1.2	0
Reagan (1981–1989)	0.5	0
G. H. W. Bush (1989–1993)	1.8	1.2
Clinton (1993–2001)	0.6	1.4
G. W. Bush (2001–)	0.4	1.6

Sources: Averages calculated from Tables 1 and 3 of Martha Joynt Kumar, "Presidential Press Conferences: The Importance and Evolution of an Enduring Forum," *Presidential Studies Quarterly* 35 (March 2005): 166–191. Professor Kumar kindly updated the published series beyond 2004 in personal correspondence.

Note: President George W. Bush series stops after July 2006.

admitting television film crews in 1955. Neither practice was, it turned out, as disruptive as it might have been. When the president sought to gain the attention of the American public, he did so directly in a prepared address. Moreover,

Eisenhower's press conference sputterings were hardly telegenic. After the novelty wore off, the networks rarely broadcast the entire conference.*

Robert Pierpoint, a veteran White House correspondent for CBS television, suggested also that in the 1950s television was not yet ready to make full use of presidential coverage. The news divisions of the networks were small, and until the middle of the next decade each network's evening news ran for only fifteen minutes.[53] Eisenhower's admission of filmed television altered presidential-press relations mostly by creating a precedent.

THE KENNEDY SYSTEM: Press Relations in an Era of Direct Communication

The real break with the Roosevelt system came with John Kennedy. Everyone in Washington recognized the new president's rhetorical talents and expected him to use them. They had first been surprised when he won over Protestant voters in the West Virginia primary; they next had witnessed the way his addresses on college campuses ignited enthusiasm among students for the New Frontier; and they had judged his television performance favorably in the debates with Richard Nixon. Everyone, including the television networks, was primed for a publicly active president. They were not disappointed. Kennedy's innovations in presidential-press relations departed radically from the past and formed what may be called the Kennedy system. It remains in place today.

The Kennedy Press Conference

In early December 1960, at the behest of President-elect Kennedy, press secretary Pierre Salinger privately solicited reporters' views on the possibility of having live, nationwide televising of press conferences. We do not know their initial responses, but later in the month when Salinger announced the new policy to the regular White House correspondents, the reaction was clear. Salinger described the scene:

> I shall never forget this press conference. I went right into the live TV decision. . . . As I explained the ground rules, a storm of protest came from the assembled reporters. . . . I heard the gravelly voice of Bill Lawrence, then the White House correspondent of the *New York Times*. I do not remember his questions but the introductory phrase is sufficient: "Mr. Salinger, as you plunge deeper and deeper into matters about which you know absolutely nothing. . . ." That did it. I didn't wait for the rest of the sentence. Now I was shouting back. It was the President's press conference—not theirs—and he would run it his own way. The decision was final. They could take it or leave it.[54]

---

* The standard procedure was for press secretary James Hagerty to give permission to the network for use of a given excerpt. This gave the White House the prerogative of censoring parts of the press conference. Reportedly, it was an option rarely invoked.

New York Times correspondent James Reston called Salinger's plan for live television "the goofiest idea since the hoola hoop." [55] The president's transition team clearly had a different view. Kennedy aide Theodore Sorensen displayed a conveniently poor sense of history when he asserted that the press conference was a forum "to inform and impress the public more than the press." And television, he added, "provided a direct communication with the voters which no newspaper could alter by interpretation or omission."* During the next several years, "direct communication" would become the leitmotif of those in the White House concerned with such matters. [56]

A significant factor motivating "direct communication" was Kennedy's awareness of its value in the event he were to lose favor with the press. This better explains the urge to go public, however, than the specific form adopted. He could have instituted, as Eisenhower press secretary James Hagerty had proposed nearly a decade earlier, regularly scheduled television addresses or fireside chats from the Oval Office. Such a format would have provided this highly telegenic president with control over the program's message and exposed him to none of the vagaries of reporters' questions or his own misstatements. But such an innovation was unprecedented; there is no evidence that it or any similar alternative was ever seriously contemplated by Kennedy's transition team. The reason Pierre Salinger and others probably thought only in terms of the televised conference is that it required so little innovation. The precedent for television cameras was already well established by 1960; all that had to be done was substitute the networks' film cameras with live ones. In seeking to extricate himself from the confining Roosevelt system, Kennedy adapted existing arrangements to new purposes. The innovative use of live television in this important instance was as much a political adaptation as a technological one.

The first live telecast of a presidential press conference, in late January 1961, drew 418 correspondents to the new State Department auditorium and an estimated prime-time audience of sixty-five million viewers. Virtually everyone who expressed an opinion agreed that the new president had done well. There was little doubt that live television would be a fixture in Kennedy's press conferences. The networks' news offices were happy. Even some of the newspaper correspondents extolled this innovation. Lester Markel in a *New York Times Magazine* article advocated more public activities by the president and the creation of a Department of Public Opinion within the White House. [57]

By summer, however, many newspaper reporters began to complain on grounds readily understandable to those who appreciate the virtues of the "private" press conference of an earlier era. Peter Lisagor of the *Chicago Daily News* compared the Kennedy press conference to "making love in Carnegie Hall."

---

* President Kennedy agreed: "I am convinced that the press will turn against me sooner or later while I am President, and I must have a way to get to the American people. So, therefore, I have to use television to get there, to speak directly to them when the press is so hostile" (cited in Blaire Atherton French, *The Presidential Press Conference* [Washington, D.C.: University Press of America, 1982], 13).

"A mess . . . disorderly, disorganized, almost chaotic" is the way he summed up the new press conference.[58] Others, like Clark Mollenhoff of the *Des Moines Register,* complained about the declining quality of the questions: "Too many of the questions are lobbed setups, and blooper balls, and there is too little effort to obtain any more than generalized information. I don't blame the President for knocking them out of the lot." He added, "Unless I have a specific question to ask, I rarely go any more." [59] A third correspondent offered the following summary assessment:

> In its new setting, blindingly lighted and amphitheatrical, . . . each reporter [tries] unvaliantly to capture the eye of the President.
> Random, inevitably, is the selection of questioners and even more random is the nature of the questions. Few significant queries are put and when one is posed, a follow-through is almost impossible.[60]

According to print journalists, television reporters "hammed it up" with long-winded questions, "thus cheapening the conference." [61] Lisagor added, the press had become merely "one of the props." [62]

Almost a decade later newspaper reporters would still be voicing many of the same complaints. A survey of prominent Washington journalists found most of them dissatisfied with the modern press conference, and television received much of the blame.[63] The complaints were chronic because the problem was structural. As background briefings and sustained questioning on issues gave way to presidential position taking and evasion, the print journalists lost their hard news. With television providing instantaneous transmission to the country, whatever fresh news came out of a press conference was stale by the time their stories were printed.

The press conference consequently matured into something quite different from the biweekly gatherings of Roosevelt. Robert Pierpoint's description of his preparation for the modern televised conference makes this clear:

> The presence of a vast audience magnifies the significance of any possible errors in questioning or in commentary afterward, and I always feel a slight sickness in the stomach and a sweatiness of the palms and forehead.
> After more than twenty years, I still go through a "psyching up" period, similar to that of a professional athlete before the big game. I read the morning newspapers and follow the news on radio and television, concentrating on the questions I will ask and the issues that could emerge at that day's conference. This means writing down a half dozen questions which the President should answer that day. I try to anticipate how each might be answered, phrasing the question carefully so the President cannot evade it. At the same time, questions must be designed to elicit genuine information or reactions of national importance. And finally, the questions cannot be so obscure or so

simple as to risk making me look foolish or to waste my colleagues' and the public's limited press-conference time.[64]

Expanded television coverage of the presidency has made celebrities of those who cover the White House for the networks.* Many of these men and women come to Washington after being newscasters for local television. On arrival they commonly draw six-figure salaries. To them "professionalism" is as likely to mean free agency as any collective interests of correspondents. The advent of live television brought into the press conference new participants who promptly became stars.[65] They assumed front-rank positions at the conference and vied aggressively with one another as well as with the newspaper correspondents for recognition from the president. And since they were the conduits through which he gained a spot on the evening news, they generally got it.

Another change, which makes the modern press conference more eventful, is its relative infrequency. Since Roosevelt, presidents have wondered how often they could go before the public and retain its attention. This consideration led Salinger to move Kennedy's press conferences off prime time to a normal midafternoon schedule. More generally, it has meant that they are conducted less frequently. Table 4-2 shows that in employing the conference to speak directly to the American people, Kennedy conducted fewer conferences on average per month than Eisenhower, and, more to the point, less than a third as many as Roosevelt. Since Kennedy, the average number of conferences per month has further declined. Full realization of the diminished status of the press conference had occurred during the Nixon presidency. Initially, his failure to meet with the press on average no more than once every two months was widely viewed as being a result of the particular circumstances of his administration—an early, muted suspicion that matured into an ardent hostility between the president and the press. But the continued erosion of the formal press conference under Ford, Carter, and Reagan and its virtual replacement with impromptu, brief, question-answer sessions under Bush and Clinton suggest that the reduced status of the press conference has resulted more from changes in the system of presidential-press relations than from personal styles or transient political conditions.

Once the news conference failed to provide a steady diet of hard news, it quickly lost standing among print correspondents. Over the years journalists have offered numerous proposals to resurrect aspects of the FDR system.[66] For their daily stories, however, they began to look elsewhere in the White House and in the agencies for presidential stories. Consequently, when the press con-

---

* According to Alan L. Otten ("Whose Conference?" 44):

> With televised press conferences, every reporter sees himself as a television personality. Since he doesn't want to boot his moment in the camera's eye by stumbling over a spontaneously phrased question, he usually has his query prepared long in advance—often not so much a question as a long speech—and he asks it even if it is completely irrelevant to everything that's gone before and even if some earlier answer is crying for clarification.

ference became moribund for long stretches under Nixon and Reagan, who preferred political travel and nationally televised addresses, the complaints came most heavily from among network correspondents rather than print journalists.

The Local Press and the Private Interview

As the press conference became yet more formal under the glare of studio lights, Kennedy introduced other avenues of access to the press. For the most part, these innovations gave the president greater control over the content of information the press received. One such innovation was special, informal news conferences with publishers and reporters of papers from a particular state or region. With Kennedy these generally took the form of White House luncheons. Every subsequent president has adopted some variant of Kennedy's innovation.

Another innovation, if it may be called that, was the frequent use of the private interview. As senator, Kennedy was reputed to have had more friends in the press than in the Senate. As president, he continued his close personal associations with Charles Bartlett of the *Chattanooga Times* and Ben Bradlee, then with *Newsweek*. He also conducted private interviews with such notables as James Reston of the *New York Times* and columnist Joseph Alsop. A perquisite of friendship with Kennedy was special access to stories. According to one source, "Any of a dozen Washington hands have access to the President's Oval Office . . . where, in the old days, an [Ernest K.] Lindley or an Arthur Krock could count on guidance 'at the highest level' only on the rarest occasions, the newsmen count on it almost weekly." [67] Network correspondents were not to be excluded. Before long, Kennedy opened the Oval Office to television crews for taped interviews.

Initially, this practice—a single instance of which had put FDR's "head on the block"—raised the ire of many members of the writing press more than did the televised press conference. Reston had personally warned the president-elect that private interviews might generate too much ill will. (Later, after becoming a favored insider, he recanted.)[68] Lisagor, whose distaste for the Kennedy system has already been recorded, called it "a baneful thing—a reporter ought to keep a public official at an arm's length." [69]

As Kennedy's sessions with the press neared the end of the first year, the expected question finally surfaced: Did not the president think it unfair to feed stories to the favored few? Obviously groping, Kennedy replied: "I think—yes, I will let them [his staff] know, and I think I ought to. I don't think there should be discrimination because of size or sex or another reason." [70] Spoken like lip service.

Routine use of the exclusive interview, cultivation of the press outside Washington, and live telecasts of news conferences constitute the Kennedy system. Each feature violates some ground rule of institutionalized pluralism upon which its predecessor, the FDR system, had been founded. Exclusive interviews with correspondents frustrate the profession's collective interests, at least as the Washington press corps was formerly constituted. Special attention to publishers and reporters from outside Washington denies the insularity of community relations and may arouse suspicion that the president is trying to replace negotiation with public pressure. From the perspective of institution-alized pluralism, the live telecast of news conferences is the most objectionable of all. Its antithetical nature was summed up earlier in Sorensen's naive remark that the forum was intended more to inform the public than the press. With television, the Kennedy system corrupted this centerpiece of the FDR system. And by introducing new—and, from the perspective of the White House, more manageable—avenues of contact with the press, the Kennedy system depreci-ated the status of the news conference.

THE KENNEDY SYSTEM AS A MODEL FOR PRESIDENTS WHO GO PUBLIC

During the past forty-five years, encompassing nine presidents, the Kennedy system has remained the working model of presidential-press relations. To the degree it has changed at all, the system reflects more the forces it set in motion than any new ideas of Kennedy's successors. As the formal press conference has withered, Kennedy's alternative forms of press relations have thrived. Precise numbers for each administration are difficult to come by, but Ronald Reagan's 194 press interviews and 150 special White House briefings of the press from outside Washington during his first three years indicate sharply increased growth in the use of this news outlet since the Johnson administration.*

The development of satellite communications permitting instantaneous transmissions from the White House to local news stations around the coun-try has created a booming market for White House communications beyond Washington. The business between local Washington television producers and stations throughout the country has been burgeoning as well. Local television news coverage offers several advantages over presidents' traditional news out-lets. First, it allows the White House to segment the market—"to narrowcast its

---

* The figures for personal interviews come from Lou Cannon, "Phantom of the White House," *Washington Post,* December 24, 1984, 25. In Mark Hertsgaard, "How Reagan Seduced Us," *Village Voice,* September 18, 1984, 12, a White House aide offered the following description of a typical briefing:

> You'd bring in 80 or 90 [journalists], maybe from a certain part of the country . . . and invite anchormen or news directors from major markets and the editors of major newspa-pers. And this is how some press people from a little town in North Dakota or somewhere like that come to see things. And they're thrilled to come. We take them up to our main briefing room and have maybe 25 camera crews from local stations and then put on a real good program for them. . . . Then we take them over to the State Dining Room for a real good lunch with the president, and they are all very pleased to come to the White House, it's a nice trick.

message to a very specific audience," in the words of one Reagan staffer.[71] Second, these newscasters are interested in presidential activities to which the networks and even local press pay little attention. The presidency is a ceremonial office. From it flows an endless stream of medals, commendations, and sometimes just salutations. Private citizens from all over the country come to the White House daily to receive the president's congratulations. For local television bureaus, these happy, often sentimental rituals offer wonderful local color. Of importance to the White House, the president is invariably cast as a sympathetic figure. The third advantage of local television coverage over traditional news outlets is that journalists for these bureaus, as recent arrivals with few prerogatives and an uncertain mandate, abide by White House instructions. The head of one of the largest local bureaus observed:

> The regular White House press corps is adversarial with the President in ways the locals are not. If the President is giving an award to a kid from Michigan for starting a community library, that is a good human-interest story for us. But if you get Sam Donaldson of ABC in on one of these things, he's going to ask the President . . . something. It becomes difficult for the President, and the White House doesn't like that.[72]

Many of the local bureaus began setting up shop during Jimmy Carter's administration. Given their special attraction, Carter was understandably quick to invite them to the White House. It was left to the Reagan administration, however, to incorporate local television reporters fully into the ongoing routines of White House media relations. This innovation, wholly consistent with the premises of the Kennedy system, was one of the established routines of presidential-press relations under Presidents Bush and Clinton.

Presidents have adapted the Kennedy system to their personal styles in other ways as well, but none has altered the system's basic structure. As noted earlier, Lyndon Johnson constructed a television studio in the White House and obliged the networks to outfit it with cameras ready to broadcast on a moment's notice. Richard Nixon dismantled the studio, but to offset his numerous, rough dealings with the television networks and particularly the *Washington Post*, he dramatically expanded press relations outside of Washington.[73] Jimmy Carter went to the public in his own way, with informal but well-orchestrated town meetings. Ronald Reagan showed a special fondness for the radio. His Saturday afternoon broadcasts from the Oval Office were frequently compared with Roosevelt's famous fireside chats. As important as these and other practices have been to a given president's overall public relations program, they amount to little more than personal and ultimately transient enhancements of the Kennedy system.

What was lost to the press when the news conference became a forum for the president's direct communications to the country was not fully realized as gains to the White House. With the adoption of the Kennedy system, presidents extracted more from the traditional relationship founded on reciprocity than they contributed. Over time correspondents established a new equilibrium. No longer needing to defer to the president's representation of events and policies (their side of the bargain), White House correspondents assumed a more objective and distant stance toward the President. Within a few years, they would be characterizing his version of news as "spin." Certainly, the emergence of an adversarial press during these years can be attributed in part to President Johnson's Vietnam "credibility gap" and Nixon's Watergate cover-up; it appears bound to have followed presidents' strategic reformulation of their press relations. Consequently, adversarial presidential-press relations did not disappear as memories of Vietnam and Watergate faded into history.

Live television requires the president to be ever mindful of the public audience, and this setting necessarily gives rise to posturing. The correspondent's job consequently becomes one of "isolating fact from propaganda when a president seeks to use the press as a springboard to public opinion, as he does in a televised press conference." [74] Journalists no longer pay homage to unobtrusive, objective journalism. Instead, they speak of getting at the facts behind the president's statement or press release.* Senior Washington correspondent James Deakin remarked: "The White House reporter has one accepted role—to report the news—and several self-appointed roles. . . . I feel I'm there, in part, to compel the government to explain and justify what it's doing. A lot of people don't like that, but I feel we're the permanent in-house critics of government." [75]

The adversarial aspect of presidential-press relations is an elusive quality, difficult to quantify, and the systematic evidence on the subject is inconclusive.[76] From the testimonials of the sparring partners, however, the adversarial relationship appears to be a well-established fact of life. The arrival of less deferential correspondents, some of whom were media stars in their own right, frequently has turned the conference into an occasion of irritation and embarrassment for the White House. Although no president has yet been willing to excuse himself altogether from these encounters, none has been reluctant to tamper with its format and schedule in an effort to produce more favorable results.

As the Vietnam War heated up at home, President Johnson sensed that reporters were lying in wait for him at press conferences with loaded questions. To throw them off balance, he switched to impromptu and short-notice press conferences that gave reporters little time to arm themselves. To stave off embarrassing issues, Nixon occasionally limited questions to specified policy areas. (This change, however, was generally well received by many newspaper correspondents because it gave them the opportunity to pursue newsworthy issues in depth.) In early 1982 some of Reagan's aides believed that their pres-

---

* Fred Barnes, executive editor of the *Weekly Standard,* has described one of the "operating assumptions of the press" as being the view of many Washington reporters that "their job . . . [is] one of attacking, and if a president, say, retains high popularity, they take it as an affront" (cited in "Calling the Press on the Carpet," *Wall Street Journal,* August 21, 1985, 22).

ident was suffering from unflattering network "take-outs" of his noontime press conferences. They therefore rescheduled these conferences to later in the day, nearly doubling the television audience and reducing the time available to networks to edit the president's remarks. However the president's aides tweaked the schedule and format, it still failed to provide Reagan with a satisfactory arrangement. He conducted three such sessions in 1987 and four in 1988. By the end of his second term, the formal news conference had become an endangered species.

Preservation of the press conference, which appeared on a trajectory to extinction, became a *cause célèbre* of correspondents, if not with voters, during George H. W. Bush's first campaign for the presidency. Shortly after election day, a time when presidents-to-be are susceptible to acting out their elation rather than calculated self-interest, President-elect Bush announced that he intended to sharply increase the frequency of news conferences.

This decision proved imprudent. Bush's penchant for sentence fragments and disjointed phrasing did not serve him well on television. The White House sought to repair the problem by giving the press conference format its greatest overhauling since Kennedy's innovations. Instead of prearranged, frequently prime-time sessions, Bush called brief, impromptu morning sessions in which the networks were allowed a few minutes to assemble the cameras if they were interested in covering the conference.* Frequently they were not or could not, leaving Cable News Network as the only television outlet for many of these sessions. Without advance notice, many correspondents were absent as well. The result did not prove as controversial as one might think, probably because the president rarely brought hard news to the occasion. By the end of his first year in office, President Bush had conducted nearly several dozen miniconferences, compared with only one that followed the formal, prime-time format. Another innovation that, as shown in Table 4-2, has proved popular with his successors, is the joint press conference, usually accompanied at the podium by a foreign dignitary. The president and his guest generally open these sessions with statements. These sessions tend to be much briefer, more focused on some aspect of the countries' bilateral relations, with half of the questions coming from the guest's press corps. The consensus among Bush's aides that the traditional solo conference format invited "disaster" reinforced the administration's enthusiasm for these new approaches to engaging the press. So, up until the reelection campaign, he held only one more formal news conference.

To continue the point that the modern press conference is what the president makes it, Bill Clinton proudly counted 45 press conferences during his

---

* Instead, Bush appears to have thought he could return to the golden years of Roosevelt's press relations. One morning he sought to enlist the help of White House correspondents in propelling his legislative program through the Democratic Congress. "I urge you people to join me in calling out for congressional action," he said, adding that the Democrats deserved an "editorial pounding . . . to support the President as he tries to move this country forward." Thomas B. Rosenstiel, "The Media: Bush Plays It Cozy," *Los Angeles Times,* December 9, 1989.

first year in office. Nearly half, however, were of the joint variety. The number also included a new format the White House media office dubbed "video press conferences." These were satellite-based question and answer sessions with local reporters across different regions.[77]

THE MODERN TRAJECTORY
OF PRESIDENTIAL-PRESS RELATIONS

Presidents and reporters still jointly produce news, but it is no longer a collaborative undertaking. The modern relationship is one in which each side anticipates and responds to distant possibly exploitive actions of the other. The president's staff plans events and writes speeches with an eye to shaping the evening news story. Getting out "the line for the day" is, in fact, one of the principal activities of the contemporary White House staff; by one estimate more than a quarter of the staff is dedicated in some way to producing the president's public activities.[78]

Modern network news bureaus have developed a couple of techniques to resist presidential influence and to assert their own control over the content of presidential communication. First, network news executives appear to emphasize presidents' failures over their successes. Certainly, presidents think so. In 1993, when pointedly asked in a press conference why he thought his popularity had dropped 15 percentage points in only two months, President Clinton quickly shot back: "I bet not five percent of the American people know that we passed a budget . . . and it passed at the most rapid point of any budget in 17 years. I bet not one in 20 American voters knows that because . . . success and the lack of discord are not as noteworthy as failure." [79] Although the results of content analysis are subject to alternative explanations, such research consistently finds a heavier concentration of unflattering presidential news nowadays than during the 1950s through the 1970s. Perhaps the most exhaustive and systematic evidence on this score comes from the Center for Media and Public Affairs' ongoing analysis of network news coverage of national politics. Since 1989 the center's staff has scored every sentence of every presidential news story broadcast on one of the three major television networks' evening news programs. Their findings for coverage during the first hundred days in Figure 4-2 is revealing. Only President George H. W. Bush received more favorable than unfavorable coverage during this traditional "honeymoon" period, when the new incumbent is fresh from victory and has limited opportunity to get in trouble.*

---

* A more extensive analysis of the center's news content data found George H. W. Bush and Bill Clinton garnering mostly negative coverage throughout their first three years in the White House. Only in four of the twenty-four quarters did these presidents average as much favorable as unfavorable network news. Even during the first quarter of 1991, when the Gulf War lifted Bush's Gallup Poll approval rating to 88 percent, the president still barely managed to win mostly favorable coverage. By these standards, a president who musters a 40–60 ratio of favorable to unfavorable news is doing pretty well.

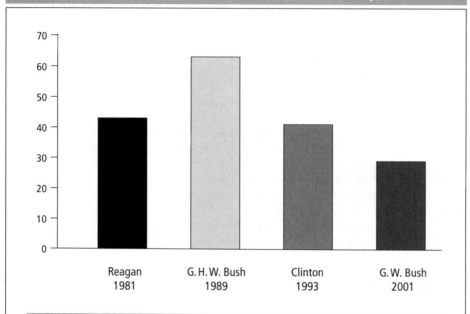

FIGURE 4-2 **Tone of Coverage for Four Presidents:**
Percent Positive Evaluations for First One Hundred Days in Office

Sources: Center for Media and Public Affairs analysis of evaluations by nonpartisan sources and reporters on the ABC, CBS, and NBC evening news; *Media Monitor* (May/June 2005): 4.

Note: Data for George H. W. Bush available only for the first fifty days.

A second network news practice that has limited recent presidents' ability to communicate with the public can be found in the way editors and reporters severely edit presidential statements and editorialize about their purposes. Reflecting this strategy is the amount of time allotted to the president on the evening network news. As late as 1968, he spoke on camera without interruption for an average of about forty seconds. Over the years this figure has dwindled to about nine seconds.[80]

At a conference of former presidential press secretaries I had occasion to raise the issue of the president's shrinking sound bite.[81] This led to an exchange between *NBC Nightly News* anchor John Chancellor and President Carter's press secretary, Jody Powell, which accurately characterizes the tension between modern presidents and the press. Compare the tenor of their remarks with that of Roosevelt's "family conference" with which we began our discussion:

> **Chancellor:** The fact is—I think television reporters out in the field, when presented with pre-packaged, pre-digested, plastic coated phrases and with no opportunity to question a president, want to get some-

thing that isn't just pre-packaged and pre-digested, and that's why you are getting a more contentious kind of reporting in the twenty seconds at the end of the spot. I had an argument with Tom Pettit during the 1988 election, and I said, "Why is it that all of our correspondents end their pieces with some little snippy, nasty saying? Why don't they just say, 'And tomorrow the president goes to Cleveland.' " And Pettit says, "It wouldn't come out that way. They would say, 'Tomorrow the president goes to Cleveland and no one knows why.' " So that you set up a kind of contest of who controls and all of this is done in a piece of television that runs about a minute-and-a-half. So you compress the political propaganda on the one hand, you increase the reactive hostility on the other hand, and that's what a minute-and-a-half television spot is today. I think both sides are probably equally responsible for it, but I think that the politicians started it.

Powell: I will just raise a logical question. Assuming that there are other things to do in a White House and now and then something else comes along that might keep you busy, why would you go to all of the trouble to do all of these things that we are talking about [in packaging the president's message] if you did not find yourself faced with a situation in which it's the way to deal with it? Why would you go to all of this trouble?

Are we supposed to believe that one morning ten, fifteen years ago somebody in the Johnson White House or the Nixon White House or whatever woke up and said, "We don't need to do this, but just for the hell of it, why don't we create this whole structure here about going out on the road and doing that sort of thing," or rather perhaps it was a reaction—maybe intelligent, maybe unwise, maybe in the public interest, maybe not. It was a reaction to a set of circumstances which they saw and said, "We've got to do something."

With presidents increasingly going public and with a more assertive press, contention over control will remain a fixture of the modern system. Pressure and competition have replaced professional reciprocity as the fabric of community relations.

Whether by cutting back the number of Washington press conferences or by minimizing their importance, modern presidents are clearly opting for more controllable means to communicate their views to the American public. Kennedy's innovations, private interviews and news conferences outside of Washington, remain prominent features of contemporary presidential media strategies. Presidents are also enlisting techniques that do not require the direct participation of reporters. Through television and speeches to gatherings of special constituencies, presidents can attract favorable news stories and direct press attention to particular issues and policies. These are venerable practices, of course, but whereas in the past they seemed to be desultorily planned outings from the White House, prompted as much by an invitation from some group as by any tactic initiated by the president, they are now part of the chief executive's weekly, almost daily, routine. In the next chapter we shall document the extraordinary growth in these news-generating activities over the past thirty years.

NOTES

1. Cited in Chalmers Roberts, "Franklin Delano Roosevelt," in *Ten Presidents and the Press*, ed. Kenneth W. Thompson (Washington, D.C.: University Press of America, 1983), 21.
2. Ibid. This incident is also reported in Olive Ewing Clapper, *Washington Tapestry* (New York: McGraw-Hill, 1946), 179–180.
3. Waldo continued as head of McClure until his death in 1943. "R. H. Waldo, Head of News Syndicate," *New York Times*, June 12, 1943, 13.
4. Roberts, "Franklin Delano Roosevelt," 22–23.
5. Clapper, *Washington Tapestry*, 180.
6. Cited in James Sterling Young, *The Washington Community: 1800–1828* (New York: Columbia University Press, 1966), 6.
7. Douglass Cater, *Power in Washington* (New York: Vintage, 1964), 224.
8. Ibid., 226.
9. Typical is Daniel J. Boorstin's "Selling the President to the People," *Commentary* (July 1955): 427.
10. See Philip Selznick, *TVA and the Grassroots* (Berkeley: University of California Press, 1948).
11. See Peter Irons, *The New Deal Lawyers* (Princeton: Princeton University Press, 1982).
12. Nelson W. Polsby, "The Institutionalization of the U.S. House of Representatives," *American Political Science Review* 62 (March 1968): 144–168; and H. Douglas Price, "The Congressional Career—Then and Now," in *Congressional Behavior*, ed. Nelson W. Polsby (New York: Random House, 1971), 14–27.
13. *The Education of Henry Adams: An Autobiography* (Boston: Massachusetts Historical Society, 1918), 253.
14. For the modern era, see Alan P. Balutis, "The Presidency and the Press: The Expanding Presidential Image," *Presidential Studies Quarterly* 7 (1977): 244–251. The findings for the nineteenth century are reported in Samuel Kernell and Gary C. Jacobson, "Congress and the Presidency as News in the Nineteenth Century," *Journal of Politics* 49 (November 1987): 1016–1035.
15. These generalizations come from the brief biographical sketches of members of the 1903 House gallery compiled by the Gridiron Club. Ralph M. McKenzie, *Washington Correspondents Past and Present* (New York: Newspaperdom, 1903).
16. Silas Bent, *Ballyhoo* (New York: Boni and Liveright, 1927), 85.
17. Ibid., 87.
18. J. Frederick Essary, "President, Congress, and Press Correspondents," *American Political Science Review* 22 (November 1928): 903.
19. Walter Lippmann, "The Job of the Washington Correspondent," *Atlantic*, January 1960, 47–49. An excellent treatment of objective reporting as an ideology can be found in Michael Schudson, *Discovering the News* (Chicago: University of Chicago Press, 1978), 121–159.
20. The modern variant of this time-honored practice is described vividly by James Deakin in *Straight Stuff* (New York: William Morrow, 1983), 131–132.
21. One president who refused to submit to press interviews was Grover Cleveland (1885–1889, 1893–1897). Instead, he communicated to the press, and through it to the public, with rou-

tine Sunday evening press releases. James E. Pollard describes how awkward exclusive reliance on this form could at times be in *The Presidents and the Press* (New York: Macmillan, 1947), 528.

22. Ibid., 558.

23. David S. Barry, *Forty Years in Washington* (Boston: Little, Brown, 1924), 270.

24. George Juergens, *News from the White House* (Chicago: University of Chicago Press, 1981), 17.

25. Ibid.

26. George H. Manning, "Liberalizing of President's Contacts with Press Hoped for from Hoover," *Editor and Publisher,* January 12, 1929, 6.

27. Juergens offers individual accounts of this requirement in operation in *News from the White House,* 23.

28. This account of Wilson's presidency relies heavily on Juergens, *News from the White House,* 126–166; and Pollard, *Presidents and the Press,* 630–696.

29. Juergens, *News from the White House,* 151.

30. Willis Sharp, "President and Press," *Atlantic Monthly,* July 1927, 240.

31. Clapper, *Washington Tapestry,* 14–15.

32. See "Editor's Ire at Coolidge Innuendo," *Literary Digest* 96 (November 12, 1927): 12; "Covering Washington," *The Nation,* June 27, 1928, 714; David Lawrence, "President and the Press," *Saturday Evening Post,* August 27, 1927, 27; O. G. Villard, "Press and the President," *Century,* December 1925, 193–200; and S. Moley, "Trials of the White House Spokesman," *Illustrated Independent Weekly,* September 19, 1925, 317–319.

33. Pollard, *Presidents and the Press,* 743.

34. Ibid.

35. Anthony Smith, *Goodbye Gutenberg* (New York: Oxford University Press, 1980), 173.

36. Leo Rosten, *The Washington Correspondents* (New York: Harcourt, Brace, 1937), 4.

37. Journalist Walter Davenport wrote in "The President and the Press," *Colliers,* January 27, 1945, 12: "A most important contributing factor to the grip that Mr. Roosevelt has on the imaginations of the Washington correspondent corps and consequently on the quality of his press [is] the enthusiasm he generated in the beginning— in 1933—[that] is still visible and still vocal."

38. Roberts, "Franklin Delano Roosevelt," 24. He adds that they applauded "because the reporters knew they were going to have access to news, the meat and potatoes of their profession."

39. The reporter quoted here is Henry M. Hyde of the *Baltimore Evening Sun.* Cited in Rosten, *The Washington Correspondents,* 50.

40. Marlan E. Pew, "Shop Talk at Thirty," *Editor and Publisher,* April 8, 1933, 36.

41. Pollard, *Presidents and the Press,* 775.

42. Rosten, *The Washington Correspondents,* 50. Arthur Krock once remarked, "He [Roosevelt] could qualify as the chief of a great copy desk" (in Rosten, *The Washington Correspondents,* 53). Heywood Broun complimented Roosevelt as "the best newspaper man who has ever been President" (in Pollard, *Presidents and the Press,* 781).

43. Raymond Clapper is cited in Pollard, *Presidents and the Press,* 780, stating, "The President and his most indefatigable critic, Mark Sullivan, still exchange pleasantries at press conferences."

44. Pollard, *Presidents and the Press,* 776.

45. Davenport, "The President and the Press," 11–12.

46. Arthur Krock, *The Consent of the Governed* (Boston: Little, Brown, 1971), 242.

47. Ibid., 243.

48. Rosten, *The Washington Correspondents,* 58–61.

49. Walter Davenport reported in *Editor and Publisher* that 45 percent of the nation's major newspapers supported Roosevelt in 1932, 34 percent in 1940, and 60 percent in 1944. "The

President and the Press," *Collier's*, February 3, 1945, 16. White's *FDR and the Press* takes a revisionist stance, arguing that Roosevelt was far more hostile to the nation's publishers than they to him. See especially chaps. 3, 4, and 5.

50. Boorstin, "Selling the President to the People," 425.

51. For another example of FDR striking a bargain by creating a relationship, see Richard Fenno's study of the appointment of Jesse Jones as Roosevelt's secretary of commerce in *The President's Cabinet* (New York: Vintage, 1959), 234–247.

52. A. L. Lorenz Jr., "Truman and the Press Conference," *Journalism Quarterly* 43 (winter 1966): 671–679, 708.

53. Robert Pierpoint, *At the White House* (New York: G. P. Putnam's Sons, 1981), 155–156.

54. Pierre Salinger, *With Kennedy* (New York: Doubleday, 1966), 57.

55. Cited in Harry Sharp Jr., "Live From Washington: The Telecasting of President Kennedy's News Conferences," *Journal of Broadcasting* 13 (winter 1968–69): 25.

56. Cited in Newton N. Minow, John Bartlow Martin, and Lee M. Mitchell, *Presidential Television* (New York: Basic Books, 1973), 39. Similarly, Nixon remarked at a press conference, "I consider a press conference as going to the people" (*Public Papers of the Presidents of the United States, Richard Nixon, 1969* [Washington, D.C.: Government Printing Office, 1971], 301). And early in the Reagan administration, NBC executive Richard S. Salant sounded the same theme: "Presidents over the past 20 years have discovered that television provides them the means to go around and over print to talk directly and simultaneously to all the people, with no reporting filter in between" ("When the White House Cozies up to the Home Screen," *New York Times*, August 23, 1981, sec. 2, 25).

57. Lester Markel, "What We Don't Know Will Hurt Us," *New York Times Magazine*, April 9, 1961, 116–117.

58. Cited in Worth Bingham and Ward S. Just, "The President and the Press," *Reporter* 26 (April 12, 1962): 20.

59. Ibid.

60. Markel, "What We Don't Know," 116.

61. James E. Pollard, "The Kennedy Administration and the Press," *Journalism Quarterly* 41 (winter 1964). See also Alan L. Otten, "Whose Conference?" *Wall Street Journal*, August 5, 1970, 44.

62. Pollard, "The Kennedy Administration and the Press," 7.

63. Jules Witcover, "Salvaging the Presidential Press Conference," *Columbia Journalism Review* 9 (fall 1970): 33.

64. Pierpoint, *At the White House*, 70–71.

65. Journalists writing about their profession appear compelled to mention the discrepancy in the salaries between broadcast and print correspondents. See, for example, James Deakin on the "star system" of broadcast journalists, *Straight Stuff*, 107–109; and Stewart Alsop, *The Center* (New York: Harper and Row, 1968), 176–177.

66. Examples are Hedrick Smith, "When the President Meets the Press," *Atlantic*, August 1970, 65–67; and Witcover, "Salvaging the Presidential Press Conference," 28.

67. Bingham and Just, "The President and the Press," 18–20. In a blistering attack on the administration's press relations, Arthur Krock charged that Kennedy had done more to "manage the news" than any president in history. Krock, who was on the "outside," took special exception to the exclusive interview, though he had taken full advantage of this practice under both Roosevelt and Truman. "Mr. Kennedy's Management of the News," *Fortune*, March 1963, 82, 199–202.

68. Bingham and Just, "The President and the Press," 18.

69. Ibid., 20.

70. Pollard, "The Kennedy Administration," 6.

71. Ibid., 18. In early 1985 the Reagan administration announced plans for a facility to allow direct television hookups from the White House to local stations around the country. Gerald M. Boyd, "White House Plans Direct TV Links," *New York Times,* January 8, 1985, 9.

72. Rosenstiel, " 'Local' News Bureaus," 18.

73. Richard Nixon's confrontations with the press have been amply documented in William E. Porter, *Assault on the Media: The Nixon Years* (Ann Arbor: University of Michigan Press, 1976); James Keogh, *President Nixon and the Press* (New York: Funk and Wagnalls, 1972); and George C. Edwards III, *The Public Presidency* (New York: St. Martin's Press, 1983), 104–133.

74. Witcover, "Salvaging the Presidential Press Conference," 28.

75. Cited in J. Anthony Lukas, "The White House Press 'Club,' " *New York Times Magazine,* May 15, 1977, 67.

76. Two studies that fail to find negative stories or hostile news conference questions are Michael Baruch Grossman and Martha Joynt Kumar, *Portraying the President* (Baltimore: Johns Hopkins University Press, 1981), chap. 10; and Jarol B. Mannheim, "The Honeymoon's Over: The News Conference and the Development of Presidential Style," *Journal of Politics* 41 (February 1979): 55–74. Dan Hallin takes exception to the notion of an adversarial press in "The Myth of the Adversary Press," *Quill* 71 (November 1983): 31–36.

77. Tom Rosentiel, *The Beat Goes On* (New York: Twentieth Century Fund), 1994.

78. "The Evolution of the White House Staff," in *Can the Government Govern?* eds. John E. Chubb and Paul E. Peterson (Washington, D.C.: The Brookings Institution, 1989), 185–237.

79. President Clinton press conference, May 7, 1993, Washington, D.C. CBS News producer Kathleen A. Frankovic acknowledged the general validity of Clinton's suspicions when she observed that "when [the president's] approval ratings go down, it's considered more news-worthy than when they go up. . . . Similarly, there seems to have been more coverage of the slippage in support for President Clinton's health care plan . . . than there was of the original post-speech levels of support." In "News Media Polling in a Changing Technological Environment" (speech delivered at Northwestern University, Evanston, Illinois, May 25, 1994).

80. Daniel C. Hallin, "Sound Bite News: Television Coverage of Elections, 1968–1988," in *We Keep America on Top of the World: Television Journalism and the Public Sphere,* ed. Daniel C. Hallin (London: TJ Press Ltd., 1994), 134.

81. "The Presidency, the Press and the People," University of California, San Diego, January 5–6, 1990. Transcript reprinted in *APIP Report* 1 (January 1991): 4–5. John Anthony Maltese provides a history of the development of White House staffing for presidential communications in *Spin Control: The White House Office of Communications and the Management of Presidential News* (Chapel Hill: University of North Carolina Press, 1992).

chapter 5

The Growth of Going Public

The preceding chapters have presented the reasons modern presidents go public. Modern technology makes it possible. Outsiders in the White House find it attractive. And the many centrifugal forces at work in Washington frequently require it. The frequency with which presidents in the past half-century have communicated directly with the American public shows that the more recent the president, the more often this strategic politician elects to go public.

The most memorable such occasions occur when the president delivers a national address on radio or television to appeal for the public's support for his legislative program stalled in Congress or to define the U.S. position in an international crisis. Although these dramatic forms of going public have become more commonplace in recent years, they still constitute only a small share of the many public activities in which modern presidents daily engage to influence the national agenda. As we found in Bill Clinton's and George W. Bush's efforts to elevate reform of health care and Social Security onto the national agenda, going public frequently involves intensive campaigns comprised of quieter overtures to targeted audiences.

There is another reason for the growth of going public. Just as bargaining presidents must continually nurture the good will of their trading partners, so too, must public-styled presidents diligently cultivate public opinion. The techniques presidents employ are called "public relations." * Like advertising generally, public relations from the White House are designed to perform the homeostatic function of maintaining public support for the president. Whenever the president's popularity begins to wane or press coverage appears to be unduly critical, the White House typically compensates by increasing the president's schedule of public activities. As much as the occasional dramatic moment when the president rallies the country behind his policies, going public is sometimes enlisted to restore the public's popular support. In the cases that follow, Presidents Nixon, Reagan, and Clinton executed carefully planned

---

* In an early study of what has become an unexceptional feature of presidents' leadership strategies, Stanley Kelley Jr. described the linkages between presidential activities (including campaigning) and professional public relations in *Professional Public Relations and Political Power* (Baltimore: Johns Hopkins University Press, 1956).

public relations strategies as though this was the most important matter confronting their presidency. Although none of these efforts fully arrested their dropping poll numbers, the first two presidents won reelection and Clinton survived impeachment.

Throughout February and March of 1971, Richard Nixon faced a barrage of criticism including large-scale, student-led protests of the U.S. invasion of Laos. To offset this opposition, the president took his case to the public. Biographers Rowland Evans and Robert Novak left little doubt that Nixon's public relations campaign was precipitated by a five-point drop in his popularity rating:

> Shortly after that Gallup finding, it was decided by Nixon's public relations experts to give the American people the largest concentrated dose of this president on television and in interviews with journalists. The purpose was to stimulate an immediate upward movement in the polls and thus prevent further deterioration of the president's position on Capitol Hill and in the nation.
>
> In quick succession, in the six weeks ending March 22, Nixon made these appearances: an interview on February 9 with conservative Peregrine Worsthorne of the *London Sunday Telegraph*; a non-televised press conference on February 17; a special televised press conference on March 4 limited to foreign policy questions; an interview on March 11 by Barbara Walters of NBC's *Today Show* for broadcast on March 15; an interview on March 11 by nine women reporters for publication on March 13; a one-hour live televised interview on March 22 by ABC's Howard K. Smith—a rate of exposure to major media outlets of more than one a week.[1]

Eleven years later, Ronald Reagan faced the same problem under different circumstances. With his approval falling as the jobless rate rose, there was little President Reagan could say or do to sell the country on unemployment. He could, however, shore up his softening support with appeals on other issues. After learning from in-house polls that he was losing the approval of blue-collar workers—many of whom were Democrats who had crossed over to vote for him in 1980—Reagan decided to target them with special appeals.*

Along with other public activities directed to this constituency, President Reagan addressed a conference of Catholic lay organizations in Chicago in

---

* Since fall 1981, Reagan's pollster, Richard Wirthlin, had been advising the president of his slipping popularity among blue-collar Democrats, many of whom were Catholic, who had supported him against Carter in 1980. See B. Drummond Ayres Jr., "G.O.P. Keeps Tabs on Nation's Mood," *New York Times*, November 16, 1981, A20; and Howell Raines, "Reagan's Gamble: Bid for Popularity," *New York Times*, March 30, 1982, A27. Similar evidence of Reagan's decline in the polls is reported by Hedrick Smith in the CBS/*New York Times* survey in "Blue-Collar Workers' Support for Reagan Declines," *New York Times*, March 8, 1982. The association between the president's decline in the polls and his tuition tax credit proposal is made by Dennis Williams, Lucy Howard, and Frank Marer, "Tax Credits for Tuition?" *Newsweek*, April 26, 1982, 86. See also Seymour Sudman, "The President and the Polls," *Public Opinion Quarterly* 46 (fall 1982): 301–310.

behalf of a proposal to have the federal government subsidize private school tuition. For the Catholic Church, financially strapped by rising costs and declining enrollments in many communities, and for parents who sent their children to these schools (or would have liked to), enactment of the president's proposal would have been a godsend. But this was highly unlikely given Reagan's penurious domestic budget that included heavy cutbacks for public education. Instead, the trip to Chicago was widely interpreted to have been inspired more by the need to shore up support with this Democratic constituency than by any expectation that it might give an impetus to his stalled legislation in Congress. It also promised an enthusiastic reception before a traditionally Democratic audience, one that would ensure prominent coverage on the networks' evening news programs. Though the reasons for Nixon's and Reagan's difficulties in the polls were quite different, both men sought remedy in rhetoric. In neither instance did the loss of popular support prompt the president to reconsider those policies that displeased the public. The loss was sufficient in each case, however, to trigger a public relations blitz. Whether either president's public relations campaign had their intended effects is hard to say. Both presidents' popular support continued to drift downward as the public's unhappiness continued to deteriorate. Perhaps their responses slowed their decline, perhaps not.

Our third case offers what might be the most dramatic instance ever of a president going public to shore up public support. In January 1998, just days before President Clinton's scheduled State of the Union address, the wire services reported that Special Prosecutor Kenneth Starr had obtained tape-recording conversations in which White House intern Monica Lewinsky confided her sexual relationship with the president to a friend that contradicted Clinton's nationally televised statement that he "did not have sex with that woman." This sudden and potentially ominous turn of events for Clinton prompted some polling firms to ratchet up their phone bank operations in a race to be the first to detect and declare the public's abandonment of the president, a prerequisite in the view of many Beltway sages for the Republican Congress to impeach and remove the president from office.

For understanding presidents' influence on public opinion, Clinton's travails, accompanied by the continuous monitoring of expectant pollsters, are a godsend. Before, during, and just after President Clinton's State of the Union address, CBS News had national surveys in the field. In his address Clinton acknowledged his personal failure and apologized to the American public. Even the normally cynical White House press corps gave the performance high marks. More important, so too did the American public. On January 22, before the speech, CBS News reported a downward drift to 55 percent approving; the next report on February 1, four days after the speech, the approval figure had jumped by 17 percentage points. Even more telling insight into the capacity of presidents to boost themselves with the public came from CBS's nimble decision to reinterview the day after the speech those survey respondents who had evaluated Clinton's job performance during the four-day period prior to the speech.* This allows us to identify who saw the speech and whether it changed their opinion of the president. In Figure 5-1 I have sorted respondents according to their party identification and job performance evaluation prior to the speech. This allows us to determine if exposure to the speech influenced subsequent opinions. First, notice that the president's earlier approvers continued to approve the president at above 90 percent whether they saw the speech or not. Second, the relationship displayed in the figure reveals a dramatic improvement in the president's job performance evaluations among those previous detractors who watched the speech. Over 40 percent of Republican and half of independent disapprovers switched to approval after watching Clinton's address. The third pattern to be gleaned from the figure and perhaps the most important in its implications for presidential opinion leadership is that evaluations of President Clinton improved sharply even among those who missed the speech. Where 90 percent or more of the president's approvers who did not watch the speech remained approving in the follow-up survey, nearly 40 percent of disapproving independents, 30 percent of Democrats, but only 10 percent of Republicans switched to a favorable evaluation of Clinton. Although the surveys are silent on the opinion dynamics that caused the shift, one can reasonably surmise that the spate of favorable news coverage of the speech reassured the public that the president remained on top of national problems and issues, and as he promised in his speech, he would not let his current political—and indeed, personal—difficulties stand in the way of performing his responsibilities.

Within a week of the speech, the president's job performance rating had surged sixteen percentage points to 71 percent approving. Although much of these gains proved ephemeral, his approval rating never fully dropped to its prespeech levels. The next year President Clinton would be impeached by the House of Representatives and tried (and acquitted) in the Senate, yet his approval rating remained above 60 percent.

With presidents' success—and occasionally even their political survival—resting ever more heavily on the public's support, presidents must pay attention to their poll numbers and cultivate the public's approbation. Consequently, modern presidents engage in continuous public relations to achieve two integrally related goals: support for their policies and support for themselves.

---

* I wish to thank Kathleen Francovic at CBS News for access to these survey data. When asked if they had seen the speech, nearly 70 percent of Clinton's admiring Democratic respondents said they had, compared to only 50 percent of independents who previously expressed their disapproval. Almost as many Republicans as Democrats claimed to have seen the speech, which is unusual. Perhaps partisans watched for sharply different reasons—Democrats to pull for the "Comeback Kid," and Republicans to witness the public hanging. These self-reports of viewing the State of the Union message appear inflated, given Nielsen Media Research's estimate that 37 percent of households with televisions on were watching the address. I suspect that many who claimed to have viewed the speech in reality had heard or read about it in the newspaper or seen excerpts on the news.

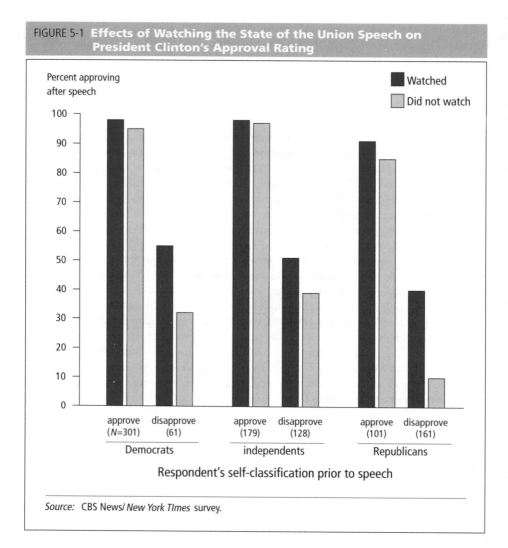

FIGURE 5-1 **Effects of Watching the State of the Union Speech on President Clinton's Approval Rating**

Percent approving after speech

■ Watched
□ Did not watch

Respondent's self-classification prior to speech

approve (N=301) disapprove (61) Democrats

approve (179) disapprove (128) independents

approve (101) disapprove (161) Republicans

Source: CBS News/*New York Times* survey.

TRENDS IN GOING PUBLIC

Going public can take a variety of forms. The most conspicuous is the formal, ceremonial occasion, such as an inaugural address or a State of the Union message, when official duty places the president prominently before the nation. Going public may, however, involve no more than a pregnant aside to a news reporter. This sort of casual, impromptu gesture eludes systematic analysis, but speeches, travel, and appearances—all of which take place in public view and therefore can be easily counted—form a good record of significant events with which to measure the rise of going public. Each of these nonexclusive activities can be further divided according to its locale or prominence.[2]

Public Addresses

Appeals for support to constituencies outside Washington are the core activities of going public. Form, audience, and content make each appeal unique. John Kennedy's October 1962 address to the nation, in which he announced a quarantine of Soviet ships laden with surface-to-surface missiles en route to Cuba, is different in each respect from Jimmy Carter's trip to Iowa in 1977 to sell his agricultural policies before a gathering of farmers. With such diversity, one may reasonably wonder what any trends discerned from a large volume of public addresses could mean.

Without delving too deeply into form, audience, and content, I shall offer a general distinction by classifying public addresses as major and minor. Major addresses are those in which the president speaks directly to a national audience over radio or television. Minor addresses, by comparison, are those the president delivers to a special audience either in person or via some broadcast medium. By these definitions, Kennedy's statement on the Cuban missile crisis qualifies as a major address and Carter's farm speech as a minor address. Beginning with Ronald Reagan, major addresses include only television broadcasts. In 1982, after becoming unhappy with press representation of his policies, Reagan initiated a series of Saturday afternoon radio broadcasts. Reagan's successors continued this practice, though not with the same regularity as the actor-president who began his career on radio. The Saturday radio broadcasts probably have a greater impact via the news directly. To include these addresses, which attract small audiences, among major appeals would misrepresent the frequency with which presidents appeared before a national audience. Nonetheless, the eight major televised addresses by Reagan in 1981 (a month of which he spent convalescing from an assassination attempt) is a first-year record for any president. The major address totals for his successors, by contrast, have returned to the level of Reagan's predecessors.

Of the major addresses, the most dramatic and potentially most effective are special reports the president delivers to the nation on prime-time television. The subjects of these television talks, listed in Table 5-1, provide a calendar of the crises and national exigencies that have preoccupied presidents since 1953.[3]

Figure 5-2 shows that until the 1960s, the average yearly numbers of major and minor addresses had grown steadily since Herbert Hoover's presidency.[4] Even though both forms of going public were on the rise, one can see as early as the Kennedy administration that minor addresses had much more upside-growth potential than did major addresses. Although major addresses may be the most dramatic and potentially most effective instrument for influencing public opinion, they also can be the most taxing. Conventional wisdom holds that the public's attentiveness corresponds to the number of such appeals. If

TABLE 5-1 Calendar of Presidential "Reports to the Nation" on National Television, Jan. 1953–Sept. 2006

	Jan	Feb	Mar	Apr	May	June	July	Aug	Sept	Oct	Nov	Dec
Eisenhower												
1953	Review											
1954				World affairs		Review		Congress				
1955		Reelection announcement		Veto–agriculture			Geneva conference					
1956		Middle East			Mutual aid							
1957									Little Rock	Middle East		
1958			Berlin					Labor reform	Europe			
1959											Science security	International peace
Kennedy												
1960		National defense	Latin America		Paris summit	Far East, Europe meetings						
1961			Nuclear tests				Berlin					
1962								Taxes	Tax cut	Cuba	Cuba	
1963						Civil rights		Test ban	Steel strike	International affairs		
Johnson												
1964				Railroad labor dispute (2)				Tonkin Gulf				

Year							
1965							
1966	Bombing North Vietnam						
1967			Dominican Rep.	Dominican Rep.			
1968	Pueblo	Vietnam; noncandidacy	Martin Luther King	Violence	Riots	Steel strike	Steel strike
Nixon							
1969	Veto–H.E.W.		S.E. Asia				Halt of bombing
1970	S.E. Asia	Postal strike	Vietnam (2)	Cambodia (2); Economy		Welfare	Vietnam-ization
1971		Busing / Economy	SALT		China trip	Peace initiative / Economy	
1972	Vietnam	Vietnam	Vietnam	Economy	China trip	Economy	
1973	Vietnam	Watergate	Economy	Economy	USSR trip (2); economy	Watergate	Energy crisis (2)
Ford							
1974	Egypt-Israel	Watergate	Middle East crisis			Pardon of Nixon	
1975	National issues	Tax cut	Mayaguez (2); energy			Tax cut	
1976							

(Continued)

TABLE 5-1 Calendar of Presidential "Reports to the Nation" on National Television, Jan. 1953–Sept. 2006 (Continued)

	Jan	Feb	Mar	Apr.	May	June	July	Aug.	Sept.	Oct.	Nov.	Dec.
Carter												
1977		Fireside chat		Energy							Energy	
1978		Panama Canal treaty										China
1979			Economy									
Reagan												
1981	Farewell (Carter)	Economy					Tax bill		Economy; budget	Inflation		Poland
1982				Budget					Middle East (2)	Economy	Arms control	Poland
1983			Defense–national security	Central America					Korean airliner	Lebanon, Grenada		
1984				Budget	Central America; Tax reform							
1985		State of the Union; National security				Economic summit	Independence Day				Soviet-U.S. summit	
1986	Space Shuttle explosion		Nicaragua						Drug abuse	Meetings with Gorbachev	Election; Iran and contra aid	Iran arms and contra aid
1987			Iran arms and contra aid					Iran arms and contra aid				
1988												Soviet-U.S. summit

Year									
1989	Farewell to the nation								
Bush									
1989	Inauguration	Administration goals						Thanksgiving	Panama
1990					Drug control strategy	Kuwait invasion	Budget agreement		
1991	Desert Storm	Persian Gulf; Iraqi withdrawal	Persian Gulf		Persian Gulf; budget deficit			Thanksgiving	Christmas
1992			Balanced Budget Amendment	L.A. riots	Nuclear weapons reduction; hurricane Andrew	Budget			Somalia crisis
Clinton									
1993	Economy (2)		Iraq		Health care	Budget	Somalia crisis	NAFTA	
1994					Haiti (2)		Iraq		Middle-Class Bill of Rights
1995		Budget deficit							Bosnia peace agreement

(Continued)

TABLE 5-1 Calendar of Presidential "Reports to the Nation" on National Television, Jan. 1953–Sept. 2006 (Continued)

	Jan	Feb	Mar.	Apr.	May	June	July	Aug.	Sept.	Oct.	Nov.	Dec.
1996												
1997												
1998											Afghan/Sud. Grand Jury Testimony	Iraq
1999						Yugoslavia			Kosovo			
2000												
Bush												
2001								Stem Cell	9/11 attacks (Sept) War on Terror (Sept)	Afghanistan (Oct.)		Homeland Sec. (Dec.)
2002										Homeland Security		
2003					Iraq							
2004												War on Terror
2005									9/11 Commemoration	Katrina		Iraqi Elections
2006					Immigration Reform							

Source: The entries from 1953 through November 1963 are from "Presidents on TV: Their Live Records," *Broadcasting*, November 8, 1965, 55–58; those from December 1963 through December 1975 are from Denis S. Rutkus, "A Report on Simultaneous Television Network Coverage of Presidential Addresses to the Nation," Congressional Research Service, (Washington, D.C., 1976), mimeograph, appendix; entries since 1976 are from the *Public Papers of the Presidents* series.

every presidential tribulation were taken to the country on prime-time television, people would soon lose interest. In private correspondence with a friend, Franklin Roosevelt said as much: "The public psychology . . . [cannot] be attuned for long periods of time to the highest note on the scale . . . people tire of seeing the same name, day after day, in the important headlines of the papers and the same voice, night after night, over the radio." * As noted earlier, Kennedy and members of his staff had similar misgivings after his first, prime-time news conference and scheduled subsequent conferences for daytime television.[5] During the Carter presidency, Gerald Rafshoon, upon assuming his duties in the rejuvenated White House Office of Communications in the summer of 1978, sent a memorandum to the president that established his media strategy for the rest of his tenure. Rafshoon cautioned, "The power of presidential communication is great, but not unlimited. You may be able to talk to the people all day . . . but the people can handle so much. *Investment of that power in too wide a range of issues will dissipate it. This has happened over the last eighteen months.*" After elaborating this theme, Rafshoon concluded, "Your involvement should always be weighed with an eye towards preventing the devaluation of presidential currency."[6] By potentially reducing the size and responsiveness of the audience for his next appeal, each prime-time address imposes opportunity costs on future appeals. Reflecting this consideration, along with emboldened network resistance to presidents commandeering prime-time television, the frequency of major presidential addresses has stabilized at a comparatively modest level.

Going public is neither premised on nor does it promote a perception of America as a "mass" society. Nor does it reduce politics to a plebiscite in which the president seeks continually to bring the weight of national opinion to bear on policy deliberation in Washington.[7] Governance under individualized pluralism remains largely a process of assembling coalitions both within party teams and across diverse interests and institutions. For this purpose, minor presidential addresses directed toward special constituencies are well suited. Not only do they avoid taxing future access to the national audience, they may succeed where an undifferentiated national appeal may not.

Aside from being more focused and less obtrusive than major addresses, minor addresses are attractive to presidents because the opportunities to give them are plentiful. The president is importuned daily to appear before graduation exercises, union conferences, and the conventions of trade and professional associations. With such advantages, minor addresses are understandably an integral component of a more general strategy of going public. George W. Bush's calendar of speaking engagements for February 2006, presented in Table

---

* Roosevelt continued, "If I had tried [in 1935] to keep up the pace of 1933 and 1934, the inevitable histrionics of the new actors, Long and Coughlin and Johnson, would have turned the eyes of the audience away from the main drama itself." Cited in Douglass Cater, "How a President Helps Form Public Opinion," *New York Times Magazine,* February 26, 1961, 12.

FIGURE 5-2 Presidential Addresses, 1929–2003 (Yearly Averages for First Three Years of First Term)

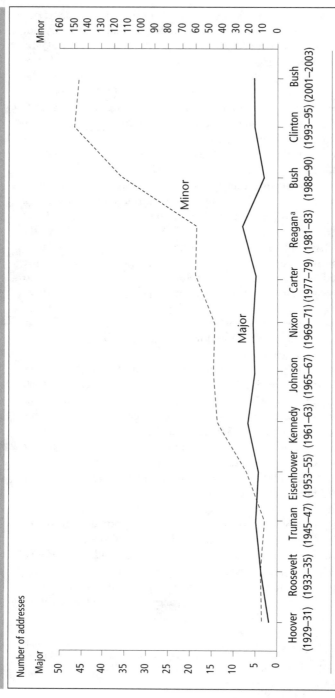

Sources: Data for Hoover, Roosevelt, Truman, Eisenhower, Nixon, and Carter are from William W. Lammers, "Presidential Attention-Focusing Activities," in *The President and the American Public*, ed. Doris A. Graber (Philadelphia: Institute for the Study of Human Issues, 1982), Table 6-1, 152. Data for Kennedy, Johnson, Reagan, Bush, and Clinton are from *Public Papers of the Presidents* series. See also Samuel Kernell, "The Presidency and the People: The Modern Paradox," in *The Presidency and the Political System*, ed. Michael Nelson (Washington, D.C.: CQ Press, 1984), 242.

Note: To eliminate public activities inspired by concerns of reelection rather than governing, only the first three years have been tabulated. For this reason, Gerald Ford's record of public activities during his two and one-half years of office have been ignored.

[a] Major addresses include television addresses only. With radio included, Reagan averaged twenty-four major addresses per year.

5-2, illustrates how these kinds of activities can dominate presidents' lives. During that month he delivered thirteen remarks and formal addresses in as many cities outside of Washington.

The real explosion in presidential talk has occurred with minor addresses. Reagan, Carter, and Nixon on average surpassed Truman, Roosevelt, and Hoover by nearly fivefold in the use of such rhetoric. George H. W. Bush managed to double these already high levels of targeted addresses. During his first three years in office he averaged a minor address every three days. Clinton did Bush one better—a minor address nearly every other day, a pace almost matched by the younger Bush.

If asked to name a president who could speak skillfully, one probably would think first of Franklin Roosevelt or perhaps John Kennedy, two men whose speeches have surpassed their time. Nixon's pronouncements—such as his prepresidential "Checkers" speech and later, his Watergate denials—will be remembered mostly as objects of ridicule and, ultimately, of historical curiosity. Carter's and both Bushes' addresses will be recalled, if at all, as instructive examples of poor elocution and tortured syntax. Of the recent class of presidents, Ronald Reagan and Bill Clinton score well as thespians. The trends in Figure 5-3 reveal that it is not success but the type of politician recruited to the office and the strategic environment within which they operate that determine the volume of presidential rhetoric.

Public Appearances

Visual images can at times convey information more effectively than talk. The audience to whom the president speaks and the location and circumstances of the event may contribute as much to his message's effectiveness as what he has to say. Shedding pomp and circumstance, Jimmy Carter's inaugural stroll down Pennsylvania Avenue hand-in-hand with his wife, Rosalyn, was choreographed to show the American public that Richard Nixon's "imperial presidency" was history. So too was the cardigan sweater he wore during his first address on national television. Similarly, the image of President Nixon donning a hard hat and waving to cheering construction workers on the scaffolding above him made a strong pitch for support among his "silent majority."

Appearances are usually accompanied by public speaking, although, as in the Nixon example, they need not be. Like minor addresses, appearances before select audiences offer the president an opportunity to target his appeals. In a preinaugural memo, Carter pollster Patrick Caddell urged the president-elect to use "his personal leadership—through visits and political contacts—to maintain his base in the South." [8] Thirty years later, Republican president Bush engaged in a similar southern strategy by making periodic appearances before conferences of fundamentalist church groups and socially conservative lay organizations.

Appearances are distinguished in Figure 5-3 by locale, those in Washington from those throughout the rest of the United States. The number

TABLE 5-2 President Bush's "Minor" Addresses, February 2006

Date	Location	Audience	Subject
Feb. 1	Nashville, Tennessee	Speech at Grand Ole Opry House	President discusses 2006 agenda
Feb. 2	Maplewood, Minnesota	3M Corporate Headquarters	President discusses American competitiveness agenda in Minnesota
Feb. 2	Washington, D.C.	Hilton Washington Hotel	Fifty-fourth Annual National Prayer Breakfast
Feb. 3	Rio Rancho, New Mexico	Intel New Mexico	American Competitiveness Panel in New Mexico
Feb. 3	Dallas, Texas	School of Engineering Yvonne A. Ewell Townview Magnet Center	President visits Science and Engineering High School in Texas
Feb. 4	Washington, D.C.	Radio address	American Competitiveness Initiative
Feb. 6	Washington, D.C.	The Federal Reserve	Swearing-in ceremony for Federal Reserve Chair Ben Bernanke
Feb. 7	Atlanta, Georgia	New Birth Missionary Church	President honors Coretta Scott King at Homecoming Celebration
Feb. 8	Manchester, New Hampshire	Radisson Hotel, Manchester	President discusses 2007 budget and deficit reduction
Feb. 9	Washington, D.C.	National Guard Building	Progress in war on terror to National Guard
Feb. 10	Cambridge, Maryland	Hyatt Regency, Chesapeake Bay	President addresses House Republican Conference
Feb. 11	Washington, D.C.	Radio address	Medicare Prescription Drug Coverage
Feb. 15	Dublin, Ohio	Wendy's International Inc.	President discusses health care
Feb. 16	Washington, D.C.	U.S. Department of Health and Human Services	Panel discussion on health care initiatives
Feb. 17	Tampa, Florida	Port of Tampa	Global War on Terror following briefing at CENTCOM
Feb. 17	Lake Buena Vista, Florida	Disney's Contemporary Resort	Remarks at Republican Party of Florida dinner
Feb. 18	Washington, D.C.	Radio address	Advanced Energy Initiative
Feb. 20	Milwaukee, Wisconsin	Johnson Controls Building Efficiency Business	President discusses advanced energy initiative in Milwaukee
Feb. 20	Auburn Hills, Michigan	United Solar Ovonic, LLC	President discusses solar technology and energy initiatives in Michigan
Feb. 21	Golden, Colorado	National Renewable Energy Laboratory	Energy Conservation and Efficiency Panel
Feb. 22	Washington, D.C.	Mandarin Oriental Hotel	President addresses Asia Society, discusses India and Pakistan
Feb. 25	Washington, D.C.	Radio address	Meeting with America's governors and health care providers
Feb. 27	Washington, D.C.	National Building Museum	Republican National Governors Association

Source: Weekly Compilation of Presidential Documents, Vol. 42, Numbers 5–8 (http://www.gpoaccess.gov/wcomp/index.html).

of public appearances outside the city generally reflects the president's non-Washington origins and divided party control of government.*

Political Travel

Generally, presidents travel in order to appear before targeted constituencies or to find locations suitable for sounding a particular theme. Reagan kicked off his tax reform proposal in 1985 in Williamsburg, Virginia, to play up his "new American Revolution" motto, an advertising theme that enjoyed a much longer run in Chevrolet commercials. Days logged in domestic travel have no importance beyond the appearances or addresses before non-Washington audiences they reflect and the telegenic evening news spots they attract. As such, they offer another useful indicator of the president's public activities represented in appearances and speeches.

When presidents travel abroad, however, they frequently do so in search of special opportunities to appear presidential. Meetings with other heads of state serve to remind the electorate of the weighty responsibilities of office and of the president's diligence in attending to them. Could future incumbents fail to notice the salutary effects of Kennedy's confrontation with Nikita Khrushchev in Vienna in 1961 and of Nixon's celebrated trip to China in 1972 on these presidents' images as national leaders? One may reasonably argue that affairs of state rather than voracious demands for publicity were the real reasons for these trips. Kennedy's biographers make clear his strongly felt need to impress the Soviet leader with America's commitments to its allies. And without the dramatic expression of national good will that Nixon's trip conveyed, the thaw in relations between the United States and China might not have been so complete. The considerable diplomatic merits of these trips notwithstanding, the fact is that both presidents thoroughly exploited their opportunities for publicity at home.

Kennedy's staff rushed film of the president with the Soviet leader to the Paris airport to give it the earliest possible airing on the networks' evening news. By the time Nixon visited China eleven years later, new technology had greatly expanded the opportunities for public relations. Hours of President Nixon's tour of famous sites and formal expressions of mutual friendship with China's leaders were televised by satellite. *Air Force One* landed in Beijing during prime time at home; the president's tour of the Great Wall and ancient palaces and the state banquet in the Great Hall were broadcast live back to the United States; and for a finale, after a timely nine-hour layover in Anchorage, *Air Force One* touched down in Washington just in time to make the evening network news. All in all, the three major networks broadcast more than forty-one hours of the

---

* An example of this genre is President Reagan's warm-up routine at a summer 1981 Jaycees convention in San Antonio while pressuring Democrats in Washington to accept his budget. To a roaring audience Reagan intoned, "Where on earth has he [Tip O'Neill] been for the last few years?" After a pause he continued, "The answer is, right in Washington, D.C." See "Reagan's Sweet Triumph," *Newsweek*, July 6, 1981, 18.

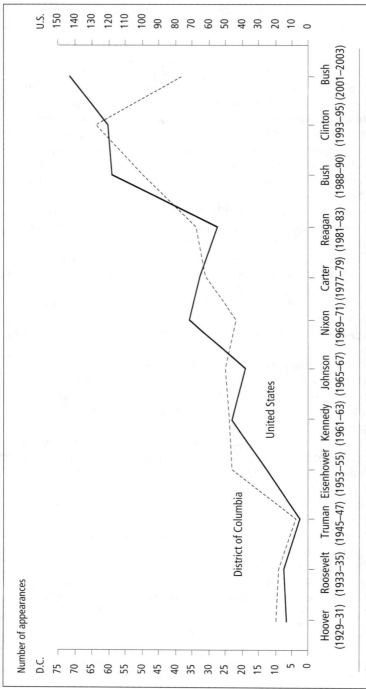

FIGURE 5-3 **Public Appearances by Presidents, 1929–2003 (Yearly Averages for First Three Years of First Term)**

Number of appearances

D.C.   U.S.

75   150
                                                                                                                      140
70   130
                                                                                                                      120
65   110
60   100
55   90
50   80
45   70
40   60
35   50
30   40
25
20   30
15   20
10
5   10
0   0

District of Columbia

United States

Hoover   Roosevelt   Truman   Eisenhower Kennedy   Johnson   Nixon   Carter   Reagan   Bush   Clinton   Bush
(1929–31)   (1933–35) (1945–47) (1953–55) (1961–63) (1965–67) (1969–71)(1977–79) (1981–83) (1988–90) (1993–95) (2001–2003)

Sources: Data for Hoover, Roosevelt, Truman, Eisenhower, Nixon, and Carter are from William W. Lammers, "Presidential Attention-Focusing Activities," in *The President and the American Public,* ed. Doris A. Graber (Philadelphia: Institute for the Study of Human Issues, 1982), Table 6-2 and 6-3, 154–156. Data for Kennedy, Johnson, Reagan, Bush, and Clinton are from *Public Papers of the Presidents* series. See also Samuel Kernell, "The Presidency and the People: The Modern Paradox," in *The Presidency and the Political System,* ed. Michael Nelson (Washington, D.C.: CQ Press, 1984), 245.

Note: To eliminate public activities inspired by concerns of reelection rather than governing, only the first three years have been tabulated. For this reason, Gerald Ford's record of public activities during his two and one-half years of office have been ignored.

seven-day trip. Afterwards, syndicated columnist Art Buchwald satirized the whole affair by reporting his wife's belief that the television set must be broken because Nixon's program was not available on any channel.[9]

The logistical planning of the visit to China is an impressive example of making the most of the opportunities for favorable publicity at home. Advances in transportation and communications, of which the China trip took full advantage, have so reduced travel time and so enhanced its public relations value that modern presidents might consider visits abroad solely for this purpose. Insiders increasingly voice suspicion that they already do.*

Modern White House correspondents, a suspicious lot, have been especially mindful of the public relations value of international political travel. During Reagan's first presidential trip to Europe, network correspondents pointed out the publicity purposes of the visual images so carefully staged by Reagan's "advance" aides. Remarkably, White House staffers openly discussed the trip's value in just these terms. Taken together, their comments reveal the motive of the visit had less to do with European comity than with the president's slipping approval rating. After assessing the poll results that shortly followed the trip, White House aides voiced delight that they had achieved their goal.

In this age of television, every president may be suspected of, and perhaps forgiven for, engaging in strategic travel and posing for the continuous "photo opportunity." The president who rests his leadership on going public will be tempted to travel frequently, in search of sympathetic audiences and "presidential images."

Because foreign and domestic travel often have different political purposes, they are measured separately in Figure 5-4. Each increased significantly in the past half-century. Domestic air travel for presidents began with Truman, but aside from brief vacation trips to his home in Independence, Missouri, he seldom took advantage of this new opportunity. Dwight Eisenhower was the first president to travel extensively around the country.[10] Not until Reagan and Bush, however, did presidents spend a total of a month on "business" travel away from Washington each year. In 1992 Clinton was the first president since Nixon in 1968 to win the office without gaining a majority of the popular vote—thus, in effect, President Clinton continued his campaign for the presidency. By the 1996 election he had averaged a visit to California, with its fifty-four electoral votes, every six weeks. In 2000 Bush won the election while receiving half a million fewer votes than did his opponent Al Gore. After nearly a month delay his victory was finally assured by a 5–4 Supreme Court decision

---

* In 1973 President Nixon went to Iceland for a special meeting with French president Georges Pompidou. No major policy decisions were made, as those privy to the trip's preparations had predicted. The *New York Times* reported the comments of one foreign service officer: "All they cared about was how things would look on television. White House aides fussed about the lighting, about who would stand where, what the background would be, and the furniture. The entire time I was assigned to the detail, no one asked me a substantive question. I'm sure they didn't care. All they seemed to care about was television." Cited in George C. Edwards III, *The Public Presidency* (New York: St. Martin's Press, 1983), 75.

favoring one set of Florida election officials' decisions over another's. He too began his presidency by returning to a campaign footing to shore up his popular support. At the moment the first plane collided into the World Trade Center, he was in a Florida elementary school classroom flanked by local television cameras promoting his education reform legislation. President Bush easily shattered Clinton's record—logging two months on *Air Force One* during his first three years despite the 9/11 terrorist attacks and two military invasions that forced him to curtail his political travel.

International political travel by presidents increased most sharply during the late 1960s. Eisenhower's 1959 "good-will" tour around the world is generally recognized to be the first international presidential travel where favorable publicity appeared to all to be the primary consideration. As the figures for subsequent presidents suggest, it was an idea whose time had come. Both Presidents Carter and Bush Sr., who enjoyed their major policy successes in foreign affairs, traveled extensively. By the close of his third year in office, Bush's overseas travels had become so conspicuous that his critics—most notably the eventual Democratic presidential nominee, Bill Clinton—found a large segment of the public agreeing with them that the president was not paying enough attention to the nation's troubles. Learning from his predecessor, Clinton stayed closer to home during his first term, especially in the early months of his presidency, when the recession remained an uppermost concern. But then again, his heavy domestic travel left little time to venture abroad.

During the past half-century, trends in presidents going public—from political travel to public addresses and appearances—have moved steadily upward. There are some revealing differences among these indicators, however, in both the overall rate of growth and the timing of the sharpest increases. The number of minor addresses, appearances outside of Washington, and domestic trips increased dramatically during President Clinton's and George W. Bush's terms. In part these sharper upward trends may reflect the special circumstances of each incumbent's initial election to the White House. And, as we found in chapter 2, they also reflect the modern president's evolving role as fund-raiser in chief. Cumulatively, these trends point toward a president today who is far more personally involved in public relations than were his predecessors thirty and forty years ago.*

THE INCREMENTAL GROWTH OF GOING PUBLIC

The rise of going public has proceeded more or less incrementally, with each president taking advantage of the precedents and extensions of public activity

---

* Because the categories of public activity are not mutually exclusive, it is not possible to obtain comparable averages for other presidents by simply adding their appearances, travel days, and speeches.

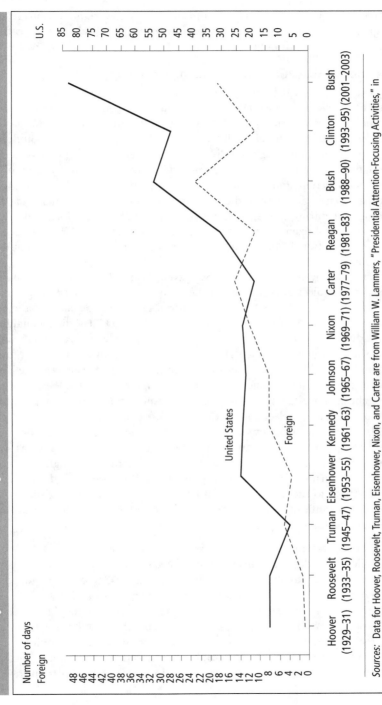

FIGURE 5-4 Days of Political Travel by Presidents, 1929–2003 (Yearly Averages for First Three Years of First Term)

Number of days

Foreign | U.S.

| Hoover
(1929–31) | Roosevelt
(1933–35) | Truman
(1945–47) | Eisenhower
(1953–55) | Kennedy
(1961–63) | Johnson
(1965–67) | Nixon
(1969–71) | Carter
(1977–79) | Reagan
(1981–83) | Bush
(1988–90) | Clinton
(1993–95) | Bush
(2001–2003) |

United States

Foreign

Sources: Data for Hoover, Roosevelt, Truman, Eisenhower, Nixon, and Carter are from William W. Lammers, "Presidential Attention-Focusing Activities," in *The President and the American Public,* ed. Doris A. Graber (Philadelphia: Institute for the Study of Human Issues, 1982), Table 6-5, 160. Data for Kennedy, Johnson, Reagan, Bush, and Clinton are from *Public Papers of the Presidents* series. See also Samuel Kernell, "The Presidency and the People: The Modern Paradox," in *The Presidency and the Political System,* ed. Michael Nelson (Washington, D.C.: CQ Press, 1984), 244.

Note: To eliminate public activities inspired by concerns of reelection rather than governing, only the first three years have been tabulated. For this reason, Gerald Ford's record of public activities during his two and one-half years of office have been ignored.

offered by his predecessors. For the purpose of discussion, the various reasons for gradual change can be classified broadly as technological and political. The former have to do with opportunity, the latter with inspiration.

Incremental Growth as a Function of Technology

Any explanation of the emergence of public strategies in the standard reper-toire of presidents must take into account the continuous technological advances in transportation and mass communications during the past six decades. Consider the difficulty a president sixty years ago would have encountered had he sought to rally the country behind his policies. By today's standards, the national transportation and communications systems of the early 1930s were primitive; barely 40 percent of all households owned radios. The president's potential audience was not only relatively small; one may assume that during the Great Depression it was also heavily skewed toward more affluent citizens. When Herbert Hoover defended his Great Depression policies on national radio—and he did so regularly—he preached mainly to the converted.[11]

Transportation in the 1930s posed even greater difficulties. Air travel for presidents would not come for another two decades, and rail transportation was so slow and arduous that one did not undertake it casually. In the early 1920s, Woodrow Wilson suffered a stroke and Warren G. Harding a fatal heart attack during long political trips. Anxious to gain the legitimacy and the audi-ence shares regular presidential broadcasts would provide, radio executives commonly cited these instances in promoting heavier presidential use of the new medium.[12] A decade later, a round trip from the East to the West Coast still took about a week.[13] Obviously, slow transportation limited a president's appearances before select audiences around the country.

International travel was even more time consuming and therefore infre-quent. Woodrow Wilson's trip to Europe in 1919 to make the peace was a rare gesture befitting the historic moment. The first international flight by a presi-dent came during World War II when Franklin Roosevelt secretly traveled to North Africa to meet with Winston Churchill. Compare the logistics of this 1943 trip with those described earlier in this chapter for Nixon's trip to China twenty-nine years later:

> The straight-line distance from Washington to Casablanca is 3,875 miles. A modern jet transport could have made the trip comfortably and without stopovers, in seven hours. But in 1943, the limited range, slower speeds, and lack of sophisticated navigational aids in the Boeing 314 and Douglas C-54 required four legs of flying, three stopovers, a change of planes, and more than three days' travel time for the President—in each direction. The circuitous route required the President to touch three continents, cross the Equator four times, and spend approximately ninety hours in the air. When his train trav-

el between Washington and Miami was included, Roosevelt had covered more than 17,000 miles before he was once more back home in the White House.[14]

The growth in presidential travel occurred piecemeal, with each new opportunity made possible by an advance in transportation technology. The eight decades of presidential travel shown in Figure 5-4 span eras in which transportation shifted from rail to air and then from prop to jet.

Technological breakthroughs in broadcast communications have had an even more profound effect on the opportunities for presidents to go public. Radio and television are, of course, the major developments, but smaller technological advances also had their effects. In 1955, for example, Kodak introduced its Tri-X film, which reduced the lighting requirements of television cameras; shortly thereafter Eisenhower admitted film crews into his news conferences.[15] The subsequent development of live satellite communications created a variety of new opportunities for live presidential television. Nixon's prime-time trip to China, Carter's town meetings at home and abroad, and Bush's and Clinton's teleconferences with national conventions in distant locales illustrate the kinds of public activities modern satellite communications make possible.[16] The steady growth of going public during the past sixty years follows the sequence of technological advances in communications as well as transportation.

Going public increased incrementally not only with the introduction of new means of communication, but also with their dissemination. One may assume that the appeal to presidents of communicating via radio and television relates to the size of the audience. President Roosevelt's participation in an experimental television broadcast at the 1939 World's Fair had no real political significance, if for no other reason than that only a minuscule audience could view the broadcast.[17] Figure 5-5 displays the rate with which radio and television entered America's homes. When FDR delivered his early fireside chats to reassure the public in the grip of the worst economic depression in the nation's history, less than half of the public could afford a radio. Although these innovative communications are justifiably credited with calming a panicky nation, there is good evidence that Roosevelt's radio addresses gained only a limited audience, at least in their initial broadcasts.* Figure 2-1 (see page 19) reproduces a wall chart found in FDR's files that plots the president's audience size. Not until the 1940s, when the nation went to war—and came out of the Depression—did radios become standard appliances and the president's audience truly became national.

By the early 1960s, the market was virtually saturated with televisions. Not coincidentally, we saw in chapter 4 that the first live-broadcast press conference

---

* Many of the fireside chats were filmed and edited into movie newsreels that ran during intermissions between feature films.

FIGURE 5-5 **Households with Radios, Televisions, and Cable TV, 1930–2005**

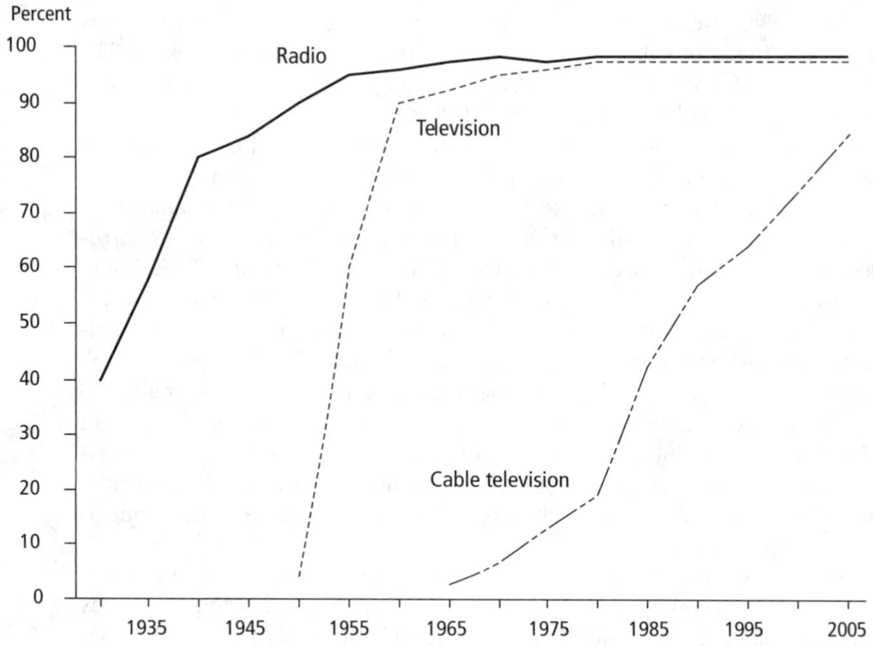

Sources: *Historical Statistics of the United States: Colonial Times to 1970,* vols. 1 and 2 (Washington, D.C.: Government Printing Office, 1975), series R104, R105, and A335. Data for 1975 through 1995 are from *Statistical Abstract of the United States* (Washington, D.C.: Government Printing Office, 1996). Subsequent figures provided by Nielsen Media Research.

occurred the next year. And during that decade presidents began more actively devising new ways to gain access to the nation's airwaves.

Although trends in going public follow the stepwise introduction and dissemination of technology, the correlation is not perfect. Presidents have adopted new technology cautiously.[18] In some instances this heed has resulted in a substantial time lag between a technology's availability and its political use. Harry Truman was the first president to go to the country on national television, but by modern standards his appearances were spare. Truman generally reserved television for moments of crisis, such as his announcement of the Korean War and seizure of the nation's steel mills. On many pressing domestic issues of the day, he spoke to the country exclusively over radio and via newsreels. In the judgment of one observer, Truman failed "to use broadcasting consciously as a lever for increasing his influence on the Congress." [19]

Presidential television came of age in the 1952 election when Eisenhower became the first candidate for president to use television commercials heavily in his campaign.* In the postelection euphoria, press secretary James Hagerty referred to the advent of presidential television as a "new age" and raised the prospect of a regularly scheduled, monthly television program from the White House. Nothing came of this idea, however. During his eight years in office, Eisenhower instead continued Truman's practice of reserving television addresses mainly for international crises. Not until the administrations of Lyndon Johnson and Richard Nixon did routine affairs of state become the subjects of presidential, prime-time television.

There is a similar time lag between technology and practice in presidential travel. Harry Truman valued the mobility offered by a plane designated for presidential use, but more for personal reasons (returning home to Missouri) than for possible political advantage. One might think that Truman, having assumed office on the death of FDR, would also have found good reason to travel around the country to gain national exposure and build support among local party organizations. But, as shown in Figure 5-4, Truman took few political trips. Eisenhower in turn was tardy in using jet transportation to travel abroad. It was left to his successors, principally Nixon, to make foreign travel a standard feature of the president's public repertoire and to discover, notably in the case of Bush, that the political limitations of extensive travel are more severe than the physical. These instances of a time lag between the availability of an innovation and its use suggest that something other than availability enters a president's decision to exploit new technology in going public.

Incremental Growth as a Function of Politics

Going public is a strategic choice grounded as much in contemporary political relations as in available technology. The decline of institutional pluralism and with it the insulation of leaders from public oversight rendered Washington's politicians increasingly susceptible to public opinion and pressure. These same forces rendered bargaining both more difficult and less likely to suffice. Moreover, presidential selection reforms are sending politicians to the White House who are neither trained nor interested in learning the "ways" of Washington. These outsiders frequently prefer to go public rather than engage in quiet diplomacy. Technology has offered ever-expanding opportunities, but the motivation to exploit them is rooted in the way politics are conducted in present-day Washington.

The decision to bargain or to go public is based upon a comparison of the relative costs and benefits of each strategy at a particular moment. Technology and evolving political relations have made the public approach increasingly attractive. But real costs may attend innovation in going public, which at times have applied a brake on the rapid expansion of public strategies. During an era

---

* Eisenhower spent $800,000 on television time, compared with $77,000 spent by the Democratic candidate, Adlai Stevenson. See Kathleen Hall Jamieson, *Packaging the Presidency* (New York: Oxford University Press, 1984), 43.

of entrenched leaders, going public would generally be construed as an exercise in pressure politics, and unless practiced delicately could easily backfire. Any public activity—but especially innovation—runs this risk of violating established expectations and triggering hostile reactions from other political elites in Washington.

Franklin Roosevelt's Court-packing campaign illustrates this well. Fresh from a landslide reelection victory and perhaps suffering from euphoria, Roosevelt early in 1937 unveiled at a press conference his proposal for legislation to increase the number of Supreme Court justices and thereby gain more sympathetic treatment of New Deal programs.[20] In doing so, he broke with existing protocol by failing to brief key members of Congress before making a public announcement of a legislative initiative. In the opinion of many participants and commentators, this early mistake contributed critically to the proposal's eventual defeat. Even Roosevelt's staunchest supporters in Congress were taken aback; his detractors predictably were outraged. The Court-packing proposal was FDR's most stunning legislative failure in his twelve years in office. It was also the only time he used one of his famous fireside chats to ask the public to pressure Congress in behalf of his policies.* From the Senate, Harry Truman witnessed firsthand the ill will sowed by Roosevelt's innovative use of the press conference. Citing it a decade later, Truman as president would refuse to use the press conference for unveiling congressional initiatives.[21]

The Court-packing episode is instructive in two ways. First, it shows that in the realm of public opinion, where politicians will understandably be quite sensitive, departures from established practices can easily backfire, even for someone as popular as Franklin Roosevelt with a Congress controlled by his party. Second, Truman's response reveals how the experiences of one president become lessons for the next. Whether learned firsthand or observed from the sidelines, the negative reactions of other politicians serve to bring presidential strategy into conformity with expectations founded upon established practice. To the degree these forces impress themselves on political behavior, one president's activity will not much differ from that of his predecessor. Innovation occurs "at the margin." The results can be seen in the aggregate trends—both in the steady growth of direct communication and, as was shown in chapter 4, in the gradual decline of the traditional press conference.

Political Forces Opposing Growth in Going Public

A president's decision to go public by enlisting a new technology or by employing an old one in a novel fashion brings forces of change into conflict with those of stability. New opportunities made possible by advances in technology

---

* Although, as a *New York Times* commentary on earlier fireside addresses pointed out, the implications of the direct public approach in motivating Congress were clear: "His use of this new instrument of political discussion is a plain hint to Congress of a recourse which the president may employ if it proves necessary to rally support for legislation which he asks and which legislators might be reluctant to give him." Cited in Becker, "Presidential Power," 15.

and rising incentives brought on by changing political circumstances run up against the established prerogatives of other politicians. When the choice favors innovation, the president can try to minimize the political costs by having it conform to, or at least resemble, existing practices as closely as possible. Presidents may summon precedents for some novel form of public activity, or they may simply do a lot more of a familiar public activity. Both are venerable strategies of incremental politics. In chapter 4 we encountered an instance of the former in President Kennedy's introduction of the televised news conference. By allowing the networks to replace film with "live" cameras, he adapted existing institutional arrangements to a radically new purpose—direct communication with the public—and thereby managed to undo the old order even as he conformed to its expectations.

Examples of incrementally expanding the base can be found in the gradually rising trends in going public presented in this chapter. Presidents have tended to increase their public activities only marginally beyond levels of accepted practice. As long as a president can credibly argue that his activity does not much differ from that of his predecessor, he should be able to blunt criticism from those who are adversely affected by his successful public appeals. The greater the departure of current from past practice, of course, the less credible the president's claim becomes and the greater the likelihood of criticism and resistance. The easiest way to discern this dynamic is the exceptional instance where the president pushes too far beyond the edge of current practices and consequently elicits an equally forceful counterforce. A good illustration of this process is President Nixon's decision shortly after entering office to sharply expand his television presence over past practice. By one count Nixon appeared on national television seventeen times within nine months beginning in late 1969. On eleven of these occasions, he preempted evening commercial television.[22] The sudden surge in presidential television appearances generated complaints from various quarters and assumed the status of a prominent news story in its own right. During the summer of 1970, Washington correspondents began pressing Nixon at news conferences with pointed questions about his television strategy. The White House responded by arguing that the president was simply subscribing to the practices of past presidents. Aide John Ehrlichman compiled figures on the television appearances of Presidents Kennedy and Johnson, as well as Nixon, arguing that his president had been on television less than Kennedy and about as often as Johnson. (His tally conveniently did not distinguish evening prime time from daytime appearances.)

Ehrlichman's reasoning did little to allay criticism, however, which was soon picked up by the president's adversaries. A group of antiwar activists, citing repeated instances of Nixon's use of television to promote his Vietnam policies, petitioned the Federal Communications Commission (FCC) for network time to respond to the president's remarks under the fairness doctrine. The Democratic National Committee appealed directly to the networks for a similar opportunity to rebut the president. In midsummer the FCC ruled for the first time that a president's repeated addresses on a subject had produced an imbalance in public debate and that those holding opposing views should be given network airtime to respond.[23] Independent of the FCC ruling, the networks liberalized access of Democrats to answer the president's remarks.

The idea of granting airtime to the president's opponents was not new. After President Truman blasted "greedy" steel company executives and, asserting inherent wartime constitutional authority as commander in chief, seized the mills in 1951, the networks gave rebuttal time to the president of Inland Steel Company. During the mid-1960s, networks began the practice of granting airtime to congressional opponents to answer the president's annual State of the Union message. According to archival research performed by the Congressional Research Service, opposition spokespersons—whether individuals, congressional leaders, or representatives of the opposition party—were allotted free response time on national television on only four occasions from 1961 to 1964. But from 1970 to 1974, after Nixon ratcheted up his television appearances, the opposition Democratic Party responded on fourteen occasions; from 1975 to 1984, there were thirty-four.[24] Today, response time is routinely accorded the opposition party in Congress, except during crises (e.g., Bush's first 9/11 speech).[25] Clearly, Nixon's heavy use of television helped establish strong precedents that will ensure future opposition parties their time on television.

Opposition groups were not alone in complaining about the frequency of Nixon's television appearances. After the heavy dose of prime-time television during Nixon's first year, CBS head Frank Stanton publicly began to characterize the White House strategy as an attempt to monopolize the airwaves.[26] Given the value of prime time, thirty-second commercial spots, one can easily discern the backbone of self-interest that prompted this network executive to charge the still-popular president with enjoying undue political advantage through his *carte blanche* access to the national television audience. Granting the opposition party response time did restore at least a semblance of parity, but this most likely was viewed as inadequate because it cost the networks yet more time slots for programming and commercials.

In October 1975 the networks hit upon a less expensive way to rein in presidential television: simply deny the president access to the airwaves. Although the next election was over a year away, CBS and NBC refused to carry Gerald Ford's address on tax reform on the dubious ground that they would have to provide equal time to other announced candidates. (At that early date, there was apparently only one—an obscure, perennial hopeful in Massachusetts.) Not until Reagan's second term, however, did the networks assert the prerogative to judge the appropriateness of a presidential address.*

---

* But it is apparent that this first instance made gaining access to the airwaves an important consideration for presidents and their aides. In late 1978 President Carter's communications director planned a media strategy involving unprecedented levels of national television. He advised the president to cultivate warm relations with the network heads, so that they would be less likely to balk at complying with his subsequent request for airtime. (Rafshoon to Carter, June 30, 1978.)

From mid-1986 through the fall of 1987, one or more of the networks refused to comply with President Reagan's request for airtime on at least three occasions. Two of these involved appeals for public support for aid to the Nicaraguan *contras*; the third urged the public's support for confirmation of Judge Robert Bork, Reagan's ultimately unsuccessfully nominee to the Supreme Court. During this nonelection period, the networks could not fall

Squeezed from Prime Time

President Bush received his comeuppance [for presumptuously assuming that he could speak to the American people on national television whenever he, as president, deemed national events warranted it] when he naively requested network airtime beginning at 8:30 for a press conferences on the first night of the "May sweeps." This industry phrase refers to the week when the networks trot out their best programming to win ratings points that set the advertising rates for the next year's commercials. To make prying this coveted time even more difficult, the president's representatives noted that beyond reviewing the "continuing progress in Iraq," the president would have no announcements or offer new information. With the highly popular duo of *Survivor* followed by *C.S.I.* that evening, CBS promptly demurred. Sporting a less impressive lineup, ABC was quick to sign on to do its civic duty, as was Fox. This left NBC in a bind. The 8:30 time slot was fine, but it badly wanted to preserve the 9:00 p.m. presentation of its wildly popular *Apprentice*. (Nor, one may surmise, did it want to break the news to Donald Trump that POTUS—White House speak for President of the United States—had bumped him off his normal slot.)

After temporizing into afternoon, the president's staff came up with a compromise—start earlier (to a smaller West Coast audience) at 8 and finish by 9. Relieved, NBC jumped on board, leaving CBS the only holdout. After deliberating throughout the afternoon (and consulting with this scholar for precedents allowing them to snub the president), CBS capitulated.

President Bush got his hour of prime time television but just. As the bewitching hour neared, Bush called for "the final question," explaining "I don't want to cut into any of those TV shows that are getting ready to air . . . for the sake of the economy." He need not have worried; both CBS and NBC had already cut away to their news anchors, who quickly wrapped up the presentation and referred the audience to their popular upcoming shows.

Source: Jacques Steinberg, "How White House Ended up on Prime Time," *New York Times*, April 29, 2005.

back on equal time for opponents as their rationale for denying the president's request. Instead, they introduced the criterion of newsworthiness with network executives acting as arbiters. This would appear a difficult and awkward arrangement, since presidents identified little more than the topic of the address to those making the decision. One network executive's comment struck directly at the strategy of going public: "Tonight's address is really directed at a small group of people on Capitol Hill, so my recommendation is not to interrupt our prime-time broadcast to carry that." [27] In 1993 none of these executives could pretend that President Clinton's request for airtime to unveil his much-heralded health care reform proposal before a joint session of Congress represented arcane Washington business. But when he suggested giving this address on September 22, every network executive balked. The president had requested prime time during the most important week of the season, when the networks debuted their fall lineup of sitcoms. [28]

Networks have continued to toughen presidents' access to prime time television, even though recent presidents have returned to pre-Nixon levels of addressing a national audience in major speeches (see Figure 5-2, page 122). In part, networks can more easily turn down White House requests because the profusion of cable channels affords presidents other outlets for reaching a national audience. Whatever value the presence of cable channels offers network executives as an excuse to deflect presidential requests, the growth of cable television posed a more urgent and dire consideration for these executives in dealing with White House requests for airtime. The adverse reaction to presidential television from the opposition party in Congress and network executives pales in comparison to that from a third class of participants—the viewing public.

What Technology Giveth, Technology Taketh Away

In the 1960s and 1970s, CBS, NBC, and ABC enjoyed an oligopoly. As one network executive reminisced, "when viewers turned on the TV set, they had five choices, and the networks were three of them . . . [and they] collectively accounted for about 90% of the television audience." [29] As displayed in Figure 5-5 (page 132), from 1965 to 2005 the number of households subscribing to cable television rose sharply from 6 percent to 83 percent. Moreover, in 1983 cable subscribers received, on average, less than fifteen channels; today, the average exceeds one hundred. [30] When the three networks controlled 90 percent of the audience share in most markets, the president enjoyed a seemingly captive audience for his addresses to the nation. There is no evidence, based on careful audience research, that an appreciable number of viewers ever chose to turn off their televisions.* Back in the days when several broadcast networks

---

* Nielsen estimates comparing audience size during presidential addresses and normal programming have found no significant differences. One study actually found that during President Ford's tenure, the audience grew slightly when he was on television. These findings are reported in Newton N. Minow and Lee M. Mitchell, "Incumbent Television: A Case of Indecent Exposure," *Annals of the American Academy of Political and Social Science* 425 (May 1976): 74–77.

dominated the airwaves, they agreed to suspend commercial programming and jointly broadcast the president's address; they even used the same camera feeds. This practice left voters with few programming options. That, in turn, served the networks' purposes, by preventing serious audience erosion when commercial programming resumed, and the president's purposes, by guaranteeing the largest possible audience.

Cable gives viewers choices, and for this reason, it makes the choice to watch the president more costly than when all viewers are tethered to the television antenna. As the number of alternative programs increases, so too does the likelihood that one of them will prove more attractive than the president's message, prompting the viewer to change channels. So, cable subscribers will be less likely to watch a presidential appearance than will those viewers who remain captive to the broadcast signal. As evidenced by recent presidents' weak audience ratings (see Figure 5-6), people have proven nimble at changing channels. However well they may be doing in the Gallup Polls, recent presidents are clearly slipping in A. C. Nielsen's audience ratings.[31] The figure depicts a point-a-year decline on average in percentages of households with televisions that have tuned in to presidential addresses during the past six administrations. Almost two-thirds of homes with televisions tuned in to President Nixon's 1971 State of the Union speech. Presidents Carter and Reagan nearly matched him once, in their first addresses to the nation, but by the time President George W. Bush first addressed the nation on prime-time television the audience had shrunk by nearly half.[32] Less than a quarter of America's households tuned in to his heavily promoted 9/11 commemoration in September 2006.

President Clinton managed to plumb new depths of presidential television ratings. On April 8, 1995, with the House of Representatives and the Senate poised to enact most of the provisions of the Republicans' Contract with America, Democrat Clinton summoned reporters for a rare prime-time news conference. Only CBS covered the evening event. This gave broadcast television households, as well as cable subscribers, ample alternative programming to which to tune. All but 6.5 percent of households with television chose some other option to watching the president.*

Undoubtedly, many citizens who were unenthusiastic and hence inattentive captive viewers when they had few choices now abandon the president. But since they were probably the least responsive members of the audience, their departure will not greatly affect the president's capacity to generate vocal support for his policies. Of greater strategic concern to a president is the fact that many other viewers, those whom the president seeks to persuade and mobilize on his behalf, also appear to be taking advantage of their options and fleeing presidential addresses.

---

* The president actually caught a break that few viewers tuned in. Early into the news conference a reporter asked him the pointed but expected question as to whether anyone in Washington was paying attention to him and whether he really thought he could withstand the Republican juggernaut. Clinton's response, "The President is not irrelevant here," was frequently repeated on news broadcasts during the next several days.

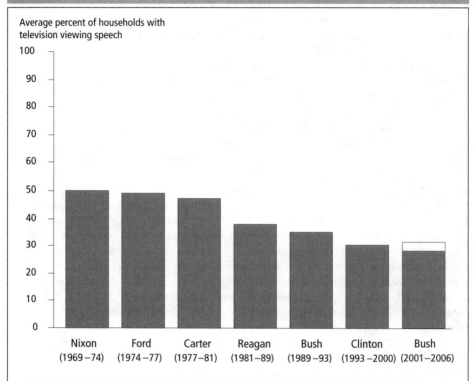

FIGURE 5-6 **The Declining Prime-Time Audience for Presidential Addresses, 1969–2006**

Average percent of households with television viewing speech

Sources: A.C. Nielsen Media Research and CBS Audience Research.

Note: The larger figure for Bush includes the two national addresses delivered immediately after September 11, 2001.

Each time the president begins an address viewers assess the attractiveness of the president's message compared to the entertainment (or informational) value of some other program. Will they benefit more from staying tuned to the president versus the most attractive option on the cable menu? So posed, this question alerts us to the possibility that cable viewers predictably separate into classes of president watchers and switchers. One important separating criterion is the viewer's assessment of the credibility of the source. Those viewers who identify with the president's party will generally regard the president as a more reliable and credible source than will those who prefer the opposition party. If so, as more households hook up to the cable, we should find those segments of the public most receptive to the president staying tuned while the rest of the audience change channels. Although Nielsen Media Research does not provide researchers with the kind of disaggregated data to test this hypothesis, we have an alternative source in the commercial polling firms that frequently ask respondents if they happened to hear or see the president's speech.* Figure 5-7 plots the percentages of party identifiers who reported watching that year's State of the Union address. As others have noticed, during the early years, when virtually everyone was held hostage by colluding networks during presidential messages, Democrats and independents watched Republican president Reagan in about the same shares as Republican viewers.[33] Note that independents were more likely than opposition identifiers to break ranks by either turning off the set or switching to one of the few independent broadcast channels. Not until the 1990s do we begin to find consistent partisan differences among viewers.† The pattern has become most pronounced during George W. Bush's presidency. In 2005, 27 percent fewer Democrats reported tuning in to that year's State of the Union message. Perhaps it reflects the continued growth of cable (and satellite) subscriptions as well as the polarizing feature of the administration.[34]

Of course, at times presidents make for compelling viewing. In late September 2001 when George W. Bush spoke before a joint session of Congress and the nation on terrorism's threat, 51 percent of American households that owned televisions—about 88 million viewers—had them tuned on one of the eight channels broadcasting the speech. Virtually everyone across the country wanted to know what the president planned to do in response to the 9/11 attacks. When Bush delivered his State of the Union address in February 2006, only 24 percent of these households tuned in to the speech despite coverage on seven outlets. Today, with uncertainty about whether the networks will decide to broadcast the president's message, and if they do, whether viewers will opt to view it, the size and makeup of the audience becomes a serious consideration in planning the president's public strategies.

CONCLUSION

A proposition of this book is that the degree to which presidents go public determines the kind of leaders they will be. Modern presidents rely upon pub-

---

* These data suffer several potential weaknesses that may render them less reliable than Nielsen's viewer logs. They are compiled from numerous polling firms with different sampling methods and some variation in question wording. Also, respondents appear to overreport watching the speech, at least when compared to the Nielsen estimates. As with self-reports of voting, a small share of respondents prefer to give a civically commendable response. In most instances I calculated the findings directly from the relevant surveys available from the Roper Center, but those for Reagan were transcribed from private reports written by pollster Richard Wirthlin to President Reagan. I wish to thank Justin Vaughan for his vigilant help in identifying and copying these records archived at the Texas A&M University library.

† Exceptions during this period, 1995 and 1998, occurred against a current backdrop of scandal —first Whitewater and then Monica Lewinsky. Perhaps Democrats stayed away rather than watch their president squirm in front of a mostly Republican audience, while more than usual shares of Republicans tuned in for the same reason.

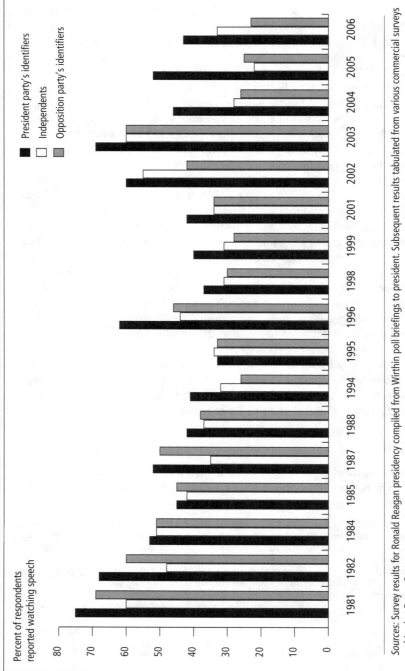

FIGURE 5-7 **Reported Viewership of State of the Union Addresses among Party Identifiers, 1981–2006**

Percent of respondents
reported watching speech

■ President party's identifiers
□ Independents
▨ Opposition party's identifiers

Sources: Survey results for Ronald Reagan presidency compiled from Wirthin poll briefings to president. Subsequent results tabulated from various commercial surveys archived at Roper Center.

lic opinion for their leadership in Washington to an extent unknown in the early 1950s. This makes for a style of leadership in the White House that was unknown to Robert A. Dahl and Charles E. Lindblom when they described the president as "an embodiment of a bargaining society" in the early 1950s or a few years later when Richard E. Neustadt predicated presidential power exclusively on bargaining.[35]

This proposition, claiming a change in the degree of going public and inferring a change in the character of leadership, is subject to rejoinder on two fronts. Because every president since Theodore Roosevelt has sought at some moment to rally public opinion to his side, and each in his public activity has drawn on the precedents and departed only marginally from the base lines of his immediate predecessor, one can easily miss the striking degree to which presidents today go public compared with the presidents of the 1930s, 1940s, or even 1950s.

Moreover, I suspect that the increasing quantity of public activity has tended to be obscured by the varying quality of public rhetoric, which is always more memorable than the quantity. To those who compared Ronald Reagan's rhetorical talents with those of Franklin Roosevelt, little appears to have changed in the past fifty years.

One misconception that results from incremental change is that the past blurs into the present. This, after all, is the purpose of the incremental strategy. A case in point is the story Arthur Schlesinger recounts of a phone call he received one morning from President Kennedy. The president asked how frequently FDR had held fireside chats. He said that *New York Times* correspondent Lester Markel was with him, complaining that he ought to go before the American people more often: "Lester . . . seems to think that Roosevelt gave a fireside chat once a week." Schlesinger subsequently reported to Kennedy that before the war, Roosevelt averaged no more than two of these now-famous radio addresses a year.* A couple of years later the issue was still current when Schlesinger passed along to Kennedy a letter from Samuel Beer, a prominent political scientist and former national chair of the Americans for Democratic Action, that said:

> I certainly do not agree, let alone sympathize, with my liberal friends
> who say that it is all the fault of the President; that if he would only
> resort to the magic of the "fire-side chat" he would create great waves

---

* Arthur M. Schlesinger Jr., *A Thousand Days* (Boston: Houghton Mifflin, 1965), 715. The following memorandum from Schlesinger to Kennedy, dated March 16, 1961, indicates that other members of the press were already forming similar expectations of the president: "There is increasing concern among friends in the press about the alleged failure of the Administration to do as effective a job of public information and instruction as it should and must. Lippmann had a column about this last week. Joe Alsop has been haranguing me about this over the telephone and plans to do some columns about it soon. Lester Markel is going to do a long piece about it in the *Times Magazine*." Cited in William E. Leuchtenburg, *In the Shadow of FDR* (Ithaca, N.Y.: Cornell University Press, 1985), 114.

of public opinion which would wash away Congressional obstruction. They simply don't remember the way FDR actually worked—e.g. the prolonged and tortured operation by which he got the Wage-Hour bill—and totally forget the political situation that gave him leverage.[36]

When it comes to collective memory of presidential performance, one seems as inclined to impose the present on the past as vice versa. Either way, the result is that nothing much *appears* to have happened.

Another counterargument accepts the trends examined in this chapter but holds that they have little bearing on the character of presidential leadership. The president may be a more familiar face on television, and he may spend more time on the road, but his public relations have not reduced the role of bargaining in presidential leadership. Against this argument, quantitative indexes of public activity, no matter how dramatic the changes they depict, stand mute.

To conclude that the multitudinous public activities of modern presidents do matter—that they have altered the character of leadership in Washington—one needs to consider more qualitative evidence, such as the transactions between the president and those he seeks to influence. The next chapter examines the ways Ronald Reagan promoted his budget with Congress during his first three years in office. The budgetary politics of these years show how a president, who took pride in his skills as a communicator, enlisted public support in his dealings with congressional leaders and how these activities substituted for and at times interfered with bargaining.

NOTES

1. Rowland Evans and Robert Novak, *Nixon in the White House* (New York: Random House, 1971), 388–389.
2. These categories of going public correspond to those developed by William W. Lammers, who was the first to systematically examine trends in presidents' public activities (William W. Lammers, "Presidential Attention-Focusing Activities," in *The President and the American Public,* ed. Doris A. Graber [Philadelphia: Institute for the Study of Human Issues, 1982], 145–171).

    To incorporate the research of Professor Lammers on the public activities of modern presidents, I adopted his coding scheme. I also consulted with him at the early stages of this study for his advice on how to code difficult cases. The present analysis, therefore, benefits from both his considerable research and good judgment.

    1. The three general categories of public activities presented in Figures 5-2, 5-3, and 5-4 are intended to be neither mutually exclusive nor together an exhaustive classification of all public behavior. Press conferences (examined in Table 5-2), purely ceremonial functions such as lighting the White House Christmas tree, vacation travel, and minor public activities such as White House receptions and brief remarks have been excluded from the analysis. The three categories of public activities are addresses, political travel, and appearances.

    Addresses. Major addresses are those generally delivered in Washington, broadcast on television or radio, and focused on more than a narrow potential audience. Inaugural and

State of the Union speeches are included in this group. Note that because of the extensive number of nationally broadcast radio addresses by President Reagan, I have separated his radio from his television addresses in Figure 5-2. The major address totals for Presidents Bush and Clinton also exclude radio addresses. Omitted from major addresses are presidential press conferences and purely ceremonial functions (for example, calls to astronauts and Christmas tree lighting ceremonies). See Table 5-2 for the decline in the use of press conferences. Minor addresses are all nonmajor statements made outside the White House in which the president spoke more than one thousand words. Question-and-answer sessions, even if conducted outside a formal press conference setting, are excluded.

Political travel. To distinguish purely vacation travel from work-related travel, only those travel days that involved public political activity are included in Figure 5-3. Moreover, to be coded as domestic political travel, the president must do more than engage in brief conversation with reporters. To be coded as political foreign travel, the travel day must include comments exceeding two hundred words, a meeting with a head of state, or attendance at an international conference, even if the president does not engage in public activity.

Appearances. Washington appearances take place away from the White House and the Executive Office Building and include all appearances in Washington and its surrounding suburbs. Brief comments with reporters are excluded from both Washington and U.S. appearances, but prepared remarks on arrival are included in the coding. Unlike Professor Lammers, who excluded President Carter's town meetings, I have coded them as constituting both days of travel and appearances.

3. As a cautionary note, in recent years the sources used to compile this list of television addresses appear to employ a more inclusive definition of "address to nation."
4. In Figures 5-2, 5-3, and 5-4, only the first three years have been tabulated in order to eliminate activities inspired by concerns for reelection rather than governing. Since Gerald Ford's tenure does not include three nonelection years, his record of public activities has been ignored.
5. Pierre Salinger, *With Kennedy* (New York: Doubleday, 1966), 138–144. For a discussion of other presidents' concerns with overexposure, see Godfrey Hodgson, *All Things to All Men* (New York: Simon and Schuster, 1980), 188–189.
6. From a memorandum to President Carter, June 30, 1978, personal papers of Gerald Rafshoon.
7. Examples of such statements are Hodgson, *All Things to All Men,* and Arthur Schlesinger Jr., *The Imperial Presidency* (Boston: Houghton Mifflin, 1973).
8. James T. Wooten, "Pre-Inaugural Memo Urged Carter to Emphasize Style Over Substance," *New York Times,* May 4, 1977, 1.
9. Newton N. Minow, John Bartlow Martin, and Lee M. Mitchell, *Presidential Television* (New York: Basic Books, 1973), 65–68.
10. J. F. terHorst and Col. Ralph Albertazzie provide a lively chronology of presidential air travel in *The Flying White House* (New York: Coward, McCann, and Geoghegan, 1979).
11. "Hoover, with 37 Radio Talks in Past Year, Made a Record," *New York Times,* December 28, 1930, 1.
12. "Health of President Coolidge Conserved by Broadcasting," *New York Times,* February 24, 1924, 15.
13. Travel time during this era is nicely displayed in the isochronic map "Rates of Travel, 1930," in Charles O. Paullin, *Atlas of the Historical Geography of the United States* (Washington, D.C.: Carnegie Institution, 1932), plate 138D.

14. terHorst and Albertazzie, *Flying White House,* 33.

15. Douglass Cater, *The Fourth Branch of Government* (Boston: Houghton Mifflin, 1959), 40–42.

16. Enlisting a new technology and enlisting it well are, of course, different matters. On the problems Bush experienced in adapting to the teleconferencing format, see Michael Wines, "In Scripts for Bush, Questions on Images," *New York Times,* November 28, 1991.

17. Roosevelt reportedly expressed to a friend his wish that the development of television would speed up. See Hodgson, *All Things to All Men,* 186.

18. See Samuel L. Becker, "Presidential Power: The Influence of Broadcasting," *Quarterly Journal of Speech* 47 (October 1961): 17.

19. Ibid.

20. Joseph Alsop and Turner Catledge, *The 168 Days* (New York: Doubleday and Co., 1938), 13–79.

21. *Memoirs by Harry S Truman: Years of Trial and Hope,* vol. 2 (Garden City, N.Y.: Doubleday and Co., 1956; reprint, New York: New American Library, 1965).

22. Minow, Martin, and Mitchell, *Presidential Television,* 69–72.

23. Denis Steven Rutkus, "President Reagan, the Opposition and Access to Network Airtime" (Congressional Research Service, Washington, D.C., 1984, Mimeographed), 69–71.

24. The figures for the years 1961–1964 come from Robert Lee Bailey, *An Examination of Prime Time Network Television Special Programs, 1948–1966,* ed. Christopher H. Sterling (New York: Arno Press, 1979), Appendix A; and for the years 1970–1984, figures come from Denis Steven Rutkus, "President Reagan, the Opposition and Access to Network Airtime," Congressional Research Service, August 1984, Appendix C.

25. Rutkus, "President Reagan," 36–59.

26. Robert B. Semple Jr., "Nixon Eludes Newsmen on Coast Trip," *New York Times,* August 3, 1970, 16.

27. Peter J. Boyer, "Networks Refuse to Broadcast Reagan's Plea," *New York Times,* February 3, 1988.

28. "Washington Insight," *Los Angeles Times,* August 23, 1993. The speech was delivered on September 19, in prime time.

29. Brian Lowry, "Cable Stations Gather Strength," *Los Angeles Times,* September 2, 1997.

30. ZdNet IT Facts, 2004: www.itfacts.biz/index.php?id=P1654.

31. This discussion is based on a systematic analysis of Nielsen ratings reported initially in Matthew A. Baum and Samuel Kernell, "Has Cable Ended the Golden Age of Presidential Television?" *American Political Science Review* 93 (March): 99–114. This analysis has been updated to include the remainder of the Clinton administration and the Bush administration through early 2006 in Matthew A. Baum and Samuel Kernell, "How Cable Ended the Golden Age of Presidential Television: From 1969 to 2006," in Samuel Kernell and Steven S. Smith, eds., *Principles and Practices of American Politics,* 3rd ed. (Washington, D.C.: CQ Press, 2007).

32. Specifically, Bush garnered a Nielsen rating of 38 percent. While the ratings graphed in Figure 5-6 do not represent all presidential prime-time addresses, they come close. I wish to thank Professor Joe Foote and Laura Kapnick at CBS News for making available the data reported here. Various statistical tests of the change in the way Nielsen monitors viewers in the fall of 1987 did not turn up a significant effect on declining presidential audience shares.

33. George C. Edwards III, *On Deaf Ears* (New Haven: Yale University Press, 2003), 203–204; Reed L. Welch, "Is Anybody Watching? The Audience for Televised Presidential Addresses," *Congress and the Presidency* 27 (spring 2000): 41–58.

34. Gary C. Jacobson has documented Bush's polarizing impact on public opinion in *A Divider, Not a Uniter* (New York: Pearson, Longman, 2007), 211–212.

35. See Robert A. Dahl and Charles E. Lindblom, *Politics, Economics, and Welfare* (New York: Harper and Row, 1960); and Richard E. Neustadt, *Presidential Power* (New York: John Wiley and Sons, 1980).

36. Cited in William E. Leuchtenburg, *In the Shadow of FDR* (Ithaca, N.Y.: Cornell University Press, 1985), 114.

6

President Reagan and His First Three Budgets: A Classic Case of Going Public in Action

Try to imagine an individual better suited by experience, temperament, and ideology to lead by going public than Ronald Reagan. It is difficult to do so. Certainly not George H. W. Bush, who served eight years as his understudy but in office proved long on motion and short on vision. Bill Clinton was better than Bush at going public but perhaps not as good as Reagan. Reagan brought to the presidency ideal qualities for this new strategy of leadership, and his performance was not disappointing. When presented at critical moments with the choice to deal or to go public, he preferred to go public—sometimes exclusively, other times in combination with bargaining. The trends in direct public appeals surveyed in chapter 4 culminated in Reagan's distinctive style of leadership, unimagined forty years ago.

Contrary to some predictions, this outsider, this public president did not fall on his face. While his legacy is already being measured in terms of the volume of red ink it incurred, judged politically—that is, according to the accomplishment of his own programmatic goals—Reagan's record of going public proved fruitful. Political elites in Washington initially expressed surprise at the president's maneuvers—during the 97th Congress the words "shock" and "bewilderment" were recurrently attributed to Democrats in Congress—but more so at their profound effects on the behavior of fellow politicians than at the acts themselves. Nearly five years later, after the president had accumulated some political bruises that invariably come with time and his approach to leadership was no longer novel to Washington politicians, they were still paying him grudging respect. One Democratic member summed up congressional sentiment toward Reagan after five years in office: "He's still formidable, no question about that. We're still a bit afraid of him." [1]

Ronald Reagan's first three years contained all the variation in prestige and legislative accomplishment necessary to study the downside as well as the upside of public leadership. Success came early and in heaping portions, but it did not last. By the beginning of his third year, with his popularity spent, the president struggled to preserve the earlier budgetary achievements of real growth in defense expenditures, reductions in social programs, and a 25 percent cut in income taxes. Although the dollar amounts varied marginally from one budget to the next, President Reagan remained consistent, both in the substance of policies as well as the strategies he employed in their behalf. The politics that ensued in each of his first three budget seasons differed greatly, however. And yet they did so in a manner altogether consistent with the theory of individualized pluralism.

Not unlike various fairy tales with famous threesomes, "President Reagan and His First Three Budgets" is a didactic story, each episode instructive in itself as well as in its overall moral. It is worth telling here, for it fleshes out the emerging features of the modern office in a way that charts and tables cannot, however steep the trends they may depict. Before beginning, however, I need to introduce the main character.

REAGAN AS AN OUTSIDER

Ronald Reagan's previous career in movies, television, and public affairs groomed him well for the role of a president who goes public routinely. Movies brought him fame, a considerable resource employed by military heroes of earlier eras in transferring laterally to a public career. Reagan's early years in Hollywood contributed incidentally to his political maturation as he waged ideological war with liberals during his tenure as president of the Screen Actors Guild.[2] Later, a decade of television spent largely as spokesman first for Borax and then for General Electric gave him mastery of the requisite techniques. In his autobiography, *Where's the Rest of Me?*, Reagan described his duties for General Electric: "I know statistics are boring, but reducing eight years of tours, in which I reached all the 135 plants and personally met with 250,000 employees, down to numbers, it turns out something like this: two of the years were spent traveling and with speeches sometimes running at 14 a day, I was on my feet in front of a 'mike' for about 250,000 minutes." [3] These ancillary public relations activities had him in training for the thirty-two-round presidential primary campaign long before the reforms had been instituted. And they gave him ample opportunity to perfect his familiar criticisms of big government and his encomiums to private enterprise.[4]

In 1967, at the age of fifty-five, Ronald Reagan embarked on a career in politics when he defeated Pat Brown for the governorship of California. Entering the public arena comparatively late in life and high on the rung of public offices also contributed to his style of leadership in the White House. If one considers a political career as a learning or developmental process where lower office not only promotes but also prepares a politician for higher office, Reagan's path to the presidency is clearly deficient. He skipped those formative experiences that take place mainly in legislatures—city councils, state assemblies, and Congress—and that expose a politician to bargaining and to compromise. Instead, as governor of California, Reagan's political tutelage occurred in peculiarly solitary yet visible environs for socialization. His tenure during years of campus unrest and Democratic legislatures gave him ample opportunity to hone his considerable rhetorical talents for the political arena. After eight years Reagan retired from office "to speak out on the issues," which meant to campaign full-time for the presidency. Being a nationally syndicated columnist and radio commentator and one of the most sought-after speakers on the Republican circuit, Reagan was better positioned than anyone else to do so.

Finally, one must consider the extensive campaign experience any candidate for the presidency invariably accumulates. Ronald Reagan may have begun a public career late and held only one office before the presidency, but he nonetheless managed to contest more than sixty-one primary and general elections, amassing a record of forty-four victories against seventeen defeats. All of them were in the national limelight.[5]

Such experience prepared Reagan to be a public president as much by what it omitted as by what it included. Other twentieth-century presidents had won the office with the thinnest of claims of insight into the ways of Washington, much less of the presidency. But with the exception of Jimmy Carter, none was so bereft of such experience as Reagan. Eisenhower, avowedly apolitical, could and did point to his "invaluable," albeit brief, service in the War Department (now Department of Defense) under George Marshall and subsequently as army chief of staff.* That Carter and Reagan should be so inexperienced is not, of course, mere coincidence. The reformed presidential nomination system coupled with lingering public memory of corruption and scandal in Washington allowed each man to convert his deprived political upbringing into a campaign asset.

Political ideology further distanced Ronald Reagan from Washington. Since his early and ardent conversion from the New Deal, Reagan had been an aggressive exponent of a traditional strain of Republican conservatism.† A favorite rhetorical device of his over the years was to decorate his attack of whatever Democratic policies were emanating from Washington at the moment with a simple, often folksy, statement of his own values and a caricature of Washington officials as "bureaucrats" and "spendthrift politicians." Reagan's insistent rhetoric helped to explain why on entering the White House he had accumulated an unusually large number of both intense followers and detractors.[6] As a conservative outsider moving to a city he perceived to be dominated by liberal insiders, Reagan was unsuited to be a pluralist president. Lou Cannon, a White House reporter and longtime Reagan watcher, attributed to him before he entered office a concept of the presidency that was consistent with his outsider status.

---

* Fred I. Greenstein attaches great significance to Eisenhower's Washington experience in arguing that his style in office, including his image among Washingtonians as a "bumbler," was actually an adroit strategic device to disarm potential adversaries and deflect responsibility. *The Hidden-Hand Presidency* (New York: Basic Books, 1982), chaps. 2, 3.

† Reagan's rhetoric over the years portrayed such consistency, as well as conviction, that his record refuted the "selling of the president" myth, which holds that television packaging requires plastic candidates whose issue positions can be molded by advertising executives guided by marketing surveys. A best-selling example of this genre is Joe McGinnis, *The Selling of the President* (New York: Trident Press, 1969).

Reagan is a modest man, but he did not object to the frequent descriptions of him as "the Great Communicator." He approvingly cited Theodore Roosevelt's description of the presidency as "a bully pulpit." With the forum of national television available to the President, Reagan was certain that his own communicative skills were sufficient to persuade Congress and the country to do whatever it was that was asked of them.[7]

As president, a politician is subjected to a brief and intense stint of decision making. Little time is available for leisurely learning. Absent is any semblance of apprenticeship, a norm that pervades virtually all other work settings including those in Washington. Rather, the president enters office with great latitude to be the kind of politician he wants to be. His definition of the presidency derives from preconceptions grounded in experience, temperament, and ideology. In Franklin Roosevelt, a man who groomed himself to serve in the office, these qualities were so configured as to present a consummate bargainer. Roosevelt's self-concept was so pure that presidential scholars have been able to glean from his performance insights into this style of pluralist leadership. So it was with Ronald Reagan. His personal qualities combined to provide similarly pristine material for the study of going public as a strategy of leadership. What other president, can one imagine, would repeatedly insist to his Soviet counterpart that he be given television time to address the Russian people?[8]

REAGAN'S THREE BUDGETS

Doonesbury's barbs about the president's laziness notwithstanding, Ronald Reagan's first three years in office were full ones. Contradicting skeptical predictions, he extracted from a Democratic House of Representatives and a narrowly Republican Senate the three major planks of his campaign platform: unprecedented budget reductions, increased military spending, and a massive three-year tax cut.* At the end of the first summer many observers were favorably comparing his legislative accomplishments with those of Franklin Roosevelt and the first New Deal and of Lyndon Johnson and the Great Society. The legacy of a massive national debt that this combination of policies would create was not yet fully realized.

As he accumulated an impressive string of victories during the summer of 1981, President Reagan increasingly appeared unbeatable. Liberal Democrats, at first stunned, gradually became more stoic. Many took solace in the rarely heard notion of letting the president have anything he wanted so he would be held responsible in the next election if the promised cornucopia of economic

---

* There were other, equally impressive victories as well. When Reagan learned that a resolution vetoing the administration's planned sale of AWACS planes to Saudi Arabia had garnered a majority of the Senate as cosponsors, he went into action. In a brief flurry of phone calls, meetings in the Oval Office, and public pronouncements, he unraveled the coalition and salvaged the sale.

benefits failed to materialize.[9] Not until September 1981, when he proposed changes in Social Security benefits—a promise he quickly retracted—did the president's fortunes begin to turn. Even so, at the close of 1981, not even the most optimistic Democratic prognosis foresaw his political discomfiture the next year.

The second session of the 97th Congress, in 1982, gave President Reagan some legislative victories, but these pale against the triumphs of the preceding year. Real growth in military spending continued despite a swelling budget deficit and louder rumblings from Democrats.[10] Congress agreed to another round of budget reductions, but this time the administration was forced to make numerous concessions after its initial budget reconciliation resolution was defeated in the House (along with every Democratic alternative). The greatest alteration of the Reagan blueprint was the tax increase of $99 billion drafted not by House Democrats but by the Republican Senate Finance Committee. This, the largest election-year tax hike in history, triggered a curious coalitional realignment in Congress.

Because midterm elections were approaching and the economy was souring quickly, the president's control over political affairs began to slip. A balanced budget became an increasingly distant goal; only record deficits and double-digit unemployment were in immediate sight. The economy manifested itself politically in the president's steady decline in the polls and, in turn, in the diminished support of politicians about to stand for election. The president was no pariah, but he was no longer the local hero.

Democratic hopes and Republican fears about the changing fortunes were confirmed in the November 1982 elections; twenty-six House seats switched over to the Democratic column, about the margin of the president's recent floor victories. From the election until the president's State of the Union message in January 1983, the foremost question among Washington politicians and bureaucrats, including many of the White House staff, was, could the president adapt to the new, harsher political realities? The answer was no. Unwilling to compromise with the Republican Senate Budget Committee, President Reagan gave up on the budget resolution and announced his intention to veto any appropriations bills that violated his budget recommendations. The story of Reagan's first three budgets spans the peaks and valleys of leadership based on going public.

Budget Politics in 1981

The early history of President Reagan's budget and tax cuts largely comprises televised presidential addresses to the nation. The first occurred on February 5 when he announced that the country faced "the worst economic mess since the Great Depression" and presented the broad contours of an economic program that resembled the tax and budget cuts on which he had campaigned. On February 18, the president returned to prime-time television to fill in the details. Addressing a televised joint session of Congress, he unveiled a package of tax cuts totaling $53.9 billion for individuals and businesses and spending reductions of $41.4 billion for fiscal year 1982. The initial response was muted, and the popular wisdom in Washington was that success would be neither quick nor easy because of the many organized constituencies opposed to reduced spending.[11] Ten days later the White House announced that an additional $13 billion cut in expenditures would be necessary to keep the budget within the targeted deficit ceiling.

As the president's economic program began wending its way through Congress's budget labyrinth, it received critical scrutiny by the press and interested constituencies. By mid-March the president's rating in the Gallup Poll stood at 59 percent approving and 24 percent disapproving, the poorest approve-to-disapprove ratio the Gallup Poll has ever recorded for a president in his second month of office. Press Secretary James Brady explained: "The fat's gotten into the fire more quickly with this [economic] proposal than in normal administrations because of [its] comprehensive nature . . . and the fact it's changing the direction of government. There's resistance to change."[12] An independent pollster concurred: "He's spending his savings [in popularity] and he has less in the bank now, that's all."[13]

The assassination attempt in late March erased his early decline in the polls. In typical fashion the public immediately rallied to his side; Reagan's approval rating went up by ten points or more in every national survey taken shortly after he was shot. More important, according to White House pollwatcher Richard Beal, the shooting and the president's unaided, almost nonchalant entry into the hospital, both of which were videotaped and reshown repeatedly on national television, "focussed uniquely on the President. It did a lot to endear the President to the people. . . . His personal attributes might never have come across without the assassination attempt."[14]

When Richard Wirthlin, the president's pollster, reported that the "resistance ratio" (a figure constructed from a battery of survey questions on the president's performance) to Reagan had improved from 2:1 to 3:1, presidential assistant Michael Deaver convened a strategy meeting to evaluate how this new "political capital" should be spent. Various options were aired, ranging from a radio address to a trip to Capitol Hill. Sensing the opportunity for high drama, they agreed on the latter course, a speech before a joint session of Congress. Journalist Sidney Blumenthal notes, "This decision was in keeping with overall strategy. To a greater extent than any other policy initiative, the President's economic program was being conducted as a national political campaign."[15]

To soften up potential allies before the president's appearance, Lyn Nofziger, the president's chief political aide, arranged for the Republican National Committee (RNC) to send party officials to the South over the Easter recess to stimulate grassroots pressure on Democratic representatives whose districts had gone heavily for Reagan in the November election.[16] By the time of his address to Congress on April 28, Reagan's surging popularity and the grassroots campaign had created a vote deficit for the Democratic opposition.

Democratic Whip Thomas Foley informed Speaker Thomas P. O'Neill Jr. on his return from an Easter trip abroad that they were already down fifty to sixty votes. Then came the president's speech.

All news accounts depict President Reagan's reception from Congress as a love feast, an ironic metaphor given that the audience was mostly Democrats who were well aware the president had come to advocate a starvation diet for many of the programs they had proudly enacted during the preceding decade. *Newsweek* reported, "His performance was a smash from the moment he entered the soaring House chamber, smiling and waving, to a three-minute thunderburst of whistles, huzzahs, and hand-clapping." [17] In the speech the president endorsed the Gramm-Latta budget reconciliation resolution (named for sponsors Phil Gramm and Delbert Latta), which carried the administration's proposals. He then attacked the Democratic alternative, calling it the "old and comfortable way." In closing his comments on the budget, President Reagan reminded the assembled legislators,

> When I took the oath of office, I pledged loyalty to only one special interest group—"We the people." Those people—neighbors and friends, shopkeepers and laborers, farmers and craftsmen—do not have infinite patience. As a matter of fact, some 80 years ago Teddy Roosevelt wrote these instructive words in his first message to the Congress: "The American people are slow to wrath, but when their wrath is once kindled, it burns like a consuming flame." [18]

A week after the speech and shortly before the budget's first major floor test, Speaker O'Neill could round up no more than 175 votes in opposition. A heated Democratic caucus followed in which O'Neill pleaded with fellow Democrats not to abandon the party and warned them: "The opinions of the man in the street change faster than anything in this world. Today, he does not know what is in this program, and he is influenced by a President with charisma and class [who] is a national hero. . . . But a year from now he will be saying, 'You shouldn't have voted that way.' " [19] For all his effort, O'Neill made but a single convert. Two days later, the House voted 253 to 176 to substitute Gramm-Latta for the Democratic bill and then promptly passed it by a wider margin. Fully a quarter of the House Democrats supported Reagan. "They say they're voting for it," reported Rep. Toby Moffett, a Connecticut liberal, "because they're afraid." [20]

It is one thing to support a general resolution that contains broad policy targets, and quite another to vote for the individual program cuts required to implement them. In mid-June, as the various House committees reported legislation implementing Gramm-Latta, the Reagan administration faced a difficult decision. With many of the spending measures departing sharply from the spending cuts mandated by the budget guidelines, should the president try to preserve his earlier victory through bargaining or going public? Each position was supported by a senior White House aide. Budget Director David Stockman urged the president to renew his public campaign to keep up the pressure on Democrats who had broken ranks with their party's leadership a month earlier. Chief of Staff James Baker and Communications Director David Gergen disagreed. Fearful of overtaxing public support, they advised the president to save his public strategy for his major tax initiative, Kemp-Roth, which was to come to a vote the next month. Stockman reports the argument this way: " 'We have to understand,' Baker warned Reagan, 'that we're running a very great risk here. If we throw down the challenge and lose, it'll sap our momentum.' " [21] The president was persuaded and instructed his aides to cut whatever deals were necessary to solidify his position with the boll weevils (southern Democrats) and gypsy moths (northern Republicans who did not favor cuts in social spending). Stockman recalls these transactions with disgust, blaming this decision for the failure of the Reagan revolution to cut back government while avoiding deficits: "[House Minority Leader Robert] Michel and I went straight from lunch to his office to preside over one of the most expensive sessions I have ever attended on Capitol Hill. I lost $20 billion in proposed three year budget savings in four hours. . . . Michel and I crammed . . . some of the worst features on the committee bills. Hour by hour I backpedaled." [22]

With mainstream House Democrats left out of the compromises, the party leadership and the House Rules Committee decided to induce second thoughts among the wayward Democrats by having the appropriations for individual programs voted on separately. By making their colleagues face up to these tough decisions, the Democratic leaders still appeared to have a chance to win.

On June 24, two days before the floor vote, President Reagan learned of this legislative maneuver while en route to San Antonio to deliver a speech. He responded with two quick public statements that made the networks' evening news on consecutive days, many phone calls to persuadable representatives, and private appeals for assistance from his business allies. According to one Reagan aide, the White House was amazed by the effectiveness of these lobbies. "Within 24 hours," he said, "one congressman had between 75 and 100 phone calls from businessmen in his district." [23] Again the president prevailed. This time by a narrow margin of 217 to 211, the full House overturned the Rules Committee's partitioning of the budget and substituted a single "up or down" vote. The House then promptly passed the president's budget by a comfortable margin of 232 to 193.

Understandably, the Democratic leaders who had just lost control over the chamber's procedures were shell-shocked. Rules Committee chair Richard Bolling added Reagan to his list of "imperial presidents" along with Johnson and Nixon. Majority Leader James Wright complained bitterly that the administration was trying to "dictate every last scintilla, every last phrase" of legislation. Summing up the Democratic gloom, Speaker O'Neill said, "I hope someday, this day is forgotten." [24]

Since early May, the taxation parts of the president's program had proceeded down a different institutional path. In late July, closely following his budget victory, President Reagan won his three-year, 25 percent income tax cut with the same coalition of Republicans and southern Democrats. His *modus operandi* was much the same and included a dramatic public appeal within a week of the House vote.

There were, however, some important differences in the budget and tax issues that made the president's task on the latter more difficult and, consequently, the need for a successful public strategy crucial. One problem clear to everyone was that the massive tax reductions contained in the Kemp-Roth bill (named for sponsors Jack Kemp and William Roth) would produce a huge shortfall in government revenues. Many of the southern Democrats who had favored reduced government expenditures were also committed to a balanced budget. Yet the president's plan moved the deficit in the opposite direction. Another difficulty was that as revenue legislation the tax bill had to pass through the House Ways and Means Committee chaired by Illinois Democrat Daniel Rostenkowski. Although this committee was no longer as formidable as it had once been under Wilbur Mills's leadership, it remained the chief fount of revenue legislation. Standing in the president's way was a committee run by northern Democrats unsympathetic to his economic philosophy and bent on protecting their prerogative to legislate tax policy.

In working with legislative sponsors to draft the Kemp-Roth bill, President Reagan agreed to the only compromise he would make during this budget session. He allowed the first-year tax cut to be reduced from 10 to 5 percent and to begin in October 1981 rather than to be retroactive to January. Both changes would reduce the growing deficit and in doing so would improve the bill's acceptability among the president's earlier congressional supporters. Unveiling the new tax package, the president announced that he would "compromise" no further.

His steadfastness was amply demonstrated in early June, when he met at the White House with Democratic leaders who were clearly looking for a deal.[25] Rostenkowski began the meeting by offering Reagan the Democrats' support for a two-year tax cut. Reagan rejected it immediately, stating that three years were "a matter of principle." Senate Minority Leader Robert Byrd then tried to sweeten the proposal with a full 10 percent cut the first year and a trigger clause allowing additional reductions later if economic conditions permitted. At this point the president reportedly glanced over to his counsel Edwin Meese, who shook his head, before replying with a simple "no." Next came House Majority Leader James Wright's turn. He tried a guaranteed three-year program of 5 percent tax cuts each year, but it drew hardly a response. Recognizing that a battle with the president was inevitable, Speaker O'Neill concluded the one-way negotiating session by telling him, "When you offer us a bill, we'll have an alternative. If you roll us, you roll us." [26]

The bravado with which the president rejected the Democrats' overtures is all the more impressive when one recognizes that all who attended the meeting knew that the administration did not then have sufficient votes to pass the

Kemp-Roth bill. Confronted with this by a reporter after the meeting, Reagan responded, "If we don't have enough votes, we'll get them." Speaker O'Neill described the situation candidly in a nationally televised interview: "If the vote were tomorrow we could win it. Right now we have the votes. Can [Reagan] take them away from us? Let's wait and see." [27]

After the bargaining session with Reagan failed, the Democratic leadership tried to woo northern Republicans and southern Democrats with special tax concessions for constituencies in their districts. This approach, it was soon discovered, had two serious limitations. First, Rostenkowski was constrained by liberal Democrats on Ways and Means who preferred to let the president win and be held responsible. The second drawback, even more serious, was the president's willingness to match everything Rostenkowski offered. By the time the bidding ended, one embarrassed White House aide joked, "There's a good argument that we gave away the store." [28]

Advised by pollster Richard Wirthlin that "if push comes to shove" the public would easily side with him over Congress, President Reagan also embarked on a public strategy with several objectives. [29] Early in June, he played an important card when he told a group of southern Democrats, "I could not in good conscience campaign against any of you Democrats who have helped me." [30] This pledge quickly circulated on Capitol Hill, and within days it had received prominent press notice. With the president fully recuperated and able to be involved more personally in the campaign to pass the Kemp-Roth bill, the White House decided against another raid on southern districts. Besides, conceded a liberal Democrat, "They don't need to do it again. The point was made." [31]

In late June, Reagan traveled to Texas (the home state of a large Democratic House delegation whose support would be necessary for victory), Colorado, and California to speak for the Kemp-Roth bill and against the Democratic alternative. But these efforts proved to be only warm-up exercises. On July 27, two days before the floor vote in the House and with the administration still short of victory, Reagan returned to national television. At first the network executives balked, arguing that the speech was too patently partisan, but after the Republican National Committee threatened to purchase airtime, they relented and reserved rebuttal time for Democratic leaders O'Neill and Rostenkowski. With visual displays that represented the administration's savings in green and the Democrats' deficit in red, the president accused the Democrats of "sleight of hand." He conceded mockingly that a working person would fare better under the opposition's legislation but "if you're only planning to live two more years." Reagan then urged the American public to join him in lobbying Congress:

> I ask you now to put aside any feelings of frustration or helplessness
> about our political institutions and join me in this dramatic but
> responsible plan to reduce the enormous burden of federal taxation
> on you and your family.
>
> During recent months many of you have asked what can you do
> to help make America strong again. I urge you again to contact your

senators and congressmen. Tell them of your support for this bipartisan proposal. Tell them you believe this is an unequaled opportunity
to help return America to prosperity and make government again the
servant of the people.[32]

Everyone in Washington who saw the speech knew that it was a block-
buster. Celebrating that evening, Treasury Secretary Donald Regan proclaimed
it "a home run with the bases loaded." The only recorded reaction to be found
from the normally garrulous O'Neill was one rueful word, "Devastating." These
early reviews were correct; the public's reaction was swift and overwhelming.
Ways and Means Democrat Richard Gephardt remarked, "The dam broke. . . .
It fell apart." [33]

House Democrats who, before the president's speech, were either undecid-
ed or had announced support of the Democratic bill came under enormous
pressure from constituents moved by Reagan's entreaty. The day after the
speech, Carroll Hubbard of Kentucky received 516 calls from his district, and
Norman Dicks of Washington received 400; each then changed his position
and voted for the Kemp-Roth bill. Bo Ginn of Georgia was encouraged to
maintain his support of the Democratic bill by Jimmy Carter, Andrew Young,
and Coretta Scott King, but 600 appeals from "less famous constituents" swept
him over to the president's side. Ralph Hall of Texas had made a deal with
House Democratic leaders—a tax break for his district's oil industry in
exchange for his support of their bill. But even Hall's pro-Reagan constituents
held sway in the end, and he, too, voted in support of the president.[34]

The experiences of these Democrats appear typical. Within hours the issue
was decided, as wavering representatives played it safe and went with the president. When the waters receded, Reagan had moved from an apparent defeat to
a sizable victory. The closest of the key votes was 238–195. Forty-eight
Democratic defections made the difference. The Democratic leadership
brought its full influence to bear on its members; it had enlisted its institutional levers of negative agenda control to the hilt—all for naught. The leadership
of the House of Representatives had been rolled. It was a historic, and for
future presidents, instructive moment in which a president armed with public
support defeated the majority party in an institution designed to prevent this
from happening.[35]

Reviewing this extraordinary first session of the 97th Congress, reporter
Steven V. Roberts found two basic reasons for Reagan's success: "Lawmakers
believed their constituents supported that program and they were afraid that
Mr. Reagan could galvanize that support through an adroit use of television
and punish any dissidents at the polls." [36] These fears were not without reason.
National polls showed strong support for Reagan as president, for increased
defense spending, for elimination of waste, and for lower taxes. Supplementing
these poll data in forms more compelling to representatives with close ties to
their home districts were the waves of mail, telegrams, and phone calls that

overwhelmed Congress after each presidential address. Reagan's public appeals generated about fifteen million more letters than normally flowed into congressional mailrooms each session.[37] What better testimony to the prowess of the president skilled at going public?

By the next budget season, in 1982, President Reagan's standing in Washington and the country had weakened considerably. His problems began in the fall of 1981 with a proposal to trim Social Security benefits that made even his own party's congressional leadership wince and stirred up an outpouring of protest from elderly voters. *Newsweek* announced in headlines, "The Runner Stumbles." [38] Quickly, President Reagan backtracked and agreed to await a report from a bipartisan commission reviewing Social Security. Shortly thereafter, in late September, he returned to the airwaves, this time calling for $24 billion in additional spending cuts. Sensing the president's vulnerability, Democrats were unsparing in their criticism. Many House Republicans were also annoyed—especially those who had reluctantly gone along with the deep reductions in domestic spending just two months earlier with the understanding that additional cuts would not be requested. Beyond Washington, the early responses were equally chilly. Bond prices fell sharply, and the Dow Jones industrial average plummeted eleven points to the lowest level since spring. Nor did representatives report a surge in their mail. On notice from his party's congressional leaders, the president quietly agreed to postpone the issue and reintroduce the cuts in his next year's budget.[39]

For many observers of the Reagan presidency, the Social Security and budget-cutting proposals of fall 1981 were the turning point. From then until after the Grenada invasion in late 1983, the president found himself dealing with Congress on its terms. An in-depth Gallup survey reveals, however, that Reagan retained much of his influence with the American public, who had served him so well in the summer.[40] Two weeks after Reagan's television address, a national survey asked, "In general are you in favor of budget cuts in addition to those approved earlier this year or are you opposed to more cuts?" More said they opposed (46 percent) further cuts than favored them (42 percent), an apparently unfavorable climate for the president's new initiative. Yet when asked specifically about the Reagan proposal three questions later, 74 percent answered that they approved the program, and only 20 percent expressed disapproval. Those who identified themselves as Democrats, a majority of whom by now were disapproving of his "job performance," gave his budget package an endorsement of 71 percent!* Clearly, the president remained a persuasive force with a broad cross section of the American public.

---

* The question was worded: "To reduce the size of the 1982 budget deficiency, President Reagan has proposed cutting $13 billion in addition to the $35 billion in cuts approved earlier this year. About $11 billion of the new cuts would come from social programs and about $2 billion from defense programs. In general, would you say you approve or disapprove of the President's proposal?" (*Gallup Opinion Index*, 6).

There were other irritants for Congress as well. Late in the legislative year the president had surprised the leadership of both parties in Congress with a veto of a continuing appropriations bill that maintained current expenditures until the normal appropriations bills could be enacted. Of all the administration's pratfalls to occur in a season full of them, the most extraordinary was a long interview published in the *Atlantic* with David Stockman, director of the Office of Management and Budget. In it the president's chief architect of the budget laid bare and even mocked the haphazard way the budget had been assembled.[41] Many within Congress felt betrayed; it seemed that they had been subjected to an ordeal for what appeared to be little more than a sham.

How much these incidents hurt the president and his policies in the polls is difficult to say.* In the fall his popularity began a descent that would continue through 1982. As for Reaganomics, Figure 6-1 shows that this neologism began to lose much of its appeal during this time. The index displayed in the figure registers the intensity as well as the direction of opinion by weighing emphatic responses twice as much. The mostly negative scores indicate that the public was never very optimistic about the personal financial rewards of Reaganomics, and by the close of 1981 was decidedly pessimistic.

Whatever the cumulative effects of presidential retractions and subordinates' confessions, one need look no further than the economy to explain the beginning of the public's loss of confidence in Reagan and his policies. During the summer and fall of 1981 unemployment rose steadily. The projected budget deficits grew apace, in part because more unemployed workers were claiming benefits. The swelling deficits meant heavy federal borrowing in the financial markets, which contributed to historically high "real" interest rates. Completing what seemed to be a self-fueling spiral of economic deterioration, high interest rates prevented recovery in the credit-sensitive auto and construction industries, which were experiencing unemployment of nearly 20 percent. Even conservative economists joined in the growing speculation that a full-fledged depression was no longer unthinkable.[42]

Budget Politics in 1982

When the president unveiled his economic program in the spring of 1982 before the same lawmakers who had the previous year given him a rousing greeting, it was clear to everyone in the audience—if perhaps not to the man at the podium—that contrary forces of political economy were at work. All of the representatives and a third of the senators would have to stand for reelection in November; this made the president's audience all the more uneasy as he called for additional domestic spending cuts, continued growth in the defense

---

* When a Gallup Poll in mid-November asked respondents if they had heard or read "about the situation in Washington involving David Stockman," 66 percent answered affirmatively. When these informed respondents were asked if it made them more or less confident in Reaganomics, 34 percent said less confident, 9 percent said more confident, and 53 percent said it had not changed their opinion. *Gallup Report* 194 (November 1981): 15.

FIGURE 6-1 **Public Opinion on the Effects of Reaganomics on Personal Finances, March 1981–March 1983**

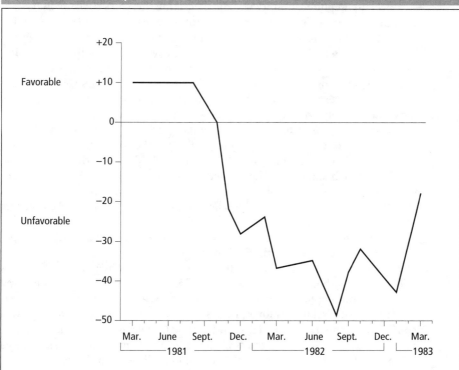

Source: Gallup Report 211 (April 1983): 14.

Note: Question: "Do you feel your financial situation will be much better, somewhat better, somewhat worse, or much worse as a result of Reagan's economic policies?" Responses are scored +2 for "much better," +1 for "somewhat better," 0 for no opinion or unsure, −1 for "somewhat worse," and −2 for "much worse." Polls were taken in March, August, October, and early and late November 1981; in February, March, June, August, September, and October 1982; and in January and March 1983.

budget, and reduced outlays for Social Security. Moreover, his proposal for a three-year, $55 billion increase in taxes seemed modest given the size of the deficit.

The president's budget found few takers. Republican senator William Armstrong, a member of the Budget Committee and a Reagan supporter, declared unequivocally, "There is no chance that Reagan's budget will pass. Very few Republicans would vote for it. I know of no one." Senate Republican Whip Ted Stevens described himself in "sort of a state of shock" from the president's proposal. House Minority Leader Robert H. Michel, who would face the toughest reelection campaign of his career within six months, agreed that the proposed deficit was "mind boggling." [43] Democrats, needless to say, were just as critical and not nearly so restrained.

Because Republican unity was disintegrating, Reagan's parliamentary-like victories of the preceding session would not be repeated. As one representative said, "If anyone thinks that this is going to be a nice, neat package, with everyone jumping up and down and passing it in a few hours, well, that's not going to happen." [44] Whether President Reagan recognized this is unclear. Press reports of anxious hand wringing by the president's advisers over his blasé intransigence were mixed with those of kudos from among this same group for the astute manner with which he was preparing for future compromise.

The latter proved to be wishful thinking, for Reagan began the task of assembling a congressional coalition by following the straitlaced, strategic prescriptions of going public. In February he toured the Midwest where he employed tough language: "The budget we propose is a line drawn in dirt"; and he challenged "paid political complainers . . . to put up or shut up." According to White House sources, these speeches were intended to shore up his crumbling congressional base. [45]

Although by early April several of his advisers were engaged in budget talks with party leaders of the House and Senate, the president continued to work Congress by going public. "He very much wants to regain the initiative," said a staffer. "The best way to do that in his estimation is to have him come directly to the people." [46] Accordingly, in mid-March the president planned two major television addresses for April; a switch from afternoon to evening press conferences, which he reasoned would double his television audience and prevent network newscasters from unfairly filtering his message; a series of live radio broadcasts on Saturdays in the vein of Franklin Roosevelt's fireside chats; and, finally, a heavy schedule of political travel. [47]

To White House political adviser Edward Rollins, the new offensive was necessary to get Republicans "back in line." He added, "It is imperative we put discipline back in this town." With the apparent blessing of the White House, Rollins initiated his own educational campaign. For those Republicans who expected difficulty in the fall elections and had begun "carping" at the president's policies, his message was simple: undermine the president and you will hurt yourself because "his strength and popularity will be a factor in [your] own elections." He went further. To make sure the association was appreciated, Rollins announced that neither President Reagan nor Vice President Bush would assist any Republican who had been "blasting the hell out of the president." [48] Little did he realize that by fall, few Republican incumbents would be soliciting help from these men.

While Reagan was busy in public posturing, his lieutenants were quietly engaged in budget negotiations with the House Democratic and Senate Republican leadership. Whether the participation of the White House in the bargaining sessions indicated genuine flexibility on Reagan's part or simply reflected the stark certainty that his initial proposal did not stand a chance in Congress is difficult to say. Two conclusions, however, may be drawn from these negotiations. First, at risk of being wholly excluded from drafting the budget, the president did finally shift from his original hard-line stance. He agreed to smaller growth in defense spending, increases for social programs, and, most significant, a near doubling of new tax receipts from $55 billion to $99 billion during the next three years.

Second, though the extensive bargaining sessions failed to yield a compromise bill, they succeeded, according to White House estimates, as a public relations coup. On April 28 with reporters trailing behind, the president traveled down Pennsylvania Avenue for a summit meeting with Speaker O'Neill. As a bargaining session it went nowhere, but it did allow President Reagan to claim in an address on prime-time television the following evening that he had "gone the extra mile."

The president's speech followed a format by now familiar: black-white presentation of the issues, visual props, and an appeal for public support. Arguing that his and not the Democrats' budget was the one of moderation, Reagan departed from the standard script to describe in detail his efforts to reach a compromise.

> In yesterday afternoon's meeting on Capitol Hill, Speaker O'Neill, Senator Howard Baker, myself, and five of the Gang of 17 participated. As I say, the figures on which the group had found some agreement were far from those we'd proposed in February. But I decided against trying to start the negotiations on the basis of that original budget.
>
> Our original cuts totaled $101 billion. They—I can't make a big enough mark to show you [referring to a chart]—but they were rejected, believe me. Our own representatives from the Congress proposed compromising at $60 billion. Their counterparts from the Democratic side of the aisle proposed 35. In our meeting yesterday, which went on for more than 3 hours, our compromise of $60 billion was rejected—now my pen is working. And then I swallowed and had volunteered to split the difference between our 60 and their 35 and settle for 48, and that was rejected. The meeting was over.[49]

After viewing the president's address, Speaker O'Neill voiced suspicion that once again he had been set up in a public relations ploy. For a president who goes public, failure at the bargaining table may be rewarded with success in the public arena.

Once again, President Reagan closed his speech by exhorting the public to "make your voice heard." [50] Unlike the previous summer, however, this appeal was not followed by major tremors on Capitol Hill. Instead, a complex sequence of legislative maneuvers ensued over which few participants—foremost among them the president—appeared to exert much control. The Republican Senate proceeded to pass its own budget containing provisions substantially different from those Reagan had originally submitted. The president promptly endorsed it; he had little choice.[51]

In the House, Minority Leader Michel rejected the Senate version as unsalable to his Republican colleagues, many of whom were facing difficult reelections. Instead, he created a special panel to formulate a Republican alternative to the budget expected from the Budget Committee, which was controlled by Democrats. Again the president endorsed the Republican product, although this one differed significantly from the Senate version. By the time of the House floor vote, there were seven different budget proposals, none of them able to muster a majority. Two weeks later, with both parties agreeing that any budget resolution was better than none, the Republican proposal, more popular than any of the others, was passed without Democratic resistance; shortly thereafter it was reconciled with the Senate version in conference committee.

Through much of the remainder of the session, as the various committees in both chambers drafted appropriations and revenue legislation in rough accord with the provisions of the budget resolution, President Reagan kept a low profile. He traveled to Europe, vacationed on his Santa Barbara ranch, and spoke to Republican gatherings.[52] Only in late August, when it became apparent that his help would be required to line up reluctant House Republicans for a $99 billion tax hike, did President Reagan return to active duty.

By that time the tax provisions of the budget differed considerably from the president's February proposals, but Reagan embraced them as if they were his own. And well he should have. They raised substantial new revenues to close a yawning deficit while preserving his three-year, 25 percent tax cut.

Congress approached the largest election-year tax increase in history with caution befitting politicians whose jobs were in jeopardy. The posturing that resulted from calculations of political survival gave rise to an interesting configuration of alliances. Three blocs of representatives and senators were decisive to the outcome: loyal House Democrats, Senate Republicans, and House Republicans. The peculiar way in which political considerations aligned these groups in support for or in opposition to the tax increase gave President Reagan one last chance to win Congress by going public.

The Democratic leaders did not want their party blamed by the electorate for the tax hike, nor, having conceded so much to the president in the preceding eighteen months, did they wish to leave themselves open for future accusations of undermining his policies. Consequently, they agreed to provide the administration the margin of victory on three conditions: (1) the legislation raising taxes would be drafted by the Republican-controlled Senate Finance Committee, and House Democrats would participate only at the conference stage; (2) a majority of House Republicans (about one hundred) would vote for it; and (3) indicative of the Democrats' queasiness, the president would write personal letters of appreciation to supportive Democrats, which could be used in the fall election to stave off criticism from Republican challengers.

As a group, Senate Republicans were unenthusiastic about the bill, but because of the swelling deficit, most realized they had little choice. They could vote higher taxes at that time—a year in which only twelve of their number were standing for reelection—or they could do so later, when more would be facing their constituents. Given the electoral calendar and the demand of House Democrats, the Republican Senate Finance Committee wrote the bill that the Republican Senate passed intact by a narrow margin.[53]

The political needs of the president, of Senate Republicans, and especially of House Democrats combined to create a serious dilemma for House Republicans. Because the Democrats were insisting that the Republicans be responsible for the tax increase, and because their Republican colleagues in the Senate and White House were willing to go along, many election-bound House Republicans felt they were being sacrificed to the deficit. Moreover, some of Washington's most fervent supply-siders came from the ranks of House Republicans. One was Rep. Jack Kemp, cosponsor of the Kemp-Roth bill, who immediately began to line up opposition to the unholy alliance. By late August, when the conference report was awaiting House ratification, Kemp could count on more Republican votes than could the White House. As the president began a public offensive to rally House Republicans, he had fewer than half the number of votes necessary to fulfill his end of the bargain with the Democrats. At this point Reagan's close friend Sen. Paul Laxalt publicly observed, "This is the most difficult legislative challenge this President has had to face. It's tight as hell." [54] One indicator of the difficulty facing a president who seeks to lead by going public is his popular standing across the country. Perhaps Laxalt had this fact in mind, for in mid-August a Gallup survey reported that the president's latest job performance rating stood at only 41 percent approving against 47 percent disapproving. Moreover, when questioned further about the president's economic performance, respondents were even more critical. Only 31 percent approved his handling of the economy overall, and because the unemployment rate was into double digits, only 23 percent were willing to endorse his handling of the unemployment problem.[55]

From such figures one might conclude that President Reagan's ratings were too thin to give him much chance of success. Had he been required to win substantial Democratic defections, as in the past session, such an assessment would be correct. In this instance, however, the political circumstances were tailored for victory. The president was simply trying to bring along fellow Republicans whose districts were generally believed to remain more favorably disposed to him and his policies than was the country overall. More important, because the Democrats had agreed to supply the rest, he had to pull only one hundred Republican votes. The peculiar coalitional requirements of the tax bill gave the increasingly unpopular Reagan a last crack at success.

As the White House cranked up its public campaign to work its magic on the 97th Congress for the fourth time, the standard operating procedures were followed. Only the target differed. Once again the president embarked on political travel in search of telegenic and sympathetic audiences. Once again the numerous White House staffers assigned to public and congressional relations got busy. Speech writers prepared another national television address and a series of presidential commercials to be broadcast in select markets across the country by the Republican National Committee; Richard Wirthlin conducted briefings for Republican House members, explaining to them that the president's leadership image would be critical to their own success in November; and other staffers busied themselves contacting more than five thousand business leaders across the country to stimulate yet another grassroots campaign.[56] (More than thirty thousand similar appeals were sent to local party leaders by the RNC.) To top it off, Rollins, posing threats as he had in the spring, spread the word that party campaign funds might be withheld from Republican representatives who bucked the president. After a congressional outcry, however, the White House retracted this form of coercion. By the time of the floor vote, more than 150 Republican House members had been escorted into the Oval Office or to Camp David for a friendly chat. All of these activities culminated with the president's prime-time address on August 16, in which he once again called on citizens to lobby Congress. Three days later the tax bill passed the House by a vote of 226 to 207. President Reagan had fulfilled his end of the bargain by bringing along 103 reluctant Republicans.

President Reagan exerted far less influence over the budget in 1982—both its substance and politics—than over the one in the preceding year. He gave concessions on taxes and expenditures, and by the end of the session he was championing a tax increase others had written that was nearly twice the figure he had proposed in February. In large part this change in fortune must be credited to his reduced political capital with Congress. The further he cut domestic spending, the fewer the number of natural allies that remained. Budget politics in 1982 reflected the president's decline in public opinion. High interest and unemployment rates and swelling projected deficits had sapped his popularity. All of these weaknesses were compounded in the minds of Washington politicians by the fall elections.

Still, the budgetary season was not as disastrous as these political conditions suggest. Reagan's fundamental economic policies survived. Real growth in the military budget continued, domestic spending was reduced further, and the tax increase did not touch his 25 percent cut in income taxes. In 1982 Ronald Reagan relinquished control of the legislative process to those with whom it properly belongs, but he was still able to set the agenda of Congress's budget deliberations. Although Reagan's weak popularity prevented him from producing the groundswells he had generated a year earlier, he did not shy away from publicly promoting his policies. The addition of his Saturday radio broadcasts gave him even greater occasion to go public than in 1981. On a more limited scale he continued to summon public support in his dealings with Congress. Judged by the budget politics of the next year, 1982 would appear successful indeed.

Budget Politics in 1983

The political context of any presidential action is defined by two realities: objective conditions and politicians' responses to those conditions. By the time

President Reagan introduced his next budget, in 1983, both realities had become distinctly unfavorable for him. The reasons were that fewer Republicans would be returning to the 98th Congress, and the president's popularity was at a historic low.

Although the Democrats narrowly failed to improve their party's share of Senate seats, they gained a net of twenty-six seats in the House of Representatives, which exceeded preelection estimates of the number required to undo Reagan's coalition of Republicans and southern Democrats. A *New York Times* survey of newly elected members, including Republicans, confirmed the widespread suspicion that the new class would be decidedly less sympathetic to the president's economic policies than the members they had replaced.[57]

President Reagan's nearly continuous decline in the polls during the campaign season further aggravated the unfavorable election results. As shown in Table 6-1, Reagan had begun 1982 with almost a majority of respondents to a Gallup Poll approving his overall performance. Even then, however, there was the prospect of subsequent decline if the economy worsened. In the same survey only 41 percent endorsed Reagan's "handling of economic conditions." During the year, unemployment climbed to a record post-depression high. Responses from a concerned public to Gallup's "most-important-problem" question shifted dramatically from inflation to unemployment.[58] At the opening of the 98th Congress, only 37 percent of the respondents registered overall approval, a figure lower than for any previous president at this stage of his first term.

Given the regional character of the president's Republican-southern Democrat coalition in the preceding Congress, the regional breakdown of his growing unpopularity is revealing. At the beginning of 1982, a majority of southerners and westerners approved his job performance; by the next year, respondents from these regions were no more supportive than respondents elsewhere. A national consensus appeared to be forming against the president.[59]

In a variety of ways, these harsh objective conditions were accentuated by politicians' strategic responses to them. During the fall congressional campaigns, Republican incumbents discovered on their own what can be seen in Figure 6-1: their association with Reaganomics was a political liability. With Democratic challengers everywhere taking up the issue, the president's Republican and boll weevil supporters found themselves forced to explain, excuse, apologize for, and in a few instances even recant their past association with these once popular policies.[60] Speaker O'Neill's prophecy of a year earlier about the fickleness of the typical voter had come to pass.

By election day 1982, so many Republican incumbents had become preoccupied with distancing themselves from Reagan and his economic policies that it was apparent before the first ballot was cast that the president's position in the next Congress would be weaker. Instead of spearheading the most active midterm campaign in recent history, as promised by political affairs aide

TABLE 6-1 **Performance Ratings of President Reagan, 1982–1983 (Percent)**										
	Jan. 1982		Aug. 1982		Nov. 1982		Dec. 1982		Jan. 1983	
Question	App.	Dis.	App.	Dis.	App.	Dis.	App.	Dis.	App.	Dis.
Do you approve of the way President Reagan is handling economic conditions in the country?	41	51	31	59	—	—	36	56	29	64
Do you approve or disapprove of the way Ronald Reagan is handling his job as president?										
National	49	40	41	47	43	47	41	50	37	54
East	43	46	40	49	42	51	36	57	35	55
Midwest	51	38	45	45	42	47	46	44	41	50
South	50	38	38	46	41	46	38	52	35	57
West	54	36	40	48	49	43	46	48	35	55

Sources: All data are from the Gallup Poll. Responses to the economic performance question as reported in *National Journal,* March 5, 1983, 524. Evaluations of President Reagan's overall job performance are from various issues of the *Gallup Report.*

Note: App. = approve; Dis. = disapprove.

Rollins in the spring of 1982, President Reagan stayed in Washington or on his Santa Barbara ranch as if sequestered there by Republican candidates. Mutual advantage dictated that he make cameo appearances in only the safest Republican districts.[61] Two weeks before the election, Rep. Guy Vander Jagt, the party's official booster and chair of the Republican National Campaign Committee, was steadfastly forecasting Republican gains in the House. Other more sober members, including House Republican Whip Trent Lott, had arrived at a different judgment. "Obviously, we won't have the same euphoria after this election we had two years ago," he told a reporter.[62]

Unfortunately, the press offers little insight into the all-important expectations of rank-and-file Republicans at the beginning of the 98th Congress. Rather, press accounts include only the comments of their leaders and of White House spokesmen about the administration's landslide victory, the better-than-expected victory, and the "moral" victory that had just occurred. Cutting through these traditional, self-serving post mortems, one may assume that instead of elation, those Republicans who were victorious sensed only relief. The 1982 midterm ended the 1980 mandate.

After the election, the boll weevils were on the move. These conservative southern Democrats who had provided President Reagan with the critical margin of victory began ambling back to the Democratic camp.[63] Rep. Buddy Roemer of Louisiana, a leader of the group and a former Reagan enthusiast, had a quick change of heart: "I don't think we need the President to write a budget," he told a reporter. Why the sudden turnaround? According to Rep. G. V. (Sonny) Montgomery of Mississippi, it was simply that the thrill of running around with the fast crowd uptown had faded.

"There was a fascination about going to the White House," Mr. Montgomery recalled. "I was down there more in two years than in the whole 14 years I've been up here. But maybe the glamour and glitter has worn off a bit.

"I think we might have gotten carried away with the White House," the Mississippian continued. "We weren't working enough with the Democratic leadership. That's the big change. We're trying to implement our philosophy through our party, not join somebody else." [64]

Although Montgomery's explanation reads more like a rationalization than a reason, it reveals that this boll weevil had returned to the ranks of his party.

One suspects the real reason these members gave up their apostasy can be found in the altered political circumstances. With the addition of twenty-six loyal Democratic members after the election, the conservative southerners no longer provided a swing vote. Even if this group voted solidly against their party, the Democratic leaders with their new 103-seat majority were generally assured victory. Consequently, confessed Representative Montgomery, "Nobody much talks to us." Another added, "Why get out there and take a bullet when you can't win anyway." [65]

Supporting the president not only was futile, and possibly injurious to their standing in the congressional party, it also had become risky at home. The midterm campaign appears to have conveyed the same messages to the boll weevils as it did to other politicians around the country. Rep. Charles Stenholm of Texas, a spokesman of the southern defectors, confessed, "We're having difficulty. There's a large amount of concern on the fairness question. The perception in the 17th District of Texas is that Reagan's program is basically unfair." [66] Testimony taken from these politicians led one reporter to conclude that the main reason for their return was "the declining support for President Reagan and his policies." [67]

It was evident early on to knowledgeable political elites in Washington that the election and the posturings of politicians had weakened President Reagan's hand with the 98th Congress. Whether it was as equally clear to the president, however, was anything but certain. As at the opening of the previous session Washington politicians were asking, did this outsider know the score? Could he adapt to the new political realities by becoming more flexible and more conciliatory toward the Democratic leadership? Such questions are appropriately asked about any president after his party has just suffered a setback; but with an outsider in the White House, especially one whose propensity to go public had been rewarded so handsomely during his first two years, these questions assumed a special poignancy.

Between the closing of the 97th Congress and the convening of the 98th, these questions were foremost among the concerns of the Washington press corps. Articles with such titles as "Midterm Malaise," "In the Event of a Presidential Power Vacuum . . . ," "The MX and Reagan's Receptivity to Compromise," and "At the Brink" proliferated in the news publications favored by those in power in Washington.[68] Nearly everyone was consulted on the matter, but nowhere did the press pry for answers more earnestly than at the White House.

The responses they received from White House insiders were as tentative and contradictory as elsewhere. No one knew how this president facing a novel situation would behave. One early prognosis, offered anonymously by a Reagan staffer, came as close to the mark as any: "He will submit a budget completely consistent with his program and philosophy, and it will probably get shot down pretty quickly."[69] Another gave a more moderate forecast that Reagan would happily agree to 75 percent of his request. A few were even more optimistic. Arguing that Reagan "has been willing to listen to people around him when they told him something would not work," one presidential adviser predicted that compromise would follow the tough proposals.[70]

With the exception of a conciliatory State of the Union address, the early signals were those of an uncompromising president who planned to spend more time in the country than at the bargaining table. The president's third budget was designed to "stay the course." Savings from additional reductions in domestic spending were to finance a 10 percent real growth in the Pentagon's budget. No major new taxes were called for, but if large deficits persisted beyond the 1985 fiscal year—and not coincidentally beyond the next election—contingency taxes were proposed.

Consistent with hanging tough on the budget, Reagan began a series of public relations maneuvers to enhance his public standing. John Herrington, an ardent Reaganite and assistant secretary of the Navy, was brought into the White House office to improve that organization's efforts in communicating his chief's positions to the American public. The president's travel budget was increased to permit more frequent trips to blue-collar constituencies with whom, his pollsters were telling him, he had experienced the greatest loss of support. Shorter, more narrowly focused news conferences were planned to give the press less opportunity to fish for negative stories.[71] A few of the president's strategists even urged him to declare his candidacy for renomination in January. This maneuver would put him on a campaign footing and "buttress his standing in current political struggles," they reasoned, adding that he could always choose not to run later.[72]

The Democratic response to the president's budget was swift and unequivocal. On March 15 after a single day of discussion, the House Budget

Committee passed the Democratic leadership's budget without changing a cent. This plan differed from the president's in limiting growth of defense spending to 4 percent rather than the president's 10 percent figure, in mandating $30 billion in additional taxes during the next fiscal year, and in restoring many of the 1981–1982 cuts in social programs. Republican leader Michel labeled the Democratic bill the "Revenge on Ronald Reagan Act of 1983." [73]

With a 103-seat majority, the Democratic leadership was again firmly in control of procedures, and it exploited its prerogatives to the fullest. The Rules Committee refused a request from southern Democrats to allow amendments to the budget resolution on the floor. Rather, the House would be permitted a vote for a single Republican alternative—presumably the president's—if one were offered. Moreover, in an effort to head off intense lobbying from the White House that had preceded floor votes in the past, the leadership scheduled the vote within the week.

The president and his staff were given little time, but by all accounts they made the most of it. On March 19 at a televised, impromptu press briefing, Reagan denounced the Democratic resolution as a "dagger aimed straight at the heart of America's rebuilding program." Of the reduced growth in the Pentagon's budget, he added, "Nothing could bring greater joy to the Kremlin." He went on to characterize the Democrats' domestic spending proposals as "a reckless return to the failed policies of the past." [74] And as for the resolution's provision for increased revenue, the president declared his readiness to veto any legislation that rescinded the third installment of his tax cut. The president served as the point man, while his staff got busy organizing constituent drives by the Chamber of Commerce and other business groups against targeted representatives. Though short on time, "our troops are fired up" and confident they could win, reported one White House staffer.[75]

The next day Speaker O'Neill fell under the grip of déjà vu. He told the press, "We thought we were in pretty good shape last week. Until this morning everybody was in accord." However, he continued, suddenly because the president and the Chamber of Commerce were out there beating the bushes, "the Democratic fissures were reopening." [76]

The Democratic majority, however, proved too great a hurdle for the administration. Three days later the House adopted the Budget Committee's resolution by a vote of 229 to 196. With Republicans in open disagreement among themselves over what an alternative budget should look like, none was offered. Despite a public invitation from the Rules Committee, the president's budget, remarkably, was never formally introduced in the House either in committee or in floor proceedings. Twenty-two of the conservative southern Democrats voted against the Democratic proposal, but this vote showed that their ranks had been thinned, and four northern Republicans further eroded their leverage by crossing over to support the Democratic resolution. For the first time since Ronald Reagan had entered office, the Democrats would take to conference a budget of their own making.

Undaunted, President Reagan returned to television within hours of the floor defeat. A national address had been scheduled to announce research into new forms of strategic weaponry. As forecast by aides, however, the president twice digressed from that subject to blast the Democratic budget. With an eye toward the Senate's upcoming markup of the legislation, he once again appealed to the public to demonstrate its continued support for his policies. "The choice is up to the men and women you have elected to Congress—and that means the choice is up to you." And later, "This is why I am speaking to you tonight—to urge you to tell your Senators and Congressmen that you know we must continue to restore our military strength." [77]

Indicative perhaps of the president's reduced status, the most noticeable response to the speech came not from the public but from congressional leaders. Even House Minority Leader Michel delivered a mild rebuke. Too much "overkill" and "macho image," he termed the performance. He further complained that since it deflected public attention away from House Republicans' criticisms of the Democratic budget, the speech "couldn't have come at a worse time." [78]

If the president expected more favorable treatment in the Senate, he was to be greatly disappointed. In a meeting with the Senate Budget Committee in early April, he was told by fellow Republicans that the projected deficit and continued military buildup were unacceptable. Reportedly, even the president's staff joined in urging him to compromise. He refused.

To give Reagan an opportunity to reconsider, Budget Committee chair Pete Domenici postponed his committee's markup for a week; and offering his president plenty of leeway, he told reporters that the president was simply assuming a "negotiation stance." [79] Meanwhile, Defense Secretary Caspar Weinberger was openly campaigning with President Reagan to ignore the budget process. In mid-April with no movement from the president, the Senate Budget Committee began the business of writing its own budget. What came out of markup was distinctly unfavorable to the White House: $30 billion in new taxes, an $11 billion increase in domestic spending over the president's figure, and a modest 5 percent growth in the defense budget.

As this resolution was presented on the floor, it remained unclear whether it or any budget bill could pass. In the absence of strong leadership from the White House, the Senate was divided into three distinct camps. On one side there were the Democrats who by and large were supporting the House bill; on the other side were the conservative Republicans who were prepared to stick with the uncompromising president. In the middle were the Republican moderates, including Majority Leader Howard Baker and most of the Republican members of the committee. Because the president was unable to unify his party "by rallying public support for his program . . . the factions have grown bolder," reported one correspondent.[80] Pessimistic forecasts were fulfilled as the Senate rejected the committee's budget. A week later, Domenici returned with a fatter military budget and a substantial tax increase. Although Reagan was hardly enthusiastic and the Democrats were calling the new budget "rinky-dink," it passed by a single vote after eleven ballots.

As the conference committee negotiations were reported daily in the press, Reagan distanced himself ever farther from the budgetary process. When the brokered budget finally passed Congress in late June, the president had retreated to threats of a veto of any appropriations bills that violated his own earlier proposal. When questioned by a reporter on the wisdom of such a course, one senior White House official replied, "I just don't know what we have to gain from playing the budget game with Congress this year." He continued saying that having shown he could work with Congress over the past two years, President Reagan could now "afford to be more confrontational." Pressed further, the official conceded that the administration would likely get the "short end of the stick" on defense spending because opinion polls were not supportive. But on social spending and taxes, he insisted, "Those are the issues he [the President] can go to the people on every time." [81] With the tax cut in place and the budget growing now from a smaller base, the president stepped back from the budget process. By the close of the 1983 budget season, President Reagan had assumed a defensive posture, threatening vetoes and promising public appeals at least on those issues where even an unpopular president might be able to elicit a favorable public response.

GOING PUBLIC AND LEADERSHIP:
The Lessons of Reagan's Budgets

President Reagan may have radically altered the strategic routines of presidential leadership, but initially these changes did not disturb the routines of the Washington press in reporting on his performance. Accustomed to explaining presidential success by digging beneath the surface and ferreting out quiet compromises and discrete logrolling, the press was especially diligent in these activities in 1981. After all, a great deal needed to be explained. For their efforts they uncovered a few truffles. A story on Rep. Lawrence DeNardis's swap of budget support for renovation of the New Haven train depot was typical. Other commodities traded during the session included sugar price supports, restoration of some energy subsidies for the poor, more funds than originally budgeted for Medicaid, and a slowdown of the conversion of industrial boilers to coal in oil-producing states.[82] Even more heavily reported were various photo sessions at the White House and the liberal distribution of such patronage as theater tickets and special $4.40 cufflinks to representatives who voted with the president.*

---

* Taking a broader view of the marketplace, Alistair Cooke inferred meaning from the two-way traffic along Pennsylvania Avenue. By his counting, the president conducted sixty-nine meetings with more than four hundred members of Congress, which Cooke cites as indicative of a president who shed the uncompromising campaign rhetoric and quickly learned to behave like a "political veteran" reminiscent of Lyndon Johnson. Cooke even discerned parliamentary-like relations in these traffic patterns. "Getting the Hang of It," *New Yorker*, March 14, 1983, 148–153.

As indications of President Reagan's leadership strategy, however, all of these minor deals and presidential gifts pale in significance when placed next to the meeting in 1981 with Democratic leaders when he rejected their entreaties to compromise even while he was still short of votes.

Reagan's record as a president who preferred going public to bargaining remained virtually unblemished. On a few occasions, however, a public appeal would be accompanied with minor, face-saving concessions or side payments to fence sitters. The bidding war with Rostenkowski for stray votes on the tax cut in 1981 offers the most prominent and substantial examples of such payments. When one considers that it was a game initiated by the Democrats and, as far as one can tell, was unanticipated by the White House, the bidding war appears more an unhappy outcome of failure to accept the generous overtures of the Democratic leaders than a planned strategy of coalition building.

One might even be tempted to find pluralist flexibility in Reagan's acceptance of the $99 billion tax hike the next year. However, the summer's sharply rising deficit projections that had so altered the fiscal environment and the public enthusiasm with which he ultimately embraced this legislation rather than try to split the difference with his original proposal suggest that the president's change of position was more a conversion than a political compromise. In accepting higher new taxes, more social spending, and less for defense than he had originally sought, President Reagan conducted himself less as a skilled bargainer than as a president who, having lost his leverage, was forced to accept more or less what others served up. Even in these episodes, he demonstrated a greater flair for going public than for negotiation. He would continue to do so in his second term. After his huge victory over Walter Mondale in November 1984, a Reagan aide announced that the president would "take advantage" of his mandate and soon tour the country "to sell this budget package. . . . We have to look at it, in many ways, like a campaign. He wants to take his case to the people." [83]

Dependence of Policy on Popularity

Undeniably, going public rewarded the president handsomely in his dealings with Congress while he remained popular. During the first session of the 97th Congress the president achieved rare mastery over both policy and the legislative process, the likes of which had not occurred since Lyndon Johnson had enjoyed a surfeit of liberal Democrats in both chambers nearly two decades earlier. True to his campaign pledge, Reagan managed to slash domestic spending, boost the Pentagon's budget, and cut taxes.

The second budget, which sought to continue or to preserve the gains of the first, was not nearly as successful. In the spring of 1982 with his popularity in steep descent and the deficit and unemployment increasing with each new report, President Reagan found his messages less inspiring to Congress and the country. His leadership style precluded resorting to pluralist methods to continue his mastery of Congress; instead, he left Washington and budget policies to others. When called upon to cast a public appeal for a tax increase—one not of his making—President Reagan still managed to provide the margin of difference at a key moment.

Largely as a consequence of his diminished popularity, Reagan's majority coalition departed in the fall 1982 election. By the beginning of the third budget season, his popularity was still down. White House staffers were wondering aloud whether the president would even be allowed to participate in the game. His budget was delivered stillborn, never to be introduced on the floor of either chamber. When the Republican Senate insisted on reduced military spending and new taxes, Reagan gave up the budget fight and announced repeatedly that he would veto appropriations bills to defeat the "credit card Congress." Fearing a street fight with the president before public opinion, the House leadership reduced its spending bills to bring them more in line with the president's initial requests. Yet in 1983, the budget was made by Congress.

From late 1982 on, the White House gradually redirected its campaign from generating public support for the president's policies to generating support for the president himself. By the summer of 1983, many political elites subscribed to the view that Reagan was prepared to sacrifice his budget to gain an issue for the next election a full year and a half away.[84] The polls show little evidence that the concerted efforts to alter public evaluations of the president's performance met with much success. A resurgence in the polls did finally occur, but only after the economy began to rebound in the fall of 1983—too late to help him with the budget.

One lesson of Reagan's record, therefore, is that the public president may perform better in the "expenditure," or transference, of popular support than in its resupply. Individualized pluralism helps to explain why he performs well in using his public support, but as a model of Washington politics, it is silent on the subject of what an unpopular president should do to restore the public's confidence. The supply of popular support rests on opinion dynamics over which the president may exercise little direct control. This is not to say that the president will not try to improve the public's estimate of him. Given who public presidents are, one suspects the temptation for self-promotion will be irresistible.

Governing as Campaigning

Whether in exploiting favorable conditions to advance policy goals or in attempting to improve the incumbent's prestige, the strategic prescriptions of going public put the office on a campaign footing. Governing, according to a Reagan staffer, amounts to little more than an extension of the campaign that brought him into office. In early 1983 aides were urging him to announce his candidacy for reelection to strengthen his hand in Congress.

President Reagan's conduct of office closely resembled his campaign for it. Both entailed heavy political travel, numerous appearances before organized constituencies, and extensive use of television—even paid commercials during nonelection periods. Moreover, both campaigning and governing required systematic planning and extensive organizational coordination. Each major television appeal by President Reagan on the eve of a critical budget vote in Congress was preceded by weeks of preparatory work. Polls were taken; speeches incorporating the resulting insights were drafted; the press was briefed, either directly or via leaks. Meanwhile in the field, the ultimate recipients of the president's message, members of Congress, were softened up by presidential travel into their states and districts and by grassroots lobbying campaigns, initiated and orchestrated by the White House but including the RNC and sympathetic business organizations. After describing some of these routines of Reagan's staff, Sidney Blumenthal drew the parallel between campaigning and governing:

> Once elected, candidates have to deal with shaky coalitions held together by momentary moods, not stable party structures. They then must try to govern through permanent campaigns. This is something more than the selling of the President—even of a telegenic President able to project an attractive image. It has become an inescapable necessity for Reagan, and probably for his successors.
>
> The President's strategists are at the center of the new political age. At the end of the day, they become spectators, seeing their performance tested by the contents of the television news programs. For the Reagan White House, every night is election night on television.[85]

As presidential governance has assumed the form of a campaign, the White House office has added trappings of a campaign organization. The available evidence indicates that Reagan's transition advisers appreciated the organizational imperatives of the public president. Although their fees were to be paid by the Republican National Committee, pollsters Richard Wirthlin and Robert Teeter were made proximate and frequent counselors to the president. Initially, the position of press secretary was downgraded to make room for an expanded Office of Communications, which was given a broad mandate to plan and coordinate all public affairs activities for the White House and executive agencies.[86]

With this office taking care of public relations, a smaller political affairs office transacted more partisan business. In addition to traditional White House political activities, such as monitoring gossip and polls and advising the president, its mandate was also to exercise the administration's political muscle. Patronage and campaign support from a variety of sources flowed to members of Congress through this office, headed for most of this period by Edward Rollins. Testimony to the office's integral role can be found in a comment by Rollins's deputy, Lee Atwater: "This shop is a new venture. I don't think the White House has ever had one before, but I think that every White House from now on will have one." [87]

Finally, as governing becomes campaigning, policy serves rhetoric. Rather than the substance of detailed scrutiny and negotiations, policy questions become overly simplified and stylized to satisfy the cognitive requirements of a largely inattentive national audience. Positions, publicly proclaimed, become fixed; intransigence among elites sets in. President Reagan's declaration before a midwestern audience that his 1982 budget was "a line drawn in dirt" is typical of what happens when partisan discussion flows through public channels.[88]

By any standard, Ronald Reagan and his three budgets constitute an extraordinary story. Extraordinary because no president in recent memory established such a presence as did Reagan vis-á-vis the 97th Congress. Extraordinary, moreover, because no president managed to exhaust his popular support so thoroughly by his first midterm election as did Reagan. And finally, extraordinary in retrospect because within a year of the budget vote in 1983, the president entered his reelection campaign generally conceded to be unbeatable and went on to amass one of the greatest landslides of this century.

These extraordinary swings in policy success and popularity reflect the volatility of a marketplace whose currency of exchange increasingly is public opinion. As exceptional as the Great Communicator's record appeared at the time, we know now that it harbingered a new era when presidents routinely go public. President Reagan's peculiar performance cast a long shadow, not unlike that of Franklin Roosevelt's, against which the performance of present and future presidents will be judged.

NOTES

1. Steven V. Roberts, "Reagan and Congress: Key Tests Ahead," *New York Times,* June 16, 1985, 14.
2. Lou Cannon, *Reagan* (New York: G. P. Putnam's Sons, 1982), 319.
3. Ronald Reagan, with Richard G. Hubler, *Where's the Rest of Me?* (New York: Duell, Sloan, and Pearce, 1965), 257.
4. Leslie H. Gelb, "The Mind of the President," *New York Times Magazine,* October 6, 1985, 4–5.
5. Reagan contested four gubernatorial primary and general elections and fifty-seven presidential primaries in the 1976 and 1980 presidential elections. Richard M. Scammon and Alice V. McGillivray, *America Votes 14: A Handbook of Contemporary American Election Statistics* (Washington, D.C.: Congressional Quarterly Inc., 1980), 27–37.
6. "Reagan Popularity below Predecessors," *Gallup Report* 186 (March 1981): 2–9.
7. Cannon, *Reagan,* 319.
8. Bernard Weinraub, "Reagan Wants to Voice Views on Russian TV," *New York Times,* September 4, 1985, A1.
9. Peter Goldman, "The Reagan Steamroller," *Newsweek,* May 18, 1981, 40. Some became downright monastic. By summer, former vice president and future presidential candidate Walter Mondale had publicly embarked on a retreat to contemplate the country's needs.
10. Notable among defense issues was the MX missile program, which was greatly scaled down yet spared from what at moments appeared to be its certain demise.
11. Lynn Rosellini, "Lobbyists' Row All Alert for Chance at the Budget," *New York Times,* February 26, 1981, 9.
12. George Skelton, "Reagan Dip in Poll Tied to Spending Cuts," *Los Angeles Times,* March 19, 1981, 6.

13. Ibid.

14. Sidney Blumenthal, "Marketing the President," *New York Times Magazine,* September 13, 1981, 111. Much of the subsequent material on the budget cut comes from Blumenthal and from Elizabeth Drew, "A Reporter in Washington," *New Yorker,* June 8, 1981, 138–142.

15. Blumenthal, "Marketing the President," 112.

16. Party officials were also sent to Ohio where Republican representatives were reportedly wavering. Drew, "Reporter in Washington," 138–142.

17. David M. Alpern, "The Second Hundred Days," *Newsweek,* May 11, 1981, 23. *Time* reported that on "only a few occasions had a President enjoyed such a shouting, clapping, emotional reception from the assembled law- makers" (Ed Magnuson, "Reagan's Budget Battle," *Time,* May 11, 1981, 16).

18. "President Reagan's April Address on Economy," in *Reagan's First Year* (Washington, D.C.: Congressional Quarterly Inc., 1982), 118–119.

19. Goldman, "The Reagan Steamroller," 39.

20. Ibid. In an effort to downplay Reagan's public leadership, some scholars have searched for evidence of bargaining. And in fairness they have found important instances that went unde- tected in this book's first edition. However, on the passage of the Gramm-Latta budget reso- lution, signs of bargaining are quite thin. Some have said that agreeing to allow Phil Gramm, Democratic representative (soon to be Republican senator), to be the chief sponsor of the administration budget proposal was a major concession—a bargain, if you will. But citing decisions that will give members of Congress credit for "carrying the president's water" strike me as dubious evidence of bargaining. The second "bargain" takes the form of President Reagan's assurances to individual members of Congress that some of the proposed cuts would later be reopened for discussion, and implicitly negotiation, if they supported the president's targets in the Gramm-Latta guidelines. Here, too, the president made no substan- tive concessions in return for a budget resolution vote. Such claims of bargaining demean the concept. Marc A. Bodnick overstates the significance of these transactions in " 'Going Public' Reconsidered: Reagan's 1981 Tax and Budget Cuts, and Revisionist Theories of Presidential Power," *Congress and the Presidency* 17 (spring 1990), 13–28.

21. David Stockman, *The Triumph of Politics* (New York: Avon, 1986), 211–212.

22. Ibid., 214.

23. Blumenthal, "Marketing the President," 112.

24. Peter Goldman, "Reagan's Sweet Triumph," *Newsweek,* July 6, 1981, 20.

25. This meeting between Reagan and five Democratic leaders is described in Peter Goldman, "Tax Cuts: Reagan Digs In," *Newsweek,* June 15, 1981, 26–27; and George J. Church, "He'll Do It His Way," *Time,* June 15, 1981, 10–12.

26. Goldman, "Tax Cuts," 25. Because reporters had gathered outside to receive the visibly glum Democrats, O'Neill may have been justified in his suspicions that they had been set up by the president for a media event.

27. Irwin B. Arieff, "Conservative Southerners Are Enjoying Their Wooing as Key to Tax Bill Success," *Congressional Quarterly Weekly Report,* June 13, 1981, 1024.

28. Peter Goldman, "Rest in Peace, New Deal," *Newsweek,* August 10, 1981, 17.

29. Wirthlin likely based such an assessment on poll results that gave the GOP almost as many identifiers as Democrats and that showed more than two-thirds of the respondents approv- ing of Congress's earlier vote on the Gramm-Latta budget resolution. Elizabeth Wehr, "Reagan May Try to Block August Recess . . . If Work Unfinished on Tax Cut Measure," *Congressional Quarterly Weekly Report,* June 27, 1981, 1134–1135.

30. Goldman, "Tax Cuts," 27.

31. Wehr, "Reagan May Try," 1135.
32. "Reagan's TV Address on Tax Bill," in *Reagan's First Year,* 122–124.
33. Goldman, "Rest in Peace," 16–20.
34. Ibid.
35. Gary W. Cox and Mathew D. McCubbins, *Setting the Agenda: Responsible Party Government in the U.S. House of Representatives,* (New York: Cambridge University Press, 2005), 118–120.
36. Steven V. Roberts, "President's Coalition," *New York Times,* October 27, 1982, 13. For another case study of the politics of the 1981 budget, see Allen Schick, "How the Budget Was Won and Lost," in *President and Congress,* ed. Norman J. Ornstein (Washington, D.C.: American Enterprise Institute, 1982), 14–43.
37. The fifteen million figure was calculated by subtracting the total mailings (letter-sized and larger envelopes) in 1980 from those in 1981. The source for these figures is Norman J. Ornstein et al., *Vital Statistics on Congress, 1982* (Washington, D.C.: American Enterprise Institute, 1982), 141. The 1984–1985 edition of *Vital Statistics* notes that mailings the next year returned to the 1980 levels, but data were not provided. Norman J. Ornstein et al., *Vital Statistics on Congress, 1984–1985 Edition* (Washington, D.C.: American Enterprise Institute, 1984), 142.
38. David M. Alpern, "The Runner Stumbles," *Newsweek,* September 28, 1982, 26–27.
39. For the standard journalistic treatment of this event, see Tom Morganthau, "Running to Stay in Place," *Newsweek,* October 5, 1981, 24; and Walter Isaacson, "Rough Waters Ahead," *Time,* October 5, 1981, 8–11.
40. The data used in the following analysis came from the American Institute of Public Opinion, Survey No. 183-G, October 2–5, 1981. The overall results are described in the *Gallup Opinion Index* (November 1981): 3–8. For a more detailed examination of this survey, see Samuel Kernell, "The Presidency and the People: The Modern Paradox," in *The Presidency and the Political System,* ed. Michael Nelson (Washington, D.C.: CQ Press, 1984), 250–253.
41. William Greider, "The Education of David Stockman," *Atlantic,* December 1981, 32–43.
42. Alan Greenspan, who chaired the Council of Economic Advisers under President Gerald Ford and would later serve as chairman of the Federal Reserve under Presidents Bush and Clinton, was quoted as saying, "This scenario [of depression] still has a low probability, but it should no longer be put into the bizarre or kooky category" (George J. Church, "A Season of Scare Talk," *Time,* March 15, 1982, 12).
43. Ed Magnuson, "A Line Drawn in Dirt," *Time,* February 22, 1982, 12.
44. Ed Magnuson, "Stumbling to a Showdown," *Time,* April 26, 1982, 12.
45. Magnuson, "A Line Drawn in Dirt," 12.
46. Howell Raines, "Reagan's Gamble: Bid for Popularity," *New York Times,* March 31, 1982, A27.
47. Ibid.
48. Jack Nelson, "Administration Seeks to Stem GOP 'Potshots' against Reagan," *Los Angeles Times,* April 14, 1982, 14. Shortly thereafter, Rollins retracted the threat, but said such members of Congress would have low priority for White House assistance. Lee Atwater, Rollins's assistant, pedaled a softer line. "We'll never ask a member to vote against his own political interest, but we sure will . . . try to show them that it may be in their interest to support the President," he told reporter Dick Kirschten. See "Reagan's Political Chief Rollins," *National Journal,* June 12, 1982, 1054–1057. For congressional testimony to threats, see Jack Nelson, "President's 'Bad-Boy' List Aims for Republican Unity," *Los Angeles Times,* May 23, 1982, 11.
49. "Fiscal Year 1983 Federal Budget," *Weekly Compilation of Presidential Documents* 18 (May 3, 1982): 545–549. Speaker O'Neill and Rules Committee chair Richard Bolling disputed the president's rendition of the negotiating sessions; they claimed instead that both sets of fig-

ures used by the president were Republican in origin. "They rigged the sheet of paper we were working from," said Bolling. "This is a case where they split the difference between their figure and their figure" (Dale Tate, "Budget Battle Erupts on Hill as Compromise Talks Fizzle," *Congressional Quarterly Weekly Report,* May 1, 1982, 967–969).

50. He continued, "Let your representatives know that you support the kind of fair, effective approach I have outlined for you tonight. Let them know you stand behind our recovery program. You did it once, you can do it again. Thank you, and God bless you" ("Fiscal Year 1983 Federal Budget," 549).

51. Sen. Ernest Hollings and Sen. Daniel P. Moynihan, both Budget Committee Democrats, pressed Republican chair Pete Domenici for a vote on the president's original budget. He refused, responding, "We don't have to be subtle. The President's budget will not pass" (Tate, "Budget Battle Erupts on Hill," 968).

52. Shortly before the president's trip to Europe, two White House aides confided their anticipation to Elizabeth Drew. They "talked openly about the political fruits of the television spectacular, and the picture of the President as a leader." One said, "It's going to be great theater" (Elizabeth Drew, "A Reporter in Washington, D.C." *New Yorker,* June 21, 1982, 97). See also Karen Elliot House and Alan L. Otten, "White House Hopes Summit Will Enhance the President's Stature," *Wall Street Journal,* May 28, 1982. Richard Wirthlin would later claim that the trip improved Reagan's job performance rating the next month. "Pollster Finds a 'Pool of Patience' with Reagan Economics Program," *New York Times,* July 31, 1982. See also Jack Nelson, "Public Still Patient with Reaganomics, Poll Finds," *Los Angeles Times,* July 31, 1982, 1.

53. Martin Tolchin anticipated the inherently conflicting budget considerations six months earlier in "G.O.P. Clocks Differ on Timing of Budget Moves," *New York Times,* November 12, 1981, 26.

54. Ed Magnuson, "Reagan Says All Aboard," *Time,* August 23, 1982, 7.

55. "Gallup Survey Finds Approval of Reagan at Its Lowest Point," *New York Times,* August 19, 1982, 14.

56. A defeat on the tax bill, Wirthlin told them, "would make the President look weak and damage the party's candidates across the board." The record is unclear on the success of this argument with the House Republicans, but it certainly caught the attention of the press, which depicted Reagan's "leadership" on the line with this vote. For examples of the press buildup, see Howell Raines, "Leadership Image Risked," *New York Times,* August 17, 1982, 1; and Hedrick Smith, "Reagan's Big Victory," *New York Times,* August 20, 1982, D14. In an earlier article Howell Raines reported Wirthlin's lobbying activities: "Reagan Runs a Reverse, Collides with Right Wing," *New York Times,* August 15, 1982, E4.

57. Hedrick Smith, "New House to Back Reagan Less, Poll Shows," *New York Times,* November 4, 1982, E4.

58. The relative importance of unemployment and inflation as "the most important problem" is charted for the years 1977–1983 in *National Journal,* February 19, 1983, 401.

59. The CBS News/*New York Times* survey revealed an equally sharp decline in Reagan's support at the close of 1982. See Howell Raines, "Reagan's Policies Lose Favor in Poll," *New York Times,* January 25, 1983, 1.

60. Hedrick Smith, "Now Democrats Attacking President," *New York Times,* September 18, 1982; David S. Broder, "GOP Will Be Hurt, Both Parties Agree," *Washington Post,* October 19, 1982, A1.

61. This did not keep the president off national television, however. On October 14, 1982, he rejected Democratic criticisms and appealed to the American public to stay the course.

62. Roberts, "President's Coalition," 13. Even in the Senate where the Republicans staved off strong Democratic challenges, the message of the elections was clear. Because nineteen Republican incumbents were facing reelection in 1984, Republican senator William Cohen of Maine predicted, "The Senate is going to be more independent next year" (Walter Isaacson, "Trimming the Sails," *Time*, November 15, 1982, 16). For an assessment of the reasons Republicans lost fewer House seats than widely predicted by various statistical models of the relation between economic conditions and the congressional vote, see Gary C. Jacobson and Samuel Kernell, *Strategy and Choice in Congressional Elections*, 2nd ed. (New Haven: Yale University Press, 1983), 94–110.

63. All except one. The former head of the boll weevils, Rep. Phil Gramm of Texas, lost his committee assignment because of his collusion with Republicans and shortly thereafter changed parties.

64. Steven V. Roberts, "The Eclipse of the Boll Weevils," *New York Times*, March 26, 1983, 10.

65. Ibid.

66. Ibid. Montgomery's message from his Mississippi constituents parallels that of Stenholm: "People in my district used to say, 'support the President.' Now I'm not hearing that much."

67. Roberts, "President's Coalition," 13.

68. Rich Jaroslovsky, "Reagan's 'Revolution' Stalls as Policies Falter Both Here and Abroad," *Wall Street Journal*, December 23, 1983, 1; Leslie Gelb, "In the Event of a Presidential Power Vacuum. . . ," *New York Times*, February 23, 1983, 12; Hedrick Smith, "The MX and Reagan's Receptivity to Compromise," *New York Times*, December 16, 1982, B16; "At the Brink" is the front cover title of the *National Journal*, March 5, 1983.

69. Isaacson, "Trimming the Sails," 16.

70. Hedrick Smith, "Reagan at Midterm," *New York Times*, December 29, 1982, 1; and Smith, "The MX," B16.

71. Francis X. Clines, "An Outsider (Soon to Be an Insider) Stirs Concern," *New York Times*, February 4, 1983, 8; and Juan Williams, "Presidential Newsmaking," *Washington Post*, February 13, 1983, A18. Another tactic was to have President Reagan tape a brief statement for the nightly news whenever some economic index became favorable. See Jonathan Fuerbringer, "Good News Often Brings More News," *New York Times*, February 21, 1983, 10. See also Dick Kirschten, "Distributing Poll Data Prompting White House to Woo Alienated Voting Blocs," *National Journal*, March 5, 1983, 488–492.

72. *Wall Street Journal*, January 14, 1983, 1.

73. Edward Cowan, "Democratic Budget Is Adopted by House, 229–196," *New York Times*, March 24, 1983. For a detailed breakdown of the differences between Reagan's and the Democrats' budgets, see "Two Budget Plans with Little in Common," *National Journal*, March 26, 1983, 670.

74. Juan Williams and Helen Dewar, "President Assails House Democrats' '84 Budget Plan," *Washington Post*, March 19, 1983, A1.

75. Ibid.

76. Dennis Farney, "House Democrats Waver on 1984 Budget, Leaders Concede, after Reagan Criticisms," *Wall Street Journal*, March 22, 1983, 2.

77. "President's Speech," *New York Times*, March 24, 1983, 8.

78. Steven V. Roberts, "Bill to Make Jobs Gets Final Assent," *New York Times*, March 25, 1983, 9.

79. Martin Tolchin, "Budget Process in Peril?" *New York Times*, April 16, 1983, 5.

80. Steven V. Roberts, "The Budget Victim: G.O.P. Senate Coalition Unravels," *New York Times*, May 7, 1983, 7.

81. Steven R. Weisman, "Turning Point on Budget," *New York Times*, June 22, 1983, D23.

82. In another instance cited in the press, some Florida lawmakers, disturbed by the rising crime rate in their state, sought and won an exemption of the 4 percent cut in federal law enforcement funds. Steven V. Roberts, "How Reagan Won in Congress," *New York Times,* December 30, 1982, 11; Hedrick Smith, "Taking Charge of Congress," *New York Times Magazine,* August 9, 1981, 17.

83. Bernard Weinraub, "Reagan Sets Tone of Nation to Seek Economic Victory," *New York Times,* January 25, 1985. President Reagan hinted that he would pursue such a course the day after the election when he told reporters in Los Angeles that he would take his case "to the people" to force congressional cooperation. Jack Nelson, "Reagan Vows to Extend Conservative Agenda," *Los Angeles Times,* November 8, 1984, 1.

84. Hedrick Smith, "Budget Maneuvers: Prime Concern Is '84 Election," *New York Times,* May 11, 1983, 9; Steven R. Weisman, "Budget Tie-Up: Reagan at the Crossroads," *New York Times,* April 20, 1983, A21; and Steven V. Roberts, "Conferees and the Budget," *New York Times,* June 20, 1983, 9.

85. Blumenthal, "Marketing the President," 114.

86. Dick Kirschten, "Life in the White House Fish Bowl—Brady Takes Charge as Press Chief," *National Journal,* January 31, 1981, 180–183.

87. Dick Kirschten, "Reagan's Political Chief Rollins: 'We Will Help Our Friends First,' " *National Journal,* June 12, 1982, 1057. See also Francis X. Clines, "Propaganda, Propagation or Just Prop," *New York Times,* June 15, 1984, A16.

88. Magnuson, "A Line Drawn in Dirt." In early April 1984, President Reagan's difficulties with Congress reached a breaking point. At a nationally televised news conference the president attacked Congress on many fronts—from aid to El Salvador to Congressional Budget Office figures. With the exception of House Republican Whip Trent Lott, Democratic and Republican leaders of both chambers took umbrage. "I want to help him," House Minority Leader Michel said of the president, "but if in the process you get torpedoed without warning, I don't appreciate that. It's always one step forward and two steps backward." A Republican Senate aide summed up the common assessment: "The President is banking on the fact that the support he needs is there in the boonies. He ran against Congress in 1980, and I assume he'll run against this body again" (Steven V. Roberts, "Pointing Fingers: Lawmakers Reply to Reagan," *New York Times,* April 11, 1984, 10). For a report of President Reagan's speech, see Francis X. Clines, "Reagan Attacks Congress' Role on Many Fronts," *New York Times,* April 5, 1984, 1.

chapter 7

Opinion Leadership and Foreign Affairs

When the first plane hit the north tower of the World Trade Center on September 11, 2001, President George W. Bush was reading to a group of second graders in a public school in Florida. He had traveled there to boost his education reform initiative, "No Child Left Behind," which was stalled in Congress. A few minutes later when White House chief of staff Andrew Card whispered to the president that a second plane had slammed into the other tower, Bush instantly knew that "they had declared war on us . . . I made up my mind at that moment that we were going to war." Within the hour the president and his entourage were on Air Force One heading to Washington.[1]

Shortly after takeoff, however, the intelligence services detected a credible threat to the president's plane. The flight immediately changed course, seeking to evade a would-be attacker and picking up escort fighters along the way. First it sped to Barksdale Air Force Base in Louisiana and then to Nebraska's Offutt military base. Meanwhile, an American Airlines plane that had recently taken off from Washington's Dulles Airport was heading back to Washington and banked toward the White House. Apparently unable to locate the executive residence among the trees, the hijackers crashed into the Pentagon.*

In retrospect, the president and his administration performed capably during these early hours of the crisis. Confronted with poor information, yet required to make urgent decisions, they nonetheless seemed to have made the correct military choices. But their performance faltered when they began dealing with the public and the media. Upon seeing the televised attacks on the world trade center, the American public and the press turned immediately to the president for direction. Bush did not measure up to the challenge. A growing audience of puzzled, disappointed, and frightened Americans listened to

---

* Security whisked Vice President Dick Cheney to the protected bunker under the White House. From there Cheney and other senior advisers conferred with the president at his Air Force One command center as yet another crisis loomed: a fourth hijacked commercial jet bound for Chicago had turned around and was heading toward Washington. The president ordered the air force to shoot it down, along with any other rogue plane—a command for which the military sought repeated confirmation. Through the heroic efforts of passengers who had learned about the fate of the other hijacked planes through cell phone calls to family, United Airlines Flight 93 never got as far as Washington; instead, it crashed in a vacant field in Pennsylvania.

their president's initial comments on the attack. He vowed to "hunt down those folks." This poorly chosen euphemism for the terrorists prompted questions about the president's leadership abilities. During the next nine days, however, the president reassured the nation that he was in charge in an Oval Office address, a speech at Washington National Cathedral, and a nationally televised appearance before a joint session of Congress.

If one moment or event can be pointed to as restoring the president's leadership, it came as Bush was leaving the House chamber after his speech before Congress. In full view of a huge national television audience (over half of all households were tuned in), the top two Democratic Party leaders in Congress—House Minority Leader Richard Gephardt and Senate Majority Leader Tom Daschle—embraced Bush and vowed their party's support. This sent an unmistakable signal to the American public, as well as the nation's friends and enemies abroad, that the president had been given broad latitude to handle the war on terrorism. These events represent a specific application of the venerable American creed that "politics stops at the water's edge." [2]

By the end of September Bush's "job performance" rating soared to 90 percent approval, the highest level ever recorded by the Gallup Poll for any president since it began asking the public's evaluation in the 1930s. Just days before the attack this same rating, which had been trending downward during late summer, stood at 51 percent—the poorest mark for any president this early in a first term. By any measure this was as dramatic a public "rally" response to a national crisis as any event since the attack on Pearl Harbor in 1941. It gave the president the latitude to respond vigorously against enemies at home and abroad. Major antiterrorist legislation, the USA Patriot Act, sailed through Congress, and in October the United States invaded Afghanistan.* One can reasonably argue that the public's and politicians' early responses set the stage for Congress's acquiescence to a joint resolution allowing the administration to invade Iraq eighteen months later.

The Framers intentionally designed the office to allow the president to rise to such challenges. In debates at the Constitutional Convention, the Framers rejected a plural executive for just this reason; the presidency had to be an "energetic" office capable of responding to national emergencies. They stated plainly and with few constraints the presidency's "commander in chief" authority.† In so configuring the presidency while designing the other branches to retard quick action in favor of careful deliberation, the Framers designated the president to serve as a focal point for coordinating policy during national emergencies. The record of the early days after the 9/11 attacks is fully

---

* Daschle slightly qualified his party's support of the president's request for a supplementary $20 billion appropriation to wage the war on terror by cautioning that it would not be tantamount to a blank check such as the one that allowed the nation to become bogged down in the Vietnam War.
† Having barely survived the "war by committee" under the executiveless Articles of Confederation, the Framers fashioned what they commonly referred to as an "energetic" office that emphasized action over deliberation.

The Modern Commander in Chief Goes Public

Under a giant banner proclaiming "Mission Accomplished," President Bush landed on the aircraft carrier USS *Abraham Lincoln* to greet sailors returning from the Middle East. His arrival, chronicled by all the major television and print media, was widely proclaimed by admirers and critics alike as the "mother of all photo opportunities." Unarguably, it produced magnificently choreographed images. Even as most news outlets recognized it as a publicity stunt and characterized it as the unofficial launching of the president's reelection campaign, they could not conceal their wonderment. The *Washington Post* on May 2, 2003, marveled at "the bowlegged swagger of a top gun." Only about a third of the news sources, according to one analysis, echoed frustrated Democrats' criticism of the staged event. Three years later, with more than 2,500 American military fatalities and tens of thousands of Iraqi civilian deaths, the Democrats are more likely to mention the president's "Mission Accomplished" celebration.

Source: Global Media Analysts.

consistent with this understanding of the Constitution. Once Bush signaled that he was personally prepared to take charge, other Washingtonians quickly accepted his leadership.

The public's overwhelming support for Bush can also be viewed as recognition of the president's role as central coordinator. Instead of a reflexive expression of patriotism, as some scholars have argued, equating the public's approval with Daschle and Gephardt's embrace offers a rational explanation for the apparently paradoxical surge on approval during a national emergency.[3]* The public's response after 9/11 is extraordinary only in the magnitude of the approval. Scholars have long noted the public's rally response to international crises. Many have applauded this phenomenon. Just when the country most requires leadership, they assert, the public gives the president free, or at least a much looser, rein to act. Others, however, regard it as an opportunity for perniciousness. In retrospect, the Tonkin Gulf incident appears far too ambiguous an event to have impelled Congress to officially launch the Vietnam War with a joint resolution supporting whatever actions Lyndon Johnson deemed necessary. Storytellers with a conspiratorial bent find presidents going beyond opportunism to the actual manufacture of crises. A classic Oliver Stone–like tale, which refuses to die, has Franklin Roosevelt exposing U.S. defenses to the attack on Pearl Harbor in 1941 because it was the only way he could persuade the country to declare an all-out war on the Axis powers. One can only imagine how severely historians will rake President Bush (as well as the Democratic congressional majorities that agreed to a resolution authorizing him to take unilateral action) for Iraq's "imminently" threatening biological, chemical, and nuclear weapons of mass destruction, none of which were ever found.

Whatever one's view about the wisdom of the rally phenomenon, it undoubtedly has proved to be a major ingredient in presidential leadership during the modern era. How different would George Bush's presidency have been had 9/11 not occurred? In Figure 7-1 President Bush's popularity rating during his first four years in office can be explained as the surge and gradual decline punctuated by periodic crises. Much the same assessment can be offered for his father's popularity ratings. By their nature, each crisis poses an unpredictable roll of the dice. Yet their occurrence during the modern era is so commonplace and potentially dominant that they must be included in any assessment of the president's capacity to go public.

RALLY EVENTS AND PRESIDENTIAL APPROVAL

To say that surges in the president's job performance rating during international crises represent a rational response to the task confronting the nation still

---

* After the U.S.-sponsored invasion of Cuba ended disastrously at the Bay of Pigs in April 1961, President Kennedy's already high approval rating rose another five percentage points. This occasioned the bemused president's famous observation, "The worse I do, the more popular I get."

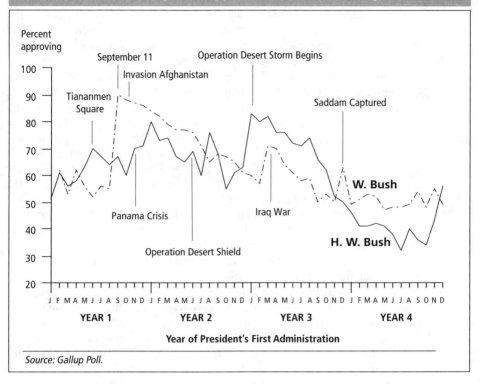

FIGURE 7-1   **Presidents' Popular Support as a Product of Rally Events**

Source: Gallup Poll.

leaves much to be explained. Many occurrences that would appear to satisfy the necessary conditions for a rally response fail to do so. When the reconnaissance ship *Pueblo* was seized by North Korea in 1968, the American public was not distracted from its steady withdrawal of approval for Lyndon Johnson as casualties mounted in Vietnam. Seven years later, however, in a strikingly similar incident, when the Cambodians seized another reconnaissance ship, the *Mayaguez*, Gerald Ford's popular support shot up eleven percentage points. What was different? Perhaps Pueblo was viewed as another incident in a long stretch of bad news during wartime.

Moreover, if, as we noted, the success or wisdom of the president's action apparently has little bearing on the magnitude of the public's rally response, what does condition it? Perhaps the drama plays a large part by galvanizing the public's attention. Jimmy Carter's failed attempt to rescue American hostages in Iran was greeted by a four-percentage-point rise in his popularity. These and other peculiarities make generalizations about the rally events hazardous. Clearly the specific details, context, and symbols enveloping these events shape the public's response.

Thus far we have considered as context only the reactions of presidents, other Washington politicians, and those who report on their activities. But the context includes another critical feature: the state of public opinion entering the crisis.[4] Since a rally event is defined by a surge in presidential support and measured by its magnitude, other things being equal, a president who already enjoys a strong public endorsement should experience smaller rallies than will one who is less popular. In early December 1979, with barely a third of the public registering its approval, President Carter faced a stiff challenge from Sen. Edward Kennedy, D-Mass. More attention was focused on whether Carter could again win the nomination than on his chances in the general election in the fall. However, the seizure of the U.S. hostages in Tehran changed his fortunes. Reinforced by the Soviet Union's invasion of Afghanistan in January, Carter's job performance ratings rose twenty-three points—at the time, the largest percentage-point change ever—and it stayed high throughout the spring presidential primaries season.

Statistical evidence based on rally events during the post–World War II era supports the conjecture that the level of prior approval predictably conditions the rally response. This relationship is not strong, however, which is not too surprising given the handicap of an unpopular president trying to frame an event.* Still, the statistical relationship is suggestive.

During normal times the public's evaluation of the president follows partisan lines. Democrats were consistently the least approving of President Bush, Republicans the most so, with independents somewhere in the middle. Consequently, there were many more Democrats than Republicans available to rally in the aftermath of 9/11, and more in fact did so. During a five-day period beginning the day before the attack, Democratic approval soared from 27 to 78 percent approving. This compares to only an eight-point change among Republicans, because 87 percent already approved Bush's performance before the attack. (Respondents calling themselves independents swung from 44 to 84 percent approving.) With the surge in crisis support occurring disproportionately among citizens who normally oppose the president, presidents may find that lofty approval ratings may buy them less influence over public opinion than they might have expected.

RALLY EVENTS AND LEADERSHIP IN WASHINGTON

Politicians will occasionally have firsthand evidence of the public's responsiveness to a president's national appeal as they assess the degree to which they should accommodate his preferences. More commonly, they must judge the president's potential prowess with the circumstantial evidence provided by his approval ratings in the polls. The president's popularity helps them gauge his

---

* The regression slope for the president's popularity in the month preceding the rally event is −.11 and not significant. The change score and prior approval are correlated at −.26.5

From Dr. New Deal to Dr. Win the War

Support for FDR among Income Subgroups: 1939–1942

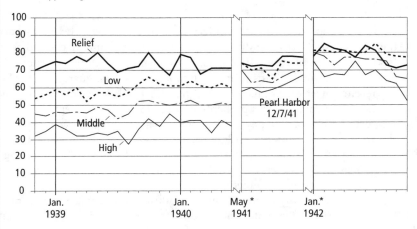

Percent approving

Source: Matthew A. Baum and Samuel Kernell, "Economic Class and Popular Support for Franklin Roosevelt in War and Peace," *Public Opinion Quarterly* (summer 2001): 198–229.

Note: For these surveys, "high," which averages 15 percent of the sample, includes those respondents earning more than $2,200 a year. The "middle" (40 percent of the sample) includes those earning greater than $1,285 a year but less than $2,200. The "low" (35 percent) includes those earning less than $1,285 a year. The "relief" (10 percent) includes those receiving direct relief, old age assistance, or those who are employed in a federal works program.

* No poll data are available June 1940–May 1941 and December 1941.

A compilation of approval ratings for Franklin Roosevelt before and after Japan's attack on Pearl Harbor illustrates the point that crisis support comes disproportionately from the president's detractors. In those days party identification was not a well-recognized concept, so that the best available means for measuring the partisan composition of FDR's coalition was income. Prior to the attack on Pearl Harbor, evaluation of the president adhered to class lines. After the president's detractors massively rallied, his popular support was pervasive. Acutely sensitive to the mood of the public, and armed with reports of these approval ratings (which after U.S. entry into the war were not published but privately given to him), President Roosevelt restyled his leadership, in his own words, from "Dr. New Deal" to "Dr. Win the War."[†]

† Richard W. Steele, "The Pulse of the People: Franklin D. Roosevelt and the Gauging of American Public Opinion," *Journal of Contemporary History* 9 (October 1975): 2.10–212. See also James MacGregor Burns, *Roosevelt: The Soldier of Freedom* (New York: Harcourt Brace Jovanovich, 1970).

ability to use public strategies. When crises generate surges in the president's popularity, they create leverage in his dealings with other Washingtonians across the board. Consider the following case, in which President George H. W. Bush parlayed his recent Desert Shield success in blocking Saddam Hussein from overrunning Kuwait's oil fields and the pending decision to attack Hussein's army.

On the evening of September 17, 1991, a discouraged secretary of state James Baker boarded a flight from Jerusalem to Cairo, the next leg of what was then his latest effort at shuttle diplomacy. Baker not only had failed to alter Israel's program of new settlements in the disputed occupied territories, but Israel had continued to insist on $10 billion in U.S. loan guarantees for housing recent Soviet emigrants. Prime Minister Yitzhak Shamir's bluntness with the American emissary was probably inspired to a greater extent by his strong support in the United States. Close to a majority of members of Congress had signed on as sponsors of legislation guaranteeing the loans when President Bush announced that, despite the "one thousand lobbyists" supporting the guarantees on Capitol Hill, he would veto any such legislation so long as Israel refused to freeze new settlements.

Jewish groups were quick to express outrage. California Senate candidate Dianne Feinstein represented the class of 1992 Democratic hopefuls when she called a press conference to label the president's position "reprehensible." Republicans made a similar political assessment. "I'm catching hell from the party," President Bush told a friend. "They're afraid we could lose some Senate seats out of this." [5]

Next came the Israelis. Foreign Minister David Levy's remarks seemed more threatening than reassuring to Bush: "Israel would never want to defeat the president of the United States. . . . But we also don't want to be humiliated." Then it was Shamir's turn. He could hardly have been more direct in mobilizing the formidable pro-Israeli faction when he stated that Jews in America "have learned a lesson from the Holocaust" and are therefore "now united and very active, to the surprise of political circles in their country." [6] Although several key members of the House and Senate expressed some appreciation of the president's position, and viewed the outcome of a fight with Bush as uncertain, "an early count suggest[ed] they may win." [7] Secretary Baker departed Israel empty-handed because Prime Minister Shamir appeared to hold winning cards in the U.S. Congress.

During the flight to Cairo, Baker vented his frustration to the traveling reporters. Whether by inadvertence or stratagem, he played what proved to be the administration's trump card. Baker told them he would recommend that the president go to the American people to make the administration's case, including a national television address "if that is what it takes." [8] As soon as reports of his comments filtered back to Washington, the political winds appeared to shift. The next day various unnamed aides informed correspondents that the White House staff was preparing for a national campaign that would include television. As one aide explained, "As long as this is an 'Inside-the-Beltway' issue, it plays to our disadvantage. 'Outside the Beltway,' the position that the president, not the Congress and not Israel, determines foreign policy seems eminently reasonable." [9]

During the next week, as President Bush defended his position and appeared to stiffen his resolve to use the veto, public opinion polls began recording strong support for his position. In an ABC News survey, 86 percent backed the president's position on loan guarantees, while another poll found 69 percent agreeing with the president that the decision should be postponed for six months.

These impressive numbers spawned doubts among Israel's supporters in Congress. One Democratic senator remarked, "No one wants to belly up to this buzz saw," and a House member observed in a similar metaphoric vein, "There is very little stomach to confront the President on this." Even the normally resourceful lobbyists became stoic. "If the President of the United States goes to the American people and says 'Enough already,' the Israeli lobby can't counteract that," explained a senior pro-Israel lobbyist. A week after Baker's conversation with reporters, the Associated Press distributed a photograph of a smiling Baker shaking hands with Israel's foreign minister to symbolize their agreement to postpone the loan-guarantee issue as the White House desired.[10] The benign ripples of Desert Storm continued to benefit the administration's foreign policy.*

Politicians' accommodation to President Bush's firm position followed their reading of the president's public support. Elected officeholders hesitate to get on the wrong side of a popular president. Ample evidence of accommodation has accumulated on a number of fronts. Congressional committees give legislative initiatives from popular presidents more careful consideration, and subsequently, they win more roll call votes on the floors of both the House and Senate.[11] Even the news media lightens up in its normally critical coverage of the administration.

RALLY EVENTS, APPROVAL, AND OPINION LEADERSHIP

During the past twenty years, the relationship between the president's approval level and his ability to influence public opinion has moved from an article of faith among Washington politicians to a standard research topic of political

---

* Beginning with Aaron Wildavsky's "two presidencies" thesis, political scientists have monitored and compared the legislative success of presidential appeals on foreign and domestic policies. For a thorough discussion of this argument and statistical analysis confirming presidents' domestic and foreign policy leadership, see Brandice Canes-Wrone, *Who Leads Whom? Presidents, Policy, and the Public* (Chicago: University of Chicago Press, 2006), 83–102. Canes-Wrone detects an important difference between domestic and foreign policy appeals. Presidents are more likely to promote domestic policies that already enjoy a measure of public support, while such strategic selection is less clear for foreign policy appeals.

science. Research has approached the president's opinion leadership in a number of ways. One survey study, performed during the time of a popular incumbent, found that respondents were significantly more likely to endorse a hypothetical policy when they were told that it represented the president's position.[12] Another examined public support for policies on which the president had actually staked out a clear position. It found that generally respondents who approved of the president's performance expressed more enthusiasm about the policy than did those who disapproved.[13] Finally, a few studies have sought to gauge changes in aggregate public opinion on policy questions as a function of a president's intervention. They similarly report a relation between the president's popularity at the time of a public appeal and the magnitude of opinion change that followed.[14] Although alternative explanations to the transference of support from the president to his policies are available to explain each of these findings, the similar results generated by these different research designs present compelling circumstantial support for the importance of a president's prestige on his opinion leadership.

Of course, all one is really saying is that people tend to evaluate a message according to its source. One can easily develop a rationale for such a transference from traditional consistency theory in social psychology, which maintains that individuals generally prefer consistent to inconsistent beliefs and opinions. An individual seeking to incorporate new information in a consistent fashion has a number of mechanisms available for doing so. One of particular relevance here is the congruence between source and message.[15] Alternatively, one can reasonably regard individuals' opinions about the president's job performance as a summary measure of their assessment of his reliability and trustworthiness based on past experiences. Citizens will alter their position on an issue according to the signal transmitted by this positively (approve) or negatively (disapprove) valenced referent. Approval inspires trust; disapproval breeds suspicion.

If going public is to succeed as a leadership strategy, presidential appeals must activate as well as persuade. Large numbers of citizens must be moved to contact their representatives. If the collective demonstration of support for the president's program impresses politicians, they may strategically align their public position in a way that is favorable to the president. The opinion dynamics required of going public, therefore, extend beyond mass persuasion, for which consistency between source and message is most appropriate. According to these dynamics, a national appeal will alter the preferences of sufficient numbers of politicians if the following four conditions are satisfied:

1. The president accurately communicates his preferences to the citizenry. The public recognizes the president's endorsement of a particular policy position. Past research on the public's familiarity with presidential appeals indicates that this is probably the least-demanding condition, although as we noted in chap-

ter 4, presidents are finding national audiences for such appeals increasingly elusive.[16]

2. Citizens register favorable or unfavorable responses to a policy initiative according to their evaluation of the president. Moreover, the salience and intensity of opinion are updated based on exposure to the president's message. All are conditioned by the strength of the individual's position on an issue and of his or her evaluation of the president before observing the appeal.

3. Citizens communicate support for the president's position to those politicians he hopes to influence. Ongoing communication is a commonly stipulated feature of representative democracy. Here, however, the principle takes on special emphasis, since the president will typically be trying to alter some specific behaviors of politicians over a short time. For such a result, the more casual and leisurely forms of communication that arise from the representative's continuing contact with constituents will have to be supplemented by the direct effort of many citizens to contact their representatives.

4. To secure their own welfare, politicians strategically align their preferences with those of the president. Representatives do not have to decide that the president's position commands majority support among their constituents for such a posture to make political sense. A presidential appeal may succeed in creating a vocal, intense supportive minority that will prevail over an indifferent or passive majority.

Facing these stringent conditions, a president might conclude that going public will not be worth the effort. Citing them, some observers have argued, in fact, that presidents should spurn going public as a substitute for bargaining. Nelson W. Polsby, a leading student of contemporary American politics, has said on the subject:

> Efforts to ignore, bypass, or run roughshod over [national interest] groups by appealing over their heads to the people are doomed on at least two counts. First, the appeal to public opinion itself is likely to fail because of the ephemerality of mass public attitudes on most issues and because of the non-transferability of president's popularity (when the president is popular) to the objects of a president's desires. Second, even if by some unusual combination of circumstances public opinion does for once yield to a president's entreaties, the effects may or may not reach Congress or influence congressional disposition of an issue.[17]

There are a number of ways to relax the four formal conditions and to make the transference less dependent upon Polsby's "unusual combination of circumstances." First, the position of the president in the policy-making process allows him to choose from a large menu of policy proposals circulating around Washington at any moment. For those issues that are sufficiently advanced to merit the president's attention, much of the preparatory, coalition-building work will have been completed. Rather than being truly innovative and building winning coalitions from the ground up, presidents typically take up others' ideas and work at the margin of support that will make the difference in victory or defeat. An example of this tactic is Ronald Reagan's use of national television and other public activities to swing thirty to fifty Republican House votes on the 1982 tax increase.

Further reducing the demands on the president's rhetoric, representatives also work at the margin of support within their constituencies. Even if a representative suspects that no more than 4 or 5 percent of the electorate will base its vote in the next election on his or her support of the president's program, it still might decisively alter his or her position on the issue.

The fact that marginal shifts of preferences, whether in Washington or in the rest of the country, often have major political consequences is what makes going public a viable strategy. The president makes an appeal; most citizens do not respond, but some do. A few of this latter group express their support actively. Most of the politicians who oppose the president's position will resist constituent pressure. A few whose positions are less fixed or who are electorally vulnerable will be persuaded that the president's course offers the least resistance. Frequently, this is all that is required for the president to appear to have worked his magic.

Moreover, the president possesses unusual institutional assets that may enhance his influence over public opinion well beyond that provided by his current popularity. Presidents by virtue of their office command the nation's attention. The broad constitutional mandate inherent in the office bestows upon the president the authority to speak on any policy matter; and his acknowledged institutional expertise requires that his arguments be weighed and, even if opposed, dealt with.[18] In foreign policy, particularly, these resources will put him in good stead.[19]

No president will ever persuade all of his admirers to support his cause. To the extent he fails, performance on condition 2 (transference of prestige to policy support) is weakened. But with the office's exceptional public standing, the incumbent president can also appeal to his detractors. His failure to persuade some of his admirers may be partly compensated by citizens who, while disapproving his current performance, nonetheless defer to his judgment. At times, consistency theory will be violated in ways that favor the president's efforts.

The remainder of this chapter tests the consistency model of opinion leadership on the Truman Doctrine speech of March 12, 1947. It is a single case, but a remarkable one. In the opinion of contemporaries and historians alike, President Truman faced a formidable task in preventing the country from settling comfortably into postwar isolationism and from failing to recognize the

Soviet challenge to its interests. He certainly thought so. Some historians have argued that to achieve his goals Truman resorted to extraordinary rhetoric and other public activities that secured his program but also eventually unleashed an anticommunist phobia throughout the country. In this case, then, a president who set out to reshape public opinion on foreign affairs stands accused by some of having kicked off the cold war at home.

THE TRUMAN DOCTRINE SPEECH: A Case Study

Delivered to Congress and broadcast across the nation on radio, this historic address has been widely credited not only with gaining the president his policy objectives but also with establishing the temper of U.S. foreign policy for the post–World War II era. Whether sympathetic to or critical of the Truman administration, historians agree that this speech more than any other single event marked the beginning of the cold war between the United States and the Soviet Union. Moreover, its implications for the future did not require hindsight. Contemporaries in Washington and abroad grasped immediately that President Truman was advocating a fundamental change in the U.S. responsibility and posture toward the rest of the world. As Joseph Jones, a State Department official who worked on the formulation of the Truman Doctrine, recalled, "All who participated in the extraordinary developments of the period were aware that a major turning in American history was taking place." [20]

The Speech

Truman's speech to the country called for congressional authorization of $400 million in economic and military assistance to Greece and Turkey. Describing the deterioration of the Greek economy and the inability of its military to cope with communist guerrilla activities, Truman starkly predicted that if the United States did not quickly replace the evacuating British forces, Greece would fall to the communists. Turkey and the rest of the Middle East would succumb in turn. But he went beyond a simple request for aid. He described a bipolar world of democracy versus totalitarianism and called for the United States to assist "free people who are resisting attempted subjugation." Two major sections of the speech depicted the communist threat and the challenge it presented to the American people to help others, specifically Greece and Turkey, resist it. Midway through he turned his discussion from Greece and Turkey and spoke more generally:

> The peoples of a number of countries of the world have recently
> had totalitarian regimes forced upon them against their will. The
> Government of the United States has made frequent protests against
> coercion and intimidation, in violation of the Yalta agreement, in
> Poland, Rumania, and Bulgaria. I must also state that in a number
> of other countries there have been similar developments.

> At the present moment in world history nearly every nation must choose between alternative ways of life. The choice is too often not a free one.
>
> One way of life is based upon the will of the majority, and is distinguished by free institutions, representative government, free elections, guarantees of individual liberty, freedom of speech and religion, and freedom from political oppression.
>
> The second way of life is based upon the will of a minority forcibly imposed upon the majority. It relies upon terror and oppression, a controlled press and radio, fixed elections, and the suppression of personal freedoms.
>
> I believe that we must assist free people to work out their own destinies in their own way.
>
> I believe that our help should be primarily through economic and financial aid which is essential to economic stability and orderly political processes.

His peroration was even more graphic:

> The seeds of totalitarian regimes are nurtured by misery and want. They spread and grow in the evil soil of poverty and strife. They reach their full growth when the hope of a people for a better life has died.
>
> We must keep that hope alive.
>
> The free peoples of the world look to us for support in maintaining their freedoms.
>
> If we falter in our leadership, we may endanger the peace of the world and we shall surely endanger the welfare of our own nation.
>
> Greater responsibilities have been placed upon us by the swift movements of events.
>
> I am confident that the Congress will face these responsibilities squarely.[21]

At the close of the speech the assembled joint session exploded into a standing ovation, and the immediate response of most columnists and editors around the country was favorable. There was some opposition, however, and it would be months before the aid authorization would pass Congress. Henry Wallace, who the next year would run for president against Truman as a third-party candidate, went on nationwide radio to lambaste the speech and characterize Truman, for his depiction of the gravity of the Soviet threat, as "the best salesman Communism ever had." [22] A number of prominent senators spanning the ideological spectrum from Robert Taft on the right to Claude Pepper on the left publicly expressed reservations.

After having experienced the cold war rhetoric of the 1950s, one may not find much in Truman's statements that is particularly arousing or inflammatory. But it must be remembered that this was the first time a president had publicly identified the Soviet Union as an enemy and depicted so starkly the struggle between democracy and totalitarianism. Despite the disappointments after Yalta, Truman had repeatedly resisted making such public statements. Even now some of his closest advisers were disturbed by the speech's tenor. Secretary of State George C. Marshall, en route to a Moscow conference, was "somewhat startled to see the extent to which the anticommunist element . . . was stressed." [23] James Byrnes, who had recently resigned as secretary of state, complained that the speech was too general in tone and commitment.[24] George Kennan, shortly to become head of the State Department's policy-planning staff, also objected to the "sweeping nature of the commitments." [25]

It is obvious from reading the memoirs of those who participated in drafting the speech that President Truman had intended it to be hortatory. Several days earlier at a White House briefing for a number of important senators and representatives, he had viewed the chilly response accorded Secretary Marshall's humanitarian reasons for giving assistance to Greece and Turkey. Only after Undersecretary Dean Acheson's presentation of the issue in strong anticommunist terms did the lawmakers warm to the proposal.[26] And as noted in chapter 2, this is when Sen. Arthur Vandenberg, the respected foreign policy expert, is reported to have advised the president that he would have to "scare hell out of the country" if he wanted to get authorization through Congress.[27] Moreover, other recent reconstruction programs proposed by the administration had received hostile responses from Congress and clearly would never be reported out of committee. Finally, Truman's vivid account of the speech writing reveals the dramatic rhetorical style he wanted infused into the text:

> The drafting of the actual message which I would deliver to the
> Congress had meanwhile been started in the State Department. The
> first version was not at all to my liking. The writers had filled the
> speech with all sorts of background data and statistical figures about
> Greece and made the whole thing sound like an investment prospec-
> tus. I returned this draft to Acheson with a note asking for more
> emphasis on a declaration of general policy. The department's drafts-
> men then rewrote the speech to include a general policy statement,
> but it seemed to me half-hearted. The key sentence, for instance, read,
> "I believe that it should be the policy of the United States. . . ." I took
> my pencil, scratched out "should" and wrote in "must." . . . I wanted
> no hedging in this speech. This was America's answer to the surge of
> expansion of Communist tyranny. It had to be clear and free of hesi-
> tation or double talk.[28]

As Richard M. Freeland has summed up the speech, President Truman committed himself and the nation to a "broad interpretative framework" of a "global assault of the 'totalitarian' forces against the forces of 'freedom'—calculated to command immediately the maximum public support." [29] When Marshall complained to the president that he had "overstated it a bit," Truman quickly replied that such language had been necessary to receive favorable congressional treatment.[30]

After past wars the United States had withdrawn at least temporarily into an isolationist mood and policy. Despite the U.S. role in creating the United Nations, every indication from the recently elected Republican Congress was that U.S. economic and military commitments around the world would be sharply curtailed. Yet here was the president, only a year after the peace, attempting to commit a hostile Congress and an unconcerned nation to an activist, international posture.

Unlike President Reagan's use of national appeals as a bludgeon against his adversaries in Congress, President Truman's enterprise was subtler. Working in an era where such force would have in all likelihood redoubled resistance, Truman sought to create an opinion climate that would make going along with his aid program for Greece and Turkey easier for members of Congress who might otherwise discern only the political costs to supporting such a policy. In going public, Truman sought not to circumvent bargaining. Indeed, by following Vandenberg's advice he tacitly agreed to shoulder responsibility for the policy and thereby remove a formidable obstacle to negotiation.[31] Truman's success, consequently, should be measured by the degree to which the speech generated a favorable opinion climate rather than by the volume of congressional mail it inspired. As such, it is an ideal case for testing at least the first two formal conditions of opinion leadership listed above.

I have hinted at another reason why the Truman Doctrine speech is of interest here. Since the late 1960s, a number of historians (whom I shall call revisionists) have been reevaluating the Truman presidency and concluding that the United States fomented the cold war abroad and at home. Among them, Freeland identifies Truman's March 12 speech, as well as subsequent propaganda and "police" activities against subversion, as creating an opinion climate of anticommunism that made the McCarthyism of the early 1950s unavoidable.* Freeland's depiction of events, like that of other revisionist historians, is simple. He contends that President Truman raised the specter of communist subversion to prompt Congress and the nation to embrace his foreign policy. Having succeeded in linking foreign and domestic threats and getting his program enacted, Truman found himself unable to turn off the pathological fear of communism he promulgated. It is a parsimonious theory. It dismisses eventual passage of the Greco-Turkish aid program as well as the Marshall Plan; it explains away the president's pro–civil libertarian resistance to congressional investigations in the

---

* Three daily newspapers during the period were examined, and subsequent references to the news media reflect their coverage. These are the *New York Times, Chicago Daily Tribune,* and the *San Francisco Chronicle.* There are as many revisionist interpretations as there are scholars writing on the subject. In some respects Freeland's thesis is among the bolder reinterpretations. All, however, tend to agree in emphasizing the effects of elite rhetoric on the formation of mass opinion.

late 1940s and the early 1950s; and it accounts for the rise of McCarthyism. And finally there is a moral: we reap what we sow. During the 1952 presidential campaign, Truman and the Democrats were roasted for being soft on communism.

This reinterpretation of foreign affairs in the late 1940s covers a broad range of occurrences in and out of government, and findings on the effect of a single event, no matter how dramatic, can neither confirm nor deny revisionist history. Yet this history relies heavily upon the assumption that elites could easily manipulate public opinion. The Truman Doctrine speech is commonly regarded in revisionist statements as one of Truman's most prominent and successful efforts.[32] In investigating the public's response to Truman's address in a realm beyond policy support, one can test, in part, these revisionist claims and explore the limits of presidential opinion leadership.

Public Familiarity with the Speech

During the two-week interval between the March 12 address and the Gallup survey that queried the public about it, the president's remarks and proposal received continuous coverage in the nation's newspapers. As a result, an unusually large share of respondents, 84 percent, reported having heard or read about the speech. This compares with only 54 percent who would claim familiarity with the Marshall Plan in the summer at a later stage of that issue's development.*

Given the extent to which Truman's address reached its audience, it is not surprising that the speech coincided with heightened public awareness of international problems, as Table 7-1 shows. In March 1947, when a Gallup survey asked what was the nation's "most important problem," more than half of the respondents volunteered foreign affairs. Only three months earlier, barely a fifth had done so; and by late summer, pressing domestic issues would reemerge as the dominant public concerns. Although international events were occurring quickly during this period, the Truman Doctrine speech appears to have been the most prominent one between the December and March surveys and probably accounts for the brief ascent of foreign affairs as the nation's "most important problem." Because the president's address to the joint session of Congress was an important event not only in Washington but also in the rest of the country, one may consider the answers to the survey questions to be real opinions rather than merely obligatory responses.

---

* In May 1950 only 23 percent had heard of Truman's Point Four Program. Only 71 percent claimed familiarity with the Taft-Hartley legislation in mid-1948, although it was a major campaign issue. In 1963 the same percentage was familiar with the Peace Corps two years after it had been in operation. Only major international events and crises such as *Sputnik*, the U-2 incident, and the Berlin crisis in 1961 reached a higher plateau of public familiarity. David O. Sears, "Political Behavior," in *The Handbook of Social Psychology*, vol. 5, eds. Gardner Lindzey and Elliot Aronson, 2nd ed. (Reading, Mass.: Addison-Wesley, 1969), 324–328.

Date	Percent naming foreign problems as most important
Before Truman Doctrine speech	
October 1945	7
February 1946	23
June 1946	11
September 1946	23
December 1946	22
After Truman Doctrine speech	
March 1947	54
July 1947	47
September 1947	28
December 1947	30
February 1948	33

TABLE 7-1 **Public Concern over Foreign Policy before and after Truman Doctrine Speech**

Sources: Gabriel Almond, *The American People and Foreign Policy* (New York: Praeger, 1960), 73; American Institute of Public Opinion, Survey No. 393, March 26–27, 1947; Samuel Kernell, "The Truman Doctrine Speech: A Case Study of the Dynamics of Presidential Opinion Leadership," *Social Science History* 1 (fall 1976): 28.

Effects of the Speech on Public Opinion

Two aspects of the March 1947 survey indicate the success of the speech in achieving its primary goal, support for the administration's foreign aid package. First, respondents were asked whether they would like to see their representatives vote for or against Truman's aid requests of $250 million for Greece and $150 million for Turkey.[33] The distribution of opinions is displayed in Table 7-2. Given the novelty of the issue, it is somewhat surprising that 85 percent of the sample expressed a preference, and nearly half felt strongly either for or against the president's proposals. Aid for Greece was the more popular of the two requests. Among those registering an opinion, 57 percent favored aid for Greece compared with only 46 percent for Turkey. The president's speech, as well as subsequent daily news reports, clearly identified Greece as being in the more precarious position. Turkey was described as having a relatively healthy economy and being in no immediate danger unless Greece were

TABLE 7-2 **Distribution of Public Support for Foreign Aid Requests in Truman Doctrine Speech (Percent)**		
	Aid for Greece	Aid for Turkey
Strongly oppose	20	22
Weakly oppose	18	23
Uncertain (don't know)	14	16
Weakly favor	29	22
Strongly favor	20	17

Sources: American Institute of Public Opinion, Survey No. 393, March 26–27, 1947; Samuel Kernell, "The Truman Doctrine Speech: A Case Study of the Dynamics of Presidential Opinion Leadership," *Social Science History* 1 (fall 1976): 34.

Note: Percentages may not total 100 because of rounding.

to collapse. Although perhaps short of a mandate, Truman succeeded in quickly generating substantial public enthusiasm for his internationalist policy. If contemporaneous informal readings of public opinion were correct in portraying a pervasive isolationist mood throughout the country, these percentages represent a sizable turnaround in public opinion.

The second aspect of the March 1947 survey that reflects on the success of Truman's speech is the relation between source and message. Table 7-3 shows that the president's approvers were more supportive than his detractors on both policy questions but that his opinion leadership was not limited to his admirers. A third of those respondents who disapproved of Truman's job performance nonetheless agreed to his aid program for Greece, and a fourth to his aid for Turkey. Because of the president's special credibility in foreign affairs, this finding is not unusual. Overall, approximately two-thirds of the respondents in Table 7-3 held opinions of the requests consistent with their evaluations of Truman's performance in office.

I enlisted consistency theory above to create a model of presidential opinion leadership that had the citizens' evaluations of Truman shaping their preferences about the president's policies. Of course, there is no intrinsic reason why consistent opinions could not arise from a reverse causal flow—that is, responses to the speech could have altered evaluations of the president. Causation is always a slippery problem in nonexperimental settings, and it is impossible with a single survey to pin down the degree to which the president was leading public opinion or simply espousing what proved to be a popular policy. One must make educated guesses about the direction of causality from more circumstantial evidence. Since few citizens could have been so prescient

TABLE 7-3 **Relationship between Approval of President Truman and Support for His Foreign Aid Requests (Percent)**

	Aid for Greece		Aid for Turkey	
	Disapprove of Truman	Approve of Truman	Disapprove of Truman	Approve of Truman
Strongly oppose	38	13	41	16
Weakly oppose	21	16	26	21
Uncertain (don't know)	9	14	9	17
Weakly favor	24	32	14	26
Strongly favor	9	25	10	20

Sources: American Institute of Public Opinion, Survey No. 393, March 26–27, 1947; Samuel Kernell, "The Truman Doctrine Speech: A Case Study of the Dynamics of Presidential Opinion Leadership," *Social Science History* 1 (fall 1976): 38.

as to have formed opinions on this issue before the speech, when even the State Department several weeks earlier had been caught unaware, one suspects that evaluations of the president's job performance probably heavily influenced opinions about his proposal.*

Although it is impossible to shed more light on the causal direction of opinion change with these data, one can tease out some of the probable dynamics of opinion change by learning more about who responded favorably to the president's appeal. Table 7-4 partitions respondents according to their 1944 presidential vote and their education. (Because the aid questions for Greece and Turkey yield highly similar relationships, I shall limit the remainder of the analysis to opinion on aid for Greece.) For only one subgroup—poorly educated Thomas E. Dewey voters—does the overall positive relationship between evaluations of Truman's job performance and support for military aid to Greece fail to turn up.

Within each educational class, the greatest support for Truman's proposal came from respondents who had both voted for Franklin Roosevelt in 1944

---

* Another causal sequence might have individuals responding favorably or unfavorably to both the source and the message at the same time. Although such an occurrence poses no real problem for making a general case for presidential opinion leadership, it does describe a different process of opinion change that makes the policy or some other aspect of the appeal (such as acting presidential), rather than prior support, the primary basis of his success. If this is what explains the association of Truman's popularity with support for his aid program, it should show up in a surge of approval in the March 26–27, 1947, survey. From late January until this survey, Truman's job performance rating rose by 11 percentage points. This was part of a trend that had begun in October, 1946 and would continue into the fall of 1947. It is impossible to know how much the Truman Doctrine speech boosted the president's standing in the polls.

TABLE 7-4 **Relationship between Approval of President Truman and Support for Aid to Greece, Controlling for Education and Presidential Vote (Percent and Number Who Favor Aid to Greece among Respondents Who Heard or Read about the President's Speech)**

Evaluation of Truman	Low education (0–8)				Moderate education (9–12)				High education (some college +)			
	Voted for Dewey		Voted for FDR		Voted for Dewey		Voted for FDR		Voted for Dewey		Voted for FDR	
	%	(N)	%	(N)	%	(N)	%	(N)	%	(N)	%	(N)
Disapprove	48.1	(27)	23.9	(46)	46.2	(80)	33.8	(74)	57.7	(71)	35.3	(51)
Approve	47.8	(69)	59.9	(187)	64.4	(146)	64.9	(259)	74.7	(150)	86.0	(150)
Difference[1]	–0.3		+36.0		+18.2		+31.1		+17.0		+50.7	

[1] Positive percentage point differences indicate the beneficial effect of approval on favoring aid to Greece.

Sources: American Institute of Public Opinion, Survey No. 393, March 26–27, 1947; Samuel Kernell, "The Truman Doctrine Speech: A Case Study of the Dynamics of Presidential Opinion Leadership," *Social Science History* 1 (fall 1976): 39.

and approved of Truman's job performance at the time of the survey. The percentage endorsing aid to Greece varied from 60 to 86 percent depending upon educational class. Highly educated respondents who were consistently Democratic in their preferences overwhelming supported Truman's emergency aid proposals. The straightforward consistency model fails, however, to explain why Roosevelt voters who disapproved of Truman's performance consistently volunteered the least support for Truman's aid program. According to the consistency rationale, this distinction should belong to disapproving Dewey voters who had both partisanship and current opinions of Truman's performance to buttress a negative opinion. Yet controlling for education, these voters are consistently more supportive of Truman's policy than are their disapproving Democratic counterparts.

In the absence of better data, one can only speculate why this is the case. It is possible that Truman's Democratic-voting detractors disproportionately belonged to a constituency for whom military aid to Greece and Turkey was objectionable. However, there are two difficulties with this argument. First, past research has identified no major segment of the Democratic constituency that was so positioned on these issues. Former Democratic vice president Henry Wallace soon became an outspoken critic of the speech, but as he would demonstrate in garnering about 3 percent of the national vote as a third-party candidate in the next presidential election, the Wallace faction was too small—especially among voters with the least education—to produce the low support from Truman's detractors shown in Table 7-4. During these years, Republicans throughout the country as well as in Congress have been generally portrayed as more disposed to isolationism. Presumably, if any constituency's prior opinions would have led them to reject Truman's appeal, it should have been Republican voters. And yet roughly half of the Dewey voters who disapproved of Truman's job performance supported him on this issue.

Another possible explanation is the relative intensity with which Dewey and Roosevelt voters may have disapproved of Truman's performance. Many Dewey voters who disapproved of Truman may simply have been responding to partisan cues, and therefore their opinions had little intellectual basis or emotional investment. This cannot be said, however, of many Roosevelt voters who found reason to disapprove of Truman's job performance despite their shared partisanship.* Consequently, disapproving Dewey voters, on the whole, may have found it less disruptive to their prior opinions to go along with President Truman's foreign policy recommendations than would those Democratic voters who had a stronger, more substantive basis for their opinion.

Such an explanation is rooted in the intensity of presidential performance evaluations rather than in the substance of the particular appeal. If cor-

---

* One can also argue that nonsupport among Democratic disapprovers reflected dissonance reduction. Because they had decided against the president earlier, opposition to President Truman's policies offered confirmation of their prior choice. See Leon Festinger, *A Theory of Cognitive Dissonance* (Stanford: Stanford University Press, 1962).

TABLE 7-5 **Educational Differences in Support for the Truman Doctrine (Percentage Points)**

1944 vote	Truman evaluation	Difference between respondents with moderate and low education[1]	Differences between respondents with high and moderate education[1]
Dewey	Disapprove	−1.9	+11.5
Dewey	Approve	+16.6	+10.3
FDR	Disapprove	+9.9	+1.5
FDR	Approve	+5.0	+21.1

[1] Based on responses in Table 7-4. Positive signs indicate that the higher educational category was more supportive of aid to Greece.

Sources: American Institute of Public Opinion, Survey No. 393, March 26–27, 1947; Samuel Kernell, "The Truman Doctrine Speech: A Case Study of the Dynamics of Presidential Opinion Leadership," *Social Science History* 1 (fall 1976): 40.

rect, it should reappear in other issues with different presidents. Until such confirmation is available, however, only two general conclusions from the relationships in Table 7-4 are possible. First, the president's opinion leadership is associated with evaluations of his performance. Second, at least in the realm of foreign policy, the president may find a receptive audience among those citizens who would normally not number among his political allies. The findings offer empirical evidence of the familiar creed "Politics stops at the water's edge."

Another politically relevant finding embedded in these relationships is the effect of education on the public's receptivity to Truman's appeal. The subgroup differences in Table 7-4 have been rearranged in Table 7-5 to show the differences in support for aid to Greece according to education among groups who are otherwise similar. For example, where in Table 7-4, 46.2 percent of moderately well-educated and disapproving Dewey voters supported Truman's policy compared with 57.7 percent of their highly educated counterparts, in Table 7-5, this difference reappears as a difference of 11.5 percentage points in support. The positive signs indicate that in seven of the eight pairings, respondents in the higher educational category were more supportive.*

---

* The reason for this support could not have been the topic of the president's appeal; otherwise, Dewey voters would show similar levels of nonsupport. Note that the exception is for a category that includes few members and is particularly susceptible to sampling error.

One might have supposed that education would have been correlated in the opposite direction, with poorly educated citizens being more susceptible to presidential appeals. Yet the finding shown here agrees with the results from other research. John E. Mueller, for example, discovered that public support for U.S. conduct of the Korean and Vietnam Wars also came more heavily from the well-educated segments of the population.[34] In a somewhat different vein, another study found that politically attentive citizens, who also tend to be better educated, are the main source of shifts in American public opinion on emergent issues.[35]

Another basis of opinion leadership suggested earlier is that the president won support for his foreign policy by scaring hell out of the country. In doing so, the argument continues, Truman nurtured an anticommunist phobia at home. Fortunately, questions in the Gallup survey of March 26–27, 1947, make it possible to test this claim.

Anticommunism as a Basis of Truman's Opinion Leadership

Revisionist historians emphasize the fear arousal aspects of Truman's rhetoric. They maintain that the president consciously used the threat of communist aggression to frighten the nation and to mobilize this fear into public support for his policy. According to Walter LaFeber, "Insofar as public opinion was concerned this tactic worked well for the Administration." Arthur Theoharis argued that it "heightened public fears" and "contributed to a parochial, self-righteous nationalism."[36] But did it really have these effects? Could it account for the widespread endorsement of aid to Greece, especially among the president's detractors? To answer these questions, one must examine the anticommunist sentiment after the speech and the relation between these opinions and support for the Truman Doctrine program.

Although the Gallup survey did not query respondents directly about their fear of an external communist threat, several questions did measure their concerns about domestic communism. One can therefore test during this early period the presumed ultimate effects proposed by the "seeds of McCarthyism" thesis. Each survey item on the issue contained a prominent civil liberties component, and most of these items gained such a strong anticommunist endorsement, they contained too little variation from which to test the effect of Truman's message on opinion.* One item that did escape overendorsement asked the respondent simply, "Do you think the Communist Party in this country should be forbidden by law?" (I shall call this the "forbid-Communist-Party" question.) Sixty percent agreed, 30 percent disagreed, and 10 percent held no opinion. Later this question would become a standard item of Gallup and the other national opinion surveys,

---

* Although it is possible that President Truman's speech increased anticommunist sentiment on domestic affairs, the skewed responses are consistent with previously recorded anticommunism and may be in large part an artifact of question wording.

but the March 26–27, 1947, survey appears to have been its first employment in a national poll.

Did the speech arouse anticommunism on the domestic front? The figures in Table 7-6 suggest not. Of all respondents, a slightly greater share of those who had heard or read about the Truman Doctrine speech did indeed register an anticommunist opinion. At the same time, more of them also gave a pro–civil liberties response. These answers indicate only that citizens who are attentive to public affairs tend also to be more opinionated on political issues of the day. The direct effect of the speech is indicated by removing the replies of respondents who failed to offer an opinion to the forbid-Communist-Party question. Table 7-6 shows that, contrary to the revisionist hypothesis, a greater percentage of those who were familiar with the speech opposed banning the Communist Party than those who were not familiar with the speech.

The reason for this result again probably has more to do with a self-selection bias in the respondents' exposure to the address than with any independent effects of the speech itself. This bias suggests the need for control variables to measure the direct effect of the speech. In an analysis of these data reported elsewhere, responses to both the forbid-Communist-Party and "heard or read about the speech" questions were associated with education and past voting participation.[37] In Table 7-7, these variables are introduced as controls, but once again the predicted relationship between exposure to Truman's address and an anticommunist opinion fails to appear. For all but one instance (those with low education who did not vote in 1944), there was either no relationship or one opposite than predicted.*

Presidents and scholars should recognize that all segments of the public are not equally attentive to presidential messages. This may at times have important implications for the president's ability to rally public support. Before casually deriving or concluding mass attitude change from a president's appeal, one first needs to identify his audience. This should provide a clue as to how generally effective his message will be. There is some evidence in Table 7-7 that the effects suggested by revisionist historians may have been produced for the least-educated and nonparticipating segment of society. Familiarity with a speech depicting an external threat may have decreased this group's support of civil liberties for communists. The president was talking disproportion-

---

* One might argue that familiarity in itself is insufficient, and more direct exposure, such as having heard the address live over radio or having read the text in the newspaper, would have differentiated the public opinion on the civil liberties question in the predicted direction. Given the present findings, this appears unlikely. The 15 percent who claimed unfamiliarity represent a rather pure category, and the 85 percent who said they had heard or read about the speech include respondents who were directly exposed to the stimuli. Therefore, if there is an underlying relationship in the predicted direction, it may be weaker with the cruder operational measures, but there still should be some relationship. Yet there is none. Only if respondents in the middle range of familiarity are assumed to have responded in the opposite direction—which seems implausible—could this argument be maintained in the face of the slight inverse relationship for most of the subsamples.

TABLE 7-6 **Relationship between Familiarity with Truman Doctrine Speech and Response to Forbid-Communist-Party Question (Percent and Number of Respondents)**

Heard about Truman's Speech?	Forbid Communist Party?			
	Don't know	No	Yes	(*N*)
All responses				
No	24.8	18.3	56.8	(387)
Yes	8.3	31.4	60.4	(2,205)
Difference	−16.5	+13.1	+3.6	
Opinionated responses only				
No		24.4	75.6	(291)
Yes		34.2	65.8	(2,023)
Difference		+9.8	−9.8	

Sources: American Institute of Public Opinion, Survey No. 393, March 26–27, 1947; Samuel Kernell, "The Truman Doctrine Speech: A Case Study of the Dynamics of Presidential Opinion Leadership," *Social Science History* 1 (fall 1976): 35.

ately to other segments of the population, however, who were better equipped to differentiate their environment and therefore less likely to generalize in this fashion. Moreover, for highly educated and participating respondents, virtually all of whom said they were familiar with the president's address, to assume an antilibertarian stance would have probably required a significantly greater attitude change. Ample evidence has accumulated from past research to show that support for civil liberties in America is greatest among those citizens who, as found in these tables, were the most likely to have heard the speech and who offered the strongest endorsement of President Truman's proposal.[38]

There is some evidence and much argument that the public became less supportive of civil liberties from the late 1940s through the mid-1950s.[39] Although with these limited data one cannot wholly dismiss charges of Truman's culpability, one can conclude that his most forceful public expression of an anti-Soviet theme had little apparent effect on anticommunist sentiment in the country. To the extent that critics have employed this speech to indict Truman for the McCarthy era, the evidence presented here weakens the charge.

A second prediction of the revisionist model is that Truman traded upon anticommunism in mobilizing support for his foreign aid package. Although the Truman Doctrine speech does not appear to have stirred up greater anti-

TABLE 7-7 **Relationship between Familiarity with Truman Doctrine Speech and Anticommunist Opinion, Controlling for Education and Participation (Percent Who Favor Forbidding Communist Party)**

Familiarity with speech	Low education (0–8)				Moderate education (9–12)				High education (some college +)			
	Did not vote in 1944		Voted in 1944		Did not vote in 1944		Voted in 1944		Did not vote in 1944		Voted in 1944	
	%	(N)	%	(N)	%	(N)	%	(N)	%	(N)	%	(N)
No	80.0	(60)	76.6	(94)	69.4	(36)	78.0	(82)	—[1]		53.8	(13)
Yes	85.0	(113)	76.5	(433)	68.5	(178)	69.8	(738)	41.5	(53)	48.2	(508)
Difference[2]	+5.0		−0.1		−0.9		−7.8		—[1]		−5.6	

[1] Insufficient *N* for percentaging.

[2] Positive percentage point difference indicates that effects of hearing about speech are in the predicted direction.

Sources: American Institute of Public Opinion, Survey No. 393, March 26–27, 1947; Samuel Kernell, "The Truman Doctrine Speech: A Case Study of the Dynamics of Presidential Opinion Leadership," *Social Science History* 1 (fall 1976): 32.

Note: Percentaging based only on responses holding an opinion.

TABLE 7-8 **Relationship between Response to Forbid-Communist-Party Question and Support for Aid to Greece and Turkey (Percent and Number of Respondents)**

	Forbid Communist Party?		
Truman's foreign aid requests	No	Yes	Difference[1]
For Greece			
For	55.6	57.6	+2.0
Against	44.4	42.4	
(*N*)	(753)	(1,280)	
For Turkey			
For	44.5	48.1	+3.6
Against	55.5	51.9	
(*N*)	(730)	(1,249)	

[1] Neither percentage point difference is statistically significant. Positive differences are in the predicted direction.

Sources: American Institute of Public Opinion, Survey No. 393, March 26–27, 1947; Samuel Kernell, "The Truman Doctrine Speech: A Case Study of the Dynamics of Presidential Opinion Leadership," *Social Science History* 1 (fall 1976): 35.

communist sentiment, it remains possible that such opinions could, nonetheless, have served as a useful resource. If Truman's support were found to have rested in large part on anticommunist sentiment, this finding would offer at least a partial confirmation of the revisionist's depiction of events. In Table 7-8 support for aid to Greece and Turkey turns out to be weakly associated with anticommunist opinion and quite possibly the result of measurement error.

This absence of a stronger relationship between these variables may strike some readers as surprising, but it corresponds well with the results of Mueller's analysis of public support for the Korean War. Examining responses to a Gallup survey of October 1950, he also found that opinions on the same forbid-Communist-Party question were unrelated to support for the Korean War.[40] Although some attitude research during the mid-1950s found an empirical association in the public's perception of internal and external communist threats on diffuse, generalized variables, the evidence reported here should caution one against imposing a simple opinion structure on the mass public.[41]

Anticommunist sentiment at home did not necessarily strengthen the president's hand in fighting communism abroad.

CONCLUSION

The Truman Doctrine speech is an exceptional historic event, yet its success was founded on well-understood principles of opinion leadership. It is historically exceptional because it has come to be widely viewed as ushering in the cold war. It is exceptional also because contemporaries—at least those in Washington—sensed its profound significance. Finally, it is exceptional as a test case for studying opinion leadership because President Truman was so intent on reconstructing the nation's worldview.

The Truman Doctrine speech has been found here to be typical, however, in the way it influenced public opinion. Although the overall extent of exposure to his declaration was indeed high, the president's message did not equally penetrate all segments of the citizenry. Better-educated citizens were on average both more familiar with the speech and, within partisan groups, more receptive to its content. And despite the highly charged rhetoric, President Truman's influence on public opinion remained specific to the issue.

Large numbers of citizens rallied behind the president's legislative proposals, but there is little evidence that the speech triggered a massive, domestic anticommunist phobia or exploited anticommunism already prevalent in the country at the time. Instead, opinion formation seems to have followed a normal pattern characterized by consistency in evaluations of source and message. The appeal of Truman's programs varied with respondents according to their evaluations of Truman as president. Also, approval of aid to Greece and Turkey came disproportionately from among the well-educated segments of the public, which perhaps helps to explain why anticommunism failed to materialize as an important factor.

The effects of President Truman's speech on public opinion are, therefore, consonant with the conventional wisdom of politicians rather than with history. Although the information on which these conclusions are based is, as noted, less than ideal, it is probably the best that will ever be available. Taken together, the findings portray a consistent and reasonable image of opinion leadership. Dramatic events may be able to generate a national phobia, but presidential rhetoric cannot. Instead, President Truman's capacity to lead the nation into a new, foreboding era of foreign affairs reflected in large part the citizenry's trust of him as its leader. How presidents go about maintaining this trust—their popular support—so that their public appeals will be received favorably is the subject of chapter 8.

NOTES

1. This account of President Bush's response to the 9/11 terrorist attacks is drawn from Dan Balz and Bob Woodward, "America's Chaotic Road to War," *Washington Post*, January 27,

2002, A1; David E. Sanger and Don Van Natta Jr., "In Four Days, a National Crisis Changes Bush's Presidency," *New York Times,* September 16, 2001; and "Bush Looks to Rally Politicians and Allies and a Shaken Public," *Wall Street Journal,* September 13, 2001.

2. Robert A. Dahl, *Congress and Foreign Policy* (New York: Norton), 1950.

3. S. L. Parker, "Toward Understanding of 'Rally' Effects: Public Opinion in the Persian Gulf War," *Public Opinion Quarterly* 59 (1995): 526–546.

4. Matthew A. Baum, "The Constituent Foundations of the Rally-Round-the-Flag Phenomenon," *International Studies Quarterly* 46 (June 2002): 263–298.

5. Doyle McManus, "Bush Prevailing in Battle with Israeli Lobby," *Los Angeles Times,* September 30, 1991, A16.

6. Jackson Diehl, "Israeli Minister Bars Concessions," *Washington Post,* September 20, 1991, A24; and Clyde Haberman, "Shamir Unmoved by Bush's Threat," *New York Times,* September 14, 1991.

7. Christopher Madison, "A Not-So-Sure Thing," *National Journal,* September 14, 1991, 2200.

8. Thomas L. Friedman, "U.S. Links Loan Guarantees to Freeze on Settlements as Baker's Israel Trip Fails," *New York Times,* September 18, 1991, 1.

9. John E. Yang, "Bush Tries to Ease Loan Crisis," *Washington Post,* September 20, 1991, A24.

10. Ibid., and McManus, "Bush Prevailing in Battle," A16.

11. Douglas Rivers and Nancy L. Rose, 1985. "Passing the President's Program: Public Opinion and Presidential Influence in Congress," *American Journal of Political Science* 29 (1985): 183–196.

12. Carey Rosen, "A Test of Presidential Leadership of Public Opinion: The Split Ballot Technique," *Polity* 6 (winter 1973): 282–290. For a survey of this literature, see George C. Edwards III, *The Public Presidency* (New York: St. Martin's Press, 1983), 39–46. One experimental study in which the president's job performance is included in the analysis is Lee Sigelman and Carol K. Sigelman, "Presidential Leadership of Public Opinion: From 'Opinion Leader' to 'Kiss of Death'?" *Experimental Study of Politics* 7 (1981): 1022.

13. For analysis of the relation between performance evaluations and support for President Reagan's second round of budget cuts, see Samuel Kernell, "The Presidency and the People: The Modern Paradox," in *The Presidency and the Political System,* ed. Michael Nelson (Washington, D.C.: CQ Press, 1984), 250–253. See also Lee Sigelman, "The Commander in Chief and the Public: Mass Response to Johnson's March 31, 1968 Bombing Halt Speech," *Journal of Political and Military Sociology* 8 (spring 1980): 1–14.

14. Examples of this research are Eugene J. Rossi, "Mass and Attentive Opinions on Nuclear Weapons Tests and Fallout, 1954–1963," *Public Opinion Quarterly* 29 (summer 1965): 280–297; and John E. Mueller, *War, Presidents and Public Opinion* (New York: John Wiley and Sons, 1973). The most systematic and comprehensive study of this type to date is Benjamin I. Page and Robert Y. Shapiro, "Presidents as Opinion Leaders: Some New Evidence," *Policy Studies Journal* 12 (June 1984): 647–662.

15. An early exploration of the source-message relation in social psychology is C. I. Hovland and W. Weiss, "The Influence of Source Credibility on Communication Effectiveness," *Public Opinion Quarterly* 15 (1951): 635–650. An outstanding collection of conceptual and research articles on consistency theory is available in Robert P. Abelson et al., *Theories of Cognitive Consistency: A Sourcebook* (Chicago: Rand McNally, 1968).

16. In a survey of the literature Donald R. Kinder and Susan T. Fiske conclude that for public opinion about the president, "Consistency appears to be a rather unimportant determinant of information-seeking." See "Presidents in the Public Mind," in *Handbook of Political Psychology,* vol. 2, ed. M. G. Hermann (San Francisco: Jossey-Bass, 1973).

17. Nelson W. Polsby, "Interest Groups and the Presidency: Trends in Political Intermediation in America," in *American Politics and Public Policy*, eds. Walter Dean Burnham and Martha Wagner Weinberg (Cambridge: MIT Press, 1978), 51.

18. In an earlier study on diffuse support for the presidency, my colleagues and I found strong endorsement for the president as the nation's leader. See Samuel Kernell, Peter W. Sperlich, and Aaron Wildavsky, "Public Support for Presidents," in *Perspectives on the Presidency*, ed. Aaron Wildavsky (Boston: Little, Brown, 1975), 148–183. See also Fred I. Greenstein, "Popular Images of the President," *American Journal of Psychiatry* 122 (November 1965): 523–529; Roberta S. Sigel, "Image of the American Presidency: Part II of an Exploration into Popular Views of Presidential Power," *Midwest Journal of Political Science* 10 (February 1966): 123–137. For a more recent and richly analytic statement, see Kinder and Fiske, "Presidents in the Public Mind."

19. Opinion leadership in foreign policy has long been acknowledged. For examples, see Aaron Wildavsky, "The Two Presidencies," in *The Presidency*, ed. Aaron Wildavsky (Boston: Little, Brown, 1969), 230–243; and Elmer E. Cornwell Jr., *Presidential Leadership of Public Opinion* (Bloomington: Indiana University Press, 1965).

20. Joseph Jones, *The Fifteen Weeks* (New York: Vintage, 1955; reprint, Corte Madera, Calif.: Harbinger, 1964), vii. Much of the subsequent account of political conditions in Washington at the time of the Truman Doctrine speech will be drawn from Jones.

21. *Public Papers of the Presidents of the United States, Harry S Truman, 1947* (Washington, D.C.: Government Printing Office, 1963), 176.

22. Jones, *The Fifteen Weeks*, 178.

23. Charles Bohlen, *The Transformation of American Foreign Policy* (New York: Norton, 1969), 86–87.

25. Richard M. Freeland, *The Truman Doctrine and the Origins of McCarthyism* (New York: Knopf, 1972), 100–101.

25. George F. Kennan, *Memoirs: 1925–1950* (Boston: Little, Brown, 1967), 319–322.

26. Dean Acheson, *Present at the Creation* (New York: Norton, 1969), 292–294.

27. Cited in David S. McLellan and John W. Reuss, "Foreign and Military Policies," in *The Truman Period as a Research Field*, ed. Richard S. Kirkendall (Columbia: University of Missouri Press, 1967), 55–57; and in Freeland, *The Truman Doctrine*, 89.

28. *Memoirs by Harry S Truman: Years of Trial and Hope*, vol. 2 (Garden City, N.Y.: Doubleday, 1956), 105–109.

29. Freeland, *The Truman Doctrine*, 114–118.

30. Bohlen, *Transformation of American Foreign Policy*, 87. This comment has received widespread circulation in revisionist accounts; see Joyce Kolko and Gabriel Kolko, *The Limits of Power* (New York: Harper and Row, 1972), 342; and Herbert Feis, *From Trust to Terror* (New York: Norton, 1970), 193.

31. Richard E. Neustadt, *Presidential Power* (New York: John Wiley and Sons, 1980), 39.

32. Arthur G. Theoharis devotes five pages in his *Seeds of Repression* (Chicago: Quadrangle Books, 1971) to description of and excerpts from the speech. He concludes that the "over-simplified moralism of this [the speech's] rhetoric was to effectively reduce the administration's own political maneuverability" (56). See pages 47–49 and 51–53 for discussion of the speech. See also Theoharis's "The Rhetoric of Politics: Foreign Policy, Internal Security, and Domestic Politics in the Truman Era, 1945–1950," in *Politics and Policies of the Truman Administration*, ed. Barton Bernstein (Chicago: Quadrangle Books, 1970), 196–241. Walter LaFeber is more explicit in concluding the speech's effect on public opinion in *America, Russia, and the Cold War, 1945–1971*, 2nd ed. (New York: John Wiley and Sons, 1972), 43–48.

Kolko and Kolko give exhaustive attention to the speech's construction in *The Limits of Power*, 338–346. They suggest that the speech "manipulated" public opinion and "did not so much mirror the global facts as tend to transform and create them." Feis devotes two chapters (25 and 26) in *From Trust to Terror* to the Truman Doctrine speech and obliquely refers to its effect on public opinion in the following way: "Most Americans found temporary relief for their own exasperation and fears in Truman's blunt challenge to Communism and its agents in many lands" (198).

33. LaFeber, *America, Russia,* 45; and Theoharis, "The Rhetoric of Politics," 206.

34. John E. Mueller, *War, Presidents and Public Opinion* (New York: John Wiley and Sons, 1983), 122–136.

35. Johannes Pederson, "Sources of Change in Public Opinion: A Probability Model with Application to Repeated Cross-sectional Surveys" (Paper delivered at the Annual Meeting of the American Political Science Association, Washington, D.C., September 5–9, 1972), 17–21.

36. LaFeber, *America, Russia,* 45; and Theoharis, "The Rhetoric of Politics," 206.

37. See Samuel Kernell, "The Truman Doctrine Speech: A Case Study of the Dynamics of Presidential Opinion Leadership," *Social Science History* 1 (fall 1976): 20–45.

38. Samuel Stouffer, *Communism, Conformity, and Civil Liberties: A Cross Section of the Nation Speaks Its Mind* (Gloucester, Mass.: P. Smith, 1955).

39. Herbert H. Hyman, "England and America: Climates of Tolerance and Intolerance," in *The Radical Right,* ed. Daniel Bell (Garden City, N.Y.: Doubleday, 1963), 268–306.

40. Mueller, *War, Presidents,* 161–163.

41. Daniel J. Levinson, "Authoritarian Personality and Foreign Policy," *Journal of Conflict Resolution* 1 (March 1957): 37–47. The scale is described and evaluated in *Measures of Political Attitudes,* eds. John P. Robinson, Jerrold G. Rusk, and Kendra B. Head (Ann Arbor: Michigan Survey Research for Social Research, 1968), 306–308.

chapter 8

Present and Future Prospects for Going Public

Throughout this discussion I have argued that presidents' reliance on going public reflects not only the opportunities presented by advances in communication technology but also the requirements of an ever-changing Washington community. During the 1970s and 1980s, times when presidents had easy access to a national audience, members of Congress increasingly found their success in retaining office depended less on the collective products of their institutions and political parties and more on personal strategies of constituency service and massive campaign spending.[1] For these new-styled, self-reliant representatives, local constituency opinion counted for more and the preferences of party caucuses and leaders for less in deciding their votes and legislative activity. To the extent presidents were able to mobilize grass-roots opinion, they gained influence over these politicians. Recently, both of these complementary trends in the president's ability to go public and legislators' independence have abated somewhat. Since the 1990s members of Congress have become more stridently partisan and the political parties more polarized in their issue positions. With more intense party competition in Congress, members have surrendered to party leaders some of their independence to advance their party's success. At the same time, presidents have found they are losing their monopolistic access to the public. On the one hand, their television audiences have shrunk, as viewers enjoy a plethora of viewing choices via modern cable and satellite services. On the other hand, they face stiffer competition for the audience in the form of issue advertising from those who oppose their policies. Given these adverse trends, we close our discussion by asking, might strategic presidents increasingly come to decide that the rewards of going public no longer justify their costs and risks?

RESURGENT POLITICAL PARTIES

Even in its golden age, when presidents routinely commandeered national, prime-time television, going public was still a costly and risky exercise. After all, not only did the president have to mobilize public opinion, but the public in turn had to influence their representatives. As highly partisan legislators defer to their party's course of action, they become less susceptible to any political breezes the president can stir up in their constituencies. Certainly, recent congressional majorities (especially in the Republican House of Representatives) have strengthened the hand of their leaders to enforce the party caucus's decisions among members and to negotiate policy with Senate leaders and the president.

Yet the trends in chapter 5 show that the first two presidents to deal with these Congresses, Clinton and Bush, did not flinch from going public repeatedly. Perhaps they found ways to adapt and refine public strategies to better fit the resurgent partisanship in Washington. One such way, as noted in chapter 2, finds modern presidents becoming "fund-raisers in chief" for their political party. As the next election cycle begins, they extensively travel around the country to replenish their party's and their candidates' coffers. In addition to serving the party's collective interest in winning seats in Congress and the state houses, these public activities give presidents the opportunity to reward their supporters and curry favor for future initiatives.[2] Moreover, party leaders in Congress do not hesitate to insist that the president make the case for controversial policies allowing individual members of Congress to keep their heads down as their opponents attack the proposal. The familiar forms of public strategies, such as a national television address—once regarded as an application of force—have come to represent a complementary division of labor between presidents and their fellow party members in Congress.

Before concluding that going public has, indeed, become domesticated in the service of party interest, we should consider Barbara Sinclair's persuasive argument that the growing ideological gulf between congressional Democrats and Republicans makes going public even more imperative. With the median positions of these partisans far apart from each other, few legislators occupy the middle ground with whom a president might negotiate a compromise policy. Even Ronald Reagan did not find so stark a setting for bargaining; he succeeded in entreating southern "boll weevil" Democrats to bolt their party and join Republicans in a massive tax cut. Perhaps presidents will continue to go public not because the setting is especially promising, but rather because the chief alternative, compromise, has become far less so.[3]

So far, we have limited our consideration to how current relations in Washington have altered presidents' incentives to go public and the form these public strategies may take. An even thornier question for discerning the prospects for going public asks whether presidents still communicate effectively with the American public.

DECLINING EFFECTIVENESS OF NATIONAL ADDRESSES

Throughout this inquiry I have presented going public as a strategic adaptation to the communications age. The profusion of technology has continued to open new avenues for presidents and other politicians to communicate to the public. For citizens, these technologies afford them numerous and diverse options to monitor politics in Washington. Citizens enjoy so many viewing options (including the Internet), presidents may have a hard time gaining their attention.

The emergence of television as a ubiquitous household appliance in the early 1960s provided presidents with a captive audience, but only for as long as America's households were tethered to broadcast antennas. Over the next several decades, as subscriptions to cable (and satellite) services became steadily more popular (see Figure 5-5, page 132), presidents' audiences shrank commensurately. By 2006, with 88 percent of homes' televisions connected to the cable network, George W. Bush's State of the Union address garnered an anemic quarter of households with televisions, about half the audience share that routinely watched these annual speeches in the 1960s and 1970s.

As presidents lose their audience, will they invariably lose their influence on public opinion? Recent research suggests that presidents' main influence over public opinion lies in increasing the salience of problems and issues rather than in changing policy preferences. Success in arousing the public's concern forces an otherwise indifferent Congress to place the issue on its agenda.[4] One recent study, however, raises serious doubts about presidents' continuing capacity to focus public attention on issues through major, prime-time addresses. Performing a content analysis of annual State of the Union addresses to identify the president's policy emphasis, Garry Young and William B. Perkins also examined public opinion data to determine whether the public adopted the president's policy concern. Specifically, they compared the president's themes with respondents' answers to the commonly asked question on "the most important question facing the nation today." * Their results, summarized in Figure 8-1, suggest that presidents' influence on the public's attention to foreign policy issues has sharply diminished with the growth of cable subscriptions and plummeting audience ratings for presidential addresses. In the earlier period the salience of foreign affairs closely tracked the presidents' references. As the number of households plugging into cable systems grew, and increasing numbers switched channels at the first sighting of a presidential address (see chapter 5), presidents had a harder time getting their message out.[†] To see how they sought to compensate for this audience loss, we turn to the public strategies of the first two presidents under this new regime.

---

* All of the addresses in their study were televised by the major networks during prime time.

† When Young and Perkins performed this analysis on presidential statements about the economy and civil rights, the results were mixed. A modest relationship on civil rights disappeared (actually, became negative but statistically insignificant) during the more recent era. They report no difference and little overall presidential influence in public mentions of the relative importance of the economy as a problem. This is not surprising, since respondents have ample information from experience and other sources on the state of the economy.

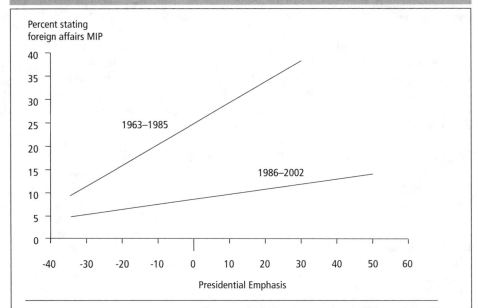

FIGURE 8-1 **Impact of Presidential Emphasis in State of the Union Messages on Public Opinion about Foreign Policy as the "Most Popular Problem"**

Source: Garry Young and William B. Perkins, "Presidential Rhetoric, the Public Agenda, and the End of Presidential Television's 'Golden Age,'" *Journal of Politics* 67 (November 2005): 1190–1205.

TWO HEROIC FAILURES

If presidents' public appeals are increasingly falling on deaf ears, someone forgot to inform Bill Clinton and George W. Bush. During their first terms, both presidents more or less continuously cultivated public support for their legislative initiatives. Each president began his term with his election team intact and poised to return to campaign mode. And their early exercises in going public earned notable legislative successes for both. Only after an intensive public relations campaign combining extensive travel and speeches with heavy commercial advertising did President Clinton win narrow passage of the NAFTA trade agreement.* President Bush waged a series of successful public cam-

---

* This treaty's provisions included government funding commitment, which required companion appropriations legislation. The narrow and decisive victory occurred not in Senate ratification but in passage of the funding legislation in the House of Representatives.

paigns to pass a major tax cut in 2001, his No Child Left Behind initiative the next year, and a second round of tax cuts in 2003.*

After these initial legislative successes, both presidents tackled what are arguably the two most serious domestic policy challenges facing the nation: Clinton proposed extension of health care to everyone through a comprehensive system of federal and private insurance, and Bush offered a fundamental Social Security reform plan that promised to fund expected future shortfalls and privatize a significant share of contributions. Both presidents waged massive, multipronged public relations campaigns on behalf of these reforms, yet neither succeeded in winning adequate public support to push the legislation past committee deliberations. In the end, both bills died quietly without committee or floor votes in either chamber.

These cases can be read as reminders of the limits of going public and perhaps, some would argue, the exercise's especially weakened state in a community of polarized politics and fragmented communications.[5] Alternatively, they can be read as reflecting the confidence with which modern presidents enlist going public to advance solutions to difficult and perhaps otherwise intractable national problems. These cases also warrant careful examination for another reason: these two presidents—one Democrat, the other Republican, poles apart ideologically—engaged in very similar campaigns. That both enlisted the same basic strategy to promote their legislative initiatives allows us to more confidently inspect them as indicating the altered circumstances that inform current techniques of going public.

Clinton's Health Care Reform

After months of behind-closed-doors deliberations by a task force of policy specialists headed by his wife, Hillary, President Clinton made good on his campaign promise by unveiling a comprehensive health care reform proposal in a September 1993 address before a joint session of Congress. The president's Health Care Security Act would have reorganized the current private and employer health care system into a comprehensive, federally managed program to ensure affordable health coverage for all citizens. Through deft timing of leaks and careful advance work with the news media, over a third of American households with televisions (an estimated forty-eight million adult viewers)

---

* Although the president's education reform was modified in various ways by the Democratically controlled Senate, the bill the president gleefully signed into law preserved all key elements of his proposal except for funding for vouchers to private schools. Similarly, the 2003 tax cut fell far short of what the president requested, but against a rising budget deficit and, apparently, an initial absence of congressional interest, the administrations' partial success was impressive. These and other instances of the Bush administration's pre- and post-9/11 efforts at going public are examined fully in George C. Edwards III, *Campaigning by Governing* (New York, Pearson Longman: 2006), 1–90. On public efforts to promote the 2003 tax cut, see Edwin Chen and Janet Hook, " 'Soggy' Economy Needs a Shot of Tax Relief, Bush Says: He's targeting home states of Democrats sympathetic to his push for $550 billion in cuts," *Los Angeles Times*, May 13, 2005.

tuned in to learn more about the president's much-rumored health plan. Afterwards, the immediate reactions of commentators and politicians attending the joint session were highly favorable. The next day's newspaper coverage generally judged the speech to be a hit. The president followed up the next evening with a nationally televised town meeting, an event designed to tell the stories behind the statistics. The early public response to the first week's campaign was enthusiastic; a late September Gallup Poll found 59 percent of the public endorsing the president's plan.*

When public opinion moves, elective officeholders are never far behind. Democratic representatives in Congress were ecstatic; for many a national health care program represented the last, unfulfilled promise of the New Deal. Although most Republican politicians became uncharacteristically taciturn, a few conceded on camera that the nation's health care system faced a crisis and urgently required congressional attention. Republican senator Bob Dole of Kansas, Clinton's opponent for the presidency two years later, lumbered aboard the health care reform bandwagon by promising to fashion a more feasible alternative to the president's legislation.

During the next month, as Clinton sought to keep up the momentum with extensive travel and sixteen minor addresses promoting his reform, newspapers and network news programs gave his policy prominent play. Instead of dissecting the particulars of this complex proposal, television news filled the airwaves with heart-wrenching stories of families left in distress medically and financially by current health care policy.

Yet even while the administration was still executing its early game plan, problems arose that deflected public attention from the president's agenda. The Justice Department subpoenaed documents from the Clintons concerning their investments in the bankrupt Whitewater Development Corporation nearly a decade earlier.† By February stories about the scandal were outnumbering health care reform by a margin of four to one.

A second development was the quick and effective response by the health care industry. Alarmed that a much larger federal role would inflict huge costs

---

* The Gallup question read: "From everything you have heard or read about the plan so far, do you favor or oppose President (Bill) Clinton's health care plan to reform health care?" For the polling, media, and presidential activities reported for this case study, I have relied heavily on the thorough analysis of Matthew Corrigan reported in two sources: "The Transformation of Going Public: President Clinton, the First Lady and Health Care Reform," *Political Communication* 17 (2000): 149–168; and "The Disconnect Between 'Going Public' and the Rational Public in Presidential Policymaking," *White House Studies* 1 (winter 2001): 3–19.

† The Whitewater scandal was the first of a series that nearly led to President Clinton's removal from office. It concerned a failed real estate development plan in Arkansas that was financed by Madison Guaranty Savings and Loan Association shortly before it went bankrupt. Insured deposits were covered by the federal government at an expense of nearly $800 million. Special Prosecutor Kenneth Starr began with this scandal but soon was taking up all charges leveled at the president. Eventually, an outside investigator and a special prosecutor issued reports more or less exonerating the Clintons.

and uncertain compensation for their businesses, pharmaceutical companies, private HMOs, hospital associations, and the American Medical Association formed an alliance to oppose the president's campaign. The most effective feature of its campaign was the production of the famous Harry and Louise television commercials. This series of ads ran mainly in Washington, New York, and selected media markets, but it attracted a far larger audience in national news coverage after the Clintons attacked them in speeches. Presenting a thoughtful suburban couple struggling at their kitchen table to figure out the implications of the president's plan for them personally, the ads proved to be enormously effective in shifting the relevant opinions from health care as a national problem to health care as a personal benefit endangered by the president's proposal. Americans grew worried that the new federal program would undermine their current coverage while creating a nightmare of paperwork.

The key insight that guided the public strategies of reform's opponents was that most Americans were personally satisfied with their medical benefits. While 86 percent of national survey respondents thought most Americans were unhappy with their health care, 78 percent stated that they personally were content, and about half expressed satisfaction with the costs. As long as the issue concerned benefits for others—say, those less fortunate—respondents endorsed the Clinton plan, but once they came to view it as costly and risky for their own health care, they turned against it.[6]

The administration responded with ads of its own—financed by the Democratic National Committee—reminding viewers of the national crisis. And in January the president emphasized the urgency of reform in his State of the Union address. Shortly thereafter Gallup reported public support had strengthened significantly to 57 percent favoring his proposal. Attempting to resuscitate his legislation stalled in Congress, President Clinton launched a second public campaign with extensive travel. Despite delivering fifty minor addresses on this issue from February through July, public interest sagged under the weight of opposition campaigning and the continuing, multipronged investigation of wrongdoing in the White House. By March public support for health care reform had dropped to 44 percent and would not recover over the next months despite the president's vigorous efforts. The public had decided that Clinton's health care reform would mostly benefit poor people while dragging their coverage, with which most Americans were well satisfied, into a morass of federal regulations. As the public turned sour, members of Congress, including the plan's former Democratic boosters, lost interest as well.

Bush's Social Security Reform

The general contours of Bush's Social Security reform campaign follow a script remarkably similar to Clinton's more than a decade earlier. The result was the same as well. In that one represented the effort of a liberal Democrat and the other a conservative Republican perhaps the fate of the plan and outcome reflects a certain logic. President Bush, like Clinton, launched his policy initiative with a national television address, in Bush's case at his first State of the Union address following his reelection. Both presidents used a joint session of Congress as a dramatic backdrop. And Bush immediately began a tour of those states that had voted for him in the presidential election but had a Democratic senator who might be persuaded to the president's position by a show of constituent enthusiasm. The speech also set the president's reelection apparatus in motion headed by advisor Karl Rove and reaching down to hundreds of thousands of neighborhood activists. Republican members of the House and Senate were briefed and given a hefty playbook that coached them in drumming up grassroots support for the president's program. Yet Social Security did not develop its reputation as the "third rail" of American politics without reason; any politician touching this popular issue, like touching the high-voltage rail from which subways draw their power, would suffer an instant, career-threatening shock. The quiet, uneventful suffocation of Bush's reform plan at the hands of Republican congressional committees later that summer confirmed the danger awaiting future presidents who set their sights on the nation's gradually bankrupting retirement system.

As Clinton had confidently launched his health care program, President Bush and his advisors enthusiastically took up reforming Social Security. Perhaps they were overconfident from the president's recent reelection victory. And, in fairness, a cursory reading of public opinion polls during this period appeared to show a public ready to support such reform. In anticipation of the president's initiative to be unveiled the next month in the president's State of the Union address, survey research firms began closely monitoring public attitudes about Social Security and alternative reforms. They found a consensus opinion that the Social Security system was in crisis. When Gallup asked respondents whether it needed fixing, only 9 percent said "no changes needed," with another 3 percent "unsure"; 49 percent assigned the issue urgency, agreeing the problem needed to be addressed in the next "year or two," and the rest said "within the next ten years." * Moreover, the public appeared poised to endorse the president's plan. Six weeks before the speech most respondents (53 percent) said they would support "a plan in which people who chose to could invest some of their Social Security contributions in the stock market." [7] To the extent that the battle over Social Security reform would be waged in public opinion, the president appeared well positioned for an early success. Nothing in the early responses to his State of the Union address or its initial reception by news analysts and politicians indicated that the proposal was already in trouble. In retrospect, we can see, however, that its State of the Union unveiling turned out to be the high point of the campaign.

---

* The question asked by Gallup in a national survey on January 7–9, 2005, read, "Do you think the federal government should make major changes in the Social Security system to ensure its long-term future in the next year or two, within the next 10 years, or do you think major changes are not needed within the next 10 years?"

After the speech President Bush traveled to a half-dozen states where he had beaten John Kerry in the election and that, not coincidentally, were served by a Democratic senator who might be susceptible to voters' demands for the president's plan. Almost immediately, Democrats, the labor movement, and AARP began a devil-in-the-details campaign questioning whether the proposal would reduce benefits and close the fund's impending deficit. As was the case with the medical industry's opposition to the Clinton health care reform plan, once the details started coming out, the public began weighing the personal costs and risks against the public good of having a fiscally sound national program. Survey questions that first informed respondents that the new personal accounts would reduce the guaranteed benefits found support dropping by six percentage points compared to support levels registered for the general plan. When the reduction in benefits was specifically tabbed at a third of currently guaranteed benefits—many analysts' estimate of the proposal's effects—support dropped another seventeen percentage points.[8]

Opponents also struck home by challenging the president's sudden enthusiasm for personal accounts as the way to fix Social Security. With a program so complex and critical features left ambiguous, ordinary citizens were poorly equipped to undertake policy analysis to figure out their preferences. Instead, they resorted to cognitive shortcuts. A favorite such shortcut is one's approval or disapproval of the message's source. Other things being equal, those who trusted the president were much more likely to accept his Social Security recommendations. One telltale sign was that respondents' assessments of the administration's performance in the Iraq war were closely correlated with their enthusiasm for the president's Social Security reform plan. Consequently, in challenging Bush's credibility, opponents sought to degrade his value as a referent in helping citizens form opinions on the issue. More generally, this is why the president's approval rating is such a useful measure for understanding public opinion on various policy questions that arise during the course of a president's term.

The relationships presented in Table 8-1 reveal just how important President Bush's association with the program was to respondents' evaluations. In a large national survey taken in May 2005, half the sample was randomly selected to answer the first question on a provision of the plan to keep current arrangements the same for the poorest recipients while introducing the personal accounts to middle- and upper-income beneficiaries. The other half was asked the same question, but with one critical difference: the wording was changed to attribute the plan to President Bush. In several ways this extra bit of information dramatically altered the respondents' views on the policy proposal. The most noticeable difference occurred among Democrats who flip-flopped from a majority favoring to a majority opposing the plan according to Bush's association with it. For Republicans the change was not quite so dramatic; those informed of their president's sponsorship were more favorably disposed by fifteen percentage points over their Republican peers who were not

TABLE 8-1 **Effect of Bush Association with Social Security Indexing**

	All	Republicans	Democrats	Independents
Described without Bush's Name[1]				
Favor	53%	47%	54%	55%
Oppose	36	41	37	36
Don't know	11	12	9	9
Described as Bush's Proposal[2]				
Favor	45	62	34	43
Oppose	43	27	57	47
Don't know	12	11	9	10
Change in Support				
Favor	−8	+15	−20	−12

[1] "One proposal for dealing with Social Security's financial situation is to keep the system as it is now for lower income retirees, but limit the growth of future benefits for wealthy and middle income retirees. Would you favor or oppose this proposal?"

[2] "George W. Bush has proposed dealing with Social Security's financial situation by keeping the system as it is now for lower income retirees, but limiting the growth of future benefits for wealthy and middle income retirees. Would you favor or oppose this proposal?"

Source: George C. Edwards III, *Governing by Campaigning: The Politics of the Bush Presidency* (New York: Longman, 2006), 262.

given this information. Among independents who presumably viewed the president as a more neutral referent, his association with the proposal reduced their support by twelve percentage points; at the time of the survey, a recent Gallup Poll had recorded only 38 percent of independents approving President Bush's job performance. Clearly, as the Iraq war and other issues weighed on the Bush presidency, these issues dragged down support for his Social Security initiative.

With public opinion trending down, the Bush administration in March announced a second, even stronger push for the president's Social Security Reform policy. Bush would embark on a "sixty stops in sixty days" marathon to sell his program to the American people. In fact, during the next two months his itinerary exceeded its target, as did those of many members of his cabinet who were assigned their own, equally ambitious, whistle-stop tours of the nation's media markets. These campaign trips attracted a lot of news attention, but little of it the kind that the president's strategists had planned. Opposition groups, led by members of the AFL-CIO, tracked the president across the country staging demonstrations. More important, it soon became apparent that attendance at Bush's "town hall" meetings had been closed to all but the president's fans, who, according to some who balked, were apparently coached with scripted questions. The clumsy staging of these encounters with "ordinary" Americans soon eclipsed Social Security as the main topic of news coverage (see box, "How Not to Orchestrate a Spontaneous Event," page 42). Network correspondents were soon ending their segments querulously asking whether the president could defend his program on its merits.

In March a full-scale air war of pro- and anti-Bush reform commercials erupted. On the president's side were business groups including major equity firms that would receive new business from the private investment accounts. The principal opponent was the thirty-five-million-member AARP, which in addition to extensive television advertising generated millions of protest phone calls to members of Congress.

Reminiscent of Clinton's effort to rejuvenate his health care reform plan with a second prime-time address several months after the campaign's initial launch, President Bush in late April scheduled another national appeal, this time in the form of a televised prime-time press conference, which he would open with a statement exhorting supporters to contact their representatives.* The event attracted next-day news coverage but failed to register so much as a blip in public opinion. By early summer the Iraq war had rendered the president less popular than at any time since his reelection. With his declining poll numbers sank the public's support for his reform package.

Despite their considerable differences in ideology and style, Presidents Clinton and Bush conducted remarkably similar campaigns to promote their ambitious policies. As their capacity to dominate the national airwaves has declined, presidents have substituted hundreds of minor appeals designed to attract local, typically less critical news coverage and to energize supporters.[9] Both presidents employed national addresses on two separate occasions: to initiate their campaigns and to reinvigorate stalled campaigns. They organized financial backing and independent advertising by private support groups, and through extensive fund-raising they filled the treasury of the national party committee to finance ads they could directly control. By sheer effort, modern presidents seek to generate the kinds of responses Ronald Reagan produced by

---

* This is the news conference where the president was squeezed by the networks resisting giving up prime time during their "May sweeps," the period when Nielsen's ratings numbers would be used to set advertising rates. (See page 137.)

simply exhorting supporters to "call, fax and mailgram" their representatives. Going public entails a lot more work than it once did.

Issue advertising emerges as a key component of both the administration's and the opposition's strategies.[10] Issue ads have been around a long time; corporate magazine and newspaper ads objecting to some pending legislation can be traced back into the 1950s.[11] Television advertising for or against issues in Congress is more recent. When opponents of Robert Bork, President Reagan's 1987 Supreme Court nominee, produced polished attack ads, as though he were some candidate for elective office, many of Bork's supporters were shocked. This Madison Avenue–style grassroots campaign's success educated the next generation of politicians and those groups that seek to influence their policies.

Until recently, when presidents enlisted public relations to boost their legislative initiatives, those opposed to their views tended to hunker down and hope that the campaign would fail or its effects would dissipate before final action needed to be taken. One misguided politician sought to beat President Reagan at his own game. He failed miserably, but his attempt instructively reminds us of the advantage presidents enjoyed until recently. In late May 1985, House Ways and Means Committee Chair Daniel Rostenkowski followed President Reagan's prime-time appeal for public support for tax reform with a national television appeal of his own. What an incongruous sight it must have been for the men and women who served with former Ways and Means chair Wilbur Mills to watch a successor telling the country that with its active support his committee would beat back the "special interests" that would be hard at work to frustrate tax reform.[12] This quintessential institutional actor closed his amazing appearance on network television by exhorting Americans to "write Rosty." *

Throughout the Clinton administration, opponents hit upon a second course of action: join the air war and try to neutralize the president's influence over public opinion. It is a tough, expensive strategy because, as we have seen, the president retains a real advantage over congressional actors. By and large, opponents must match the president's "free media" (i.e., news coverage) with "paid media" (i.e., television commercials). But when presidents take up issues for which the status quo has strong backers with deep pockets, the president's advantage in setting the public agenda can be directly challenged. President Clinton met his match in the Health Care Association; AARP was no less effective as Bush's nemesis.

Clearly, rallying public opinion remains a central ingredient in presidential leadership. Indeed, present-day members and leaders of Congress have

---

* Rostenkowski's insight was not altogether lost on the Speaker Thomas P. O'Neill, who hired a new, more publicly active press secretary. Although public relations cut against O'Neill's grain, he faced the dilemma, as observed by one congressional reporter, that "if he had not gone public, there would have been nobody at all to tell the Democratic story." Alan Ehrenhalt, "Speaker's Job Transformed under O'Neill," *Congressional Quarterly Weekly Report,* June 22, 1985, 1247.

come to expect and at times even insist that presidents publicly shoulder responsibility for difficult or unpopular policies.[13] Having the president provide political cover can entail significant costs for legislators, however. When presidents build public support for a policy or course of action, they may effectively set Congress's agenda, making it difficult for members to avoid a decision or opt for a different policy.

That both presidents failed in these efforts says less about the efficacy of public strategies than the scale of each president's aspirations. With inflationary medical care costs bankrupting the uninsured and forcing rising shares of the public to go without adequate care, and an aging population draining the Social Security fund, a consensus among the public and its representatives has long held that both systems are seriously broken and needing repair. For two decades or more, health care and Social Security have periodically flared up as serious national problems where all politicians agree that current policy is untenable but disagree on how to change it or who should take the first, politically risky move. Deciding that only with massive public demand for change would Congress act, both presidents took their case to the country. Those who opposed the reforms agreed with this assessment. Consequently, public opinion became the battlefield on which both reforms were contested and ultimately defeated.

THE POTENTIAL FOR PATHOLOGY

So long as the citizenry remains attentive to matters of peace and prosperity, so must the president. Otherwise, his popular support will suffer and with it any claim to leadership in Washington. In our separated powers system, holding the president accountable has the potential for injustice. The public will occasionally punish a hard-working president who is doing as good a job as one can reasonably expect under unfavorable circumstances, while at other times it will reward an underachiever blessed by good luck. So be it. Fairness to presidents is less important than motivating them to deal with the country's problems. The public must hold them responsible, even if at times it does so naively. To do less would encourage presidents to shirk their duties.

Consider how public opinion forced presidents to tackle the energy crisis of the 1970s. No one would deny that the production cutbacks from the emerging oil cartel, OPEC, set energy prices and inflation generally spiraling upward toward 20 percent annual increases in Americans' cost of living. Nonetheless, rather than seek refuge behind the truth that the problem was not their fault, neither President Nixon nor Carter, to their credit, hid behind excuses that they were not to blame. Instead, both actively sought a solution, even at the risk of imposing hardship on the public and facing the brunt of national frustration. The fact that energy-induced inflation ultimately took a heavy toll on the prestige of both men will undoubtedly provide future historians a basis for sympathetic revisions of their performance. But for the citizenry, such sentiments have little value.

With a class of "outsiders" who get to Washington through extensive campaigning and who base much of their leadership on public relations, it is especially important for the public to keep them pointed toward problem solving. These new-styled presidents might misinterpret weak approval ratings as a deficiency in communications, or they might come to view their standing in the polls as an end in itself. Either way, they are less than full-fledged problem solvers.

Mistaking Bad News for Bias

No matter how motivated they may be to satisfy the public, if presidents fail to appreciate the real sources of the nation's distress and their low ratings, their actions will probably miss the mark. Politicians who routinely engage in public relations to promote themselves and their policies may be especially prone to misperception. They must have abiding faith in the power of rhetoric. The way these politicians approach the electorate may well shape how they come to view it. Preceding chapters have recounted numerous instances of a modest downturn in a president's poll rating, triggering a flurry of public relations activities from the White House. Moreover, the same efficacy modern presidents assign to their own rhetoric they do not deny to others, especially members of the press. The readiness with which recent presidents have enlisted television and their attention to the nuance of public relations gives one cause to wonder whether they might fail to comprehend that the citizenry will ultimately judge them not on their rhetoric (or that of anyone else) but on their performance.

Even when they recognize that the public's disaffection reflects more than the criticism of opponents or uncharitable news coverage, they may still search for success in public relations rather than problem solving. Such myopia would be endemic—specifically, in the installation of politicians in the White House who soar or fall in Washington according to their popularity in the country. How to induce self-interested politicians to recognize the citizenry's concerns and how to structure presidents' incentives so that self-interest leads them to act in ways that promote the general welfare are related issues that have challenged political theory since the founding of the republic. They are no less relevant today as one ponders the emergence of presidents whose leadership rests heavily on the moods of the American public. Can these presidents recognize a world beyond communications and images? Will they retain the perspective that a bad press—even when it is exactly that—feeds on bad news? Do they grasp that only by solving the nation's problems will they solve their own?

The anecdotal record for recent presidents cautions against alarmism. Indeed, much of the apparatus installed in the White House for going public involves advisers who continuously monitor the public's concerns. A president's heavy investment in accurately discerning public opinion should serve as a counterweight to whatever faith he places in rhetoric. Jimmy Carter's press secretary, Jody Powell, expressed a sentiment one commonly hears from the White House: "Communications and the management of them, the impact is marginal. The substance of what you do and what happens to you over the long haul is more important, particularly on the big things like the economy." [14]

Although presidents occasionally lash out at the news media for their difficulties in the polls, there is little evidence that they have lost sight of the real sources of the public's disillusionment with them. Lyndon Johnson and Jimmy Carter suffered both in the polls and with the press; against the latter, their spokesmen sometimes railed bitterly. Yet neither man had any difficulty appreciating the effects of major issues on his popular support. Johnson observed, "I think [my grandchildren] will be proud of two things. What I did for the Negro and seeing it through in Vietnam for all of Asia. The Negro cost me 15 points in the polls and Vietnam cost me 20." [15] Carter, too, was aware of the real reason for his low standing in the polls:

> I think the Roper poll shows that I was below 60 percent, the Gallup Poll about 60 percent. Of course, I would like to have higher than either one of those, but I think that the controversial nature of some of the things that we put forward inherently causes a concern about me and reduces my standing in the polls, although I didn't want the prediction to come true. When I announced that I would put forward an energy package, I predicted my poll rating would drop 15 percent. [16]

The dependence of modern presidents on public support appears to keep them attentive to "real world" problems, even as they engage in public relations. As long as we care about an issue, so too must they.

Pandering

Another potential pathology to which those politicians who go public for a living might be especially susceptible is pandering. Might these new-styled presidents pursue policy solely to maximize their approval ratings? If so, they would be inclined to take the popular course wherever it leads policy. Some presidents strive for the public's approbation more than others. Two earlier-era examples can be found in the very different regard for public opinion held by Harry Truman and his successor, Dwight Eisenhower. Truman disdained paying attention to public opinion polls, which befit his famous motto as president, "the buck stops here." Throughout his nearly seven rocky years in office, Truman disregarded his generally dismal poll ratings and abided by the belief that by making the right policies, he would probably be rewarded by voters.*

His successor, Eisenhower, has often been depicted as a man who valued the public's approbation more than most presidents, and in the judgment of critics, to a fault. Ironically, this war-hero politician, who had never sought elective office before winning the White House, coveted the public's favor as if

---

* In his candid, highly readable memoirs Truman reminisced that his frequent and large swings in the approval ratings were "like riding a tiger."

By Bob Gorrell. © 1995 Creators Syndicate Inc.
Reprinted with special permission of Creators Syndicate Inc.

it were an end in itself. "Eisenhower's seemingly effortless facility in weaning public confidence never stopped him," observed one biographer, "from also working to find additional ways to enhance his support." [17] Eisenhower's failure to champion unpopular programs or to engage critics, his refusal "to go public as a politician, looking carefully rather than leaping," his pusillanimous defense of the State Department against Sen. Joseph McCarthy's witch hunt, and his willingness to delegate to subordinates responsibility for unhappy occurrences are all perfectly consistent with this view of a president intent on preserving his prestige as if it were an end rather than a means.[18] In this quality Truman and Eisenhower appear quite different, and for our purposes, can serve as endpoints for assessing the posture of their successors who found their leadership ever more dependent on public relations.

Early in his presidency Bill Clinton's reputation among Washingtonians suffered from accusations of pandering.* As the Republican Congress undertook welfare reform, the president initially balked, and then when this popular program appeared bound for passage, he raced to the front of the welfare reform phalanx by publicly announcing proposed legislation—and urging Congress' speedy adoption—that contained many key features of the Republican plan that he and other Democrats had previously scorned as draconian and heartless.

---

* As distinguished from charges of philandering, which came later and required even more nimble public relations, as noted in chapter 5.

Based on this and similar experiences, Republican congressional leaders ruefully came to believe that President Clinton was mostly a panderer—a politician more interested in appearances than actual leadership—and so could be manipulated to give them what they wanted and before the next election be exposed as such. They were not alone in this early impression. News pundits, both conservatives and liberals, picked up the theme: Clinton "relies too heavily on polling information"; he "follows polls slavishly"; and he "demonstrat[ed] that polling has turned leaders into followers." [19] In the 1995 appropriations battle, recounted in chapter 3, Republican leaders badly miscalculated in assuming that President Clinton could be handed minor, face-saving concessions and led to accept the Republican budget. Instead, they gave him an instant opportunity to repair his reputation in Washington and look presidential to the nation. No panderer, after all, would veto a bill that shut down the government.

Whatever their personal tolerance for public criticism, we may expect all presidents to attend to their poll ratings more vigilantly as reelection nears. At what date on the electoral calendar presidents become transfixed on husbanding and rekindling public support depends upon how popular they are entering the election cycle. With party nomination decided by caucuses and primaries, and unpopular incumbents no longer guaranteed renomination, incumbents must start paying attention to the ramifications of their decisions with public opinion much sooner now than did their predecessors.

In the spring of 1983, with President Reagan the least popular of any president by the end of his first two years, many Republican senators who had been his cheerleaders just a year earlier began carping that the president was shying away from tough budget cuts in deference to an election nearly two years away. By summer, White House aides confirmed the president's election concerns while announcing an extensive itinerary of political travel that would include a visit to China. Reflecting his unprecedented weak popularity at midterm, President Reagan's fence-mending activities appropriately began earlier than most. Spring of the election year is the season one hears politicians voicing unfamiliar concerns, in some instances the same ones to which they had turned a deaf ear only a few months earlier. [20]

In considering how much popularity is enough, Eisenhower's political adviser Bryce Harlow appeared conservative when he confided, "The trick is to get the president into the fourth year with an approval rating still over 50 percent." [21] In fact, his estimate accords well with the track record of the nine incumbents who have sought reelection since 1948. In Figure 8-2 each president's share of the vote is plotted against his job performance rating for the preceding June. The regression line crosses 50 percent of the vote within a hair of Harlow's 50 percent approving. [22] During the postwar era, no president lost who entered a reelection campaign with half or more of the public behind him. And only one president who failed to reach the golden mean won the election. That was George W. Bush, whose approval rating stood at 48 percent in June before the 2004 election.

FIGURE 8-2 **Relationship between Vote Share and Popularity of Incumbent Presidents Seeking Reelection, 1948–2004 (Percent)**

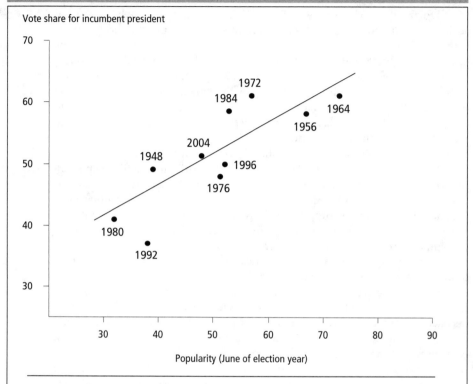

Source: Data taken from the American Presidency Project, www.presidency.ucsb.edu.

Note: The estimated equation represented in the regression line is Vote = 27.2 + .48 x Popularity. This single variable explains 70 percent of the variance in the vote share of the incumbent president.

With each approval point in the ratings accounting for about a half a percentage point in the popular presidential vote, we should expect to find presidents pandering to voters as the next election approaches. Once reelected, the personal incentive to pander should disappear. All this reflects a simple, common sense view that these elected officeholders will become especially attentive to the public's preferences on issues as reelection nears. One can imagine all sorts of mitigating issues and circumstances beyond the president's control that would interfere with the president's ability to actually behave this way. Yet the fact is, presidents do tend to become more popular during the six months preceding the beginning of the reelection campaign. One careful statistical analysis of when presidents adopt popular positions in the public confirms that all else being equal, presidents do pander as the election nears, especially when they are marginally unpopular but within striking distance of their opponent.[23]

Elections aside, presidents must answer for themselves where they belong along that Truman–Eisenhower continuum of tolerance for public disapproval. Whatever equilibrium forces may be operating within the country to prevent the president from long remaining universally beloved, one such force operates within the White House itself—namely, most presidents will spend surpluses of support in order to accomplish their and their party's commitments to core constituencies. These presidents strategically view public approval as a resource to be spent or husbanded according to its current purchasing power and future needs. As a resource—that is, as a means to other ends—they would be foolish to hoard it, and therefore they do not always automatically act to increase their popularity. When a president enjoys a surplus of popular support, he may be expected to try to convert some of it into endorsement of his policy objectives. With their approval ratings glowing from recent victory and their next election distant, newly elected presidents can afford to be as programmatic as at any time in the remainder of their term. Franklin Roosevelt, Lyndon Johnson, Ronald Reagan, and even George W. Bush when he enacted his early tax-cut legislation all exploited their initial support to advance ideological policies dear to their core constituencies.

The anecdotal record of presidents and their advisors confirms that newly elected presidents frequently seek to spend their "honeymoon" public approval to win policies. When Reagan's job performance ratings (discussed in chapter 6) began dropping just before his attempted assassination in 1981, a White House correspondent queried a Reagan aide about this emerging trend. The aide observed matter-of-factly, "The fat's gotten into the fire more quickly with this [economic] proposal than in normal administrations because of [its] comprehensive nature. . . . There's resistance to change." An independent pollster added, "He's spending his savings [in popularity] and he has less in the bank now, that's all." [24] George W. Bush was even blunter. In the first press conference after his reelection in 2004 (presumably his last candidacy for public office), the president announced, "I earned capital in the campaign, political capital, and now I intend to spend it." [25] Spend it he did; by the next summer his approval rating was plumbing historic depths (see Figure 7-1, page 187).*

So far we have treated the presidential popularity as if it were a highly liquid commodity—something that can be spent and conserved in precise, calculated amounts. It is, of course, no such thing. Calling popular support a cur-

---

* With Clinton's approval rating slumping in the low 40 percent range just six months into his administration, the president's political advisers could ill afford so casual an assessment. Instead, they sounded the alarm when they jointly wrote a memo warning, "We do not exaggerate when we say that our current course, advanced by our economic team and Congressional leaders, threatens to sink your popularity further and weaken your presidency." Bob Woodward, *The Agenda* (New York: Simon and Schuster, 1994), 243.

rency conveys its instrumental value, but once one tries to calculate the gains and losses resulting from a particular policy, the glint of this metaphor begins to fade. The exchange value of popularity will always be somewhat uncertain, depending upon the skill of the president in going public and upon only dimly understood dynamics of opinion change. At times a policy will provoke a particular constituency to withdraw its approval en masse—as in the farmers' reactions to President Carter's embargo of grain exports to the Soviet Union in 1980. At other times a seemingly risky policy will fail to register on the approval charts. Perhaps the gravest miscalculation of the public's reception of a presidential decision occurred in 1974 when Gerald Ford pardoned Richard Nixon for any possible violations of federal law deriving from the Watergate investigation. Could he, or for that matter could his pollsters, have foreseen that his brief televised announcement would precipitate a thirty-point drop in his approval rating, or that nearly two years later voters would cite it as much as anything else as the reason for their unfavorable views toward him as a candidate?[26] In a world where politicians strive for safe and certain outcomes, spending popularity can be a risky venture.

President Clinton grappled with several issues that jeopardized his public support. Should he sign or veto cutbacks on welfare benefits to children and legal immigrants? Could he generate a sufficiently large groundswell of public support for health care reform that would force congressional action? Should he sign the Republican Congress's deficit reduction proposal, or should he veto it and force the federal government to shut down? These questions did not arise principally from concern for his popularity, but one can be sure that someone among his inner circle questioned their effects and procured survey data to answer them. One may safely assume that in none of these cases did the political ramifications escape President Clinton or his staff. For a president to fail or to refuse to think about policy strategically is tantamount to a decision to spend his support inefficiently.

CONCLUSION

Throughout our discussion we have encountered trends in both politics and technology that may limit the effectiveness of going public and hence this strategy's attractiveness to presidents in the future. One is the profusion of viewing options for the television audience whenever the president speaks to the nation. When presidents speak, fewer and fewer citizens are paying attention. On the political front, increasingly polarized partisanship on Capitol Hill translates to more representatives committed to a policy alternative and, consequently, less susceptible to presidentially induced constituent communications. Both potentially raise the risks that going public will fail, thereby compounding the costs of making the attempt.

This raises the prospect that presidents might eventually turn away from going public as a leadership strategy. Despite these and other adverse developments that have removed the central pillar of going public during the 1980s and 1990s—namely, the dramatic television address to a large, prime-time audience—the record of the two most recent presidents suggests that presidents will not soon abandon public strategies. Rather, they, like the presidents before them, will continue to adapt going public to ever-changing technology and political relations.

NOTES

1. Gary C. Jacobson launched a scholarly industry analyzing the effects of campaign spending on congressional elections in *Money and Politics.* New Haven: Yale University Press, 1980. On the growth of constituency service, see Morris B. Fiorina, *Congress: Keystone of Washington Establishment* (New Haven: Yale University Press), 1989.

2. For Clinton's performance on this score, see Gary C. Jacobson, Samuel Kernell, and Jeff Lazarus, "Assessing the President's Role as Party Agent in Congressional Elections: The Case of Bill Clinton in 2000," *Legislative Studies Quarterly* 29 (2004): 159–184.

3. Barbara Sinclair, *Party Wars* (Norman: Oklahoma University Press, 2006), 306–307.

4. Brandice Canes-Wrone, "The President's Public Influence from Public Appeals," *American Journal of Political Science* 45 (July 2001): 313–329.

5. George C. Edwards III *On Deaf Ears* (New Haven: Yale University Press), 2003.

6. This explanation follows a more detailed analysis in Samuel Kernell and Gary C. Jacobson, *The Logic of American Politics,* 2nd ed. (Washington, D.C.: CQ Press, 2003), 355–357.

7. ABC News/*Washington Post* survey on December 16–19, 2004. Results posted on www.pollingreport.com/social.htm.

8. Gary C. Jacobson, *A Divider, Not a Uniter* (New York: Pearson, Longman, 2007), 211–212.

9. Elisabeth Bumiller, "Presidential Travel: It's All about Local News," *New York Times,* February 11, 2002.

10. Janet Hook, "An Unlikely Face to Bush's Tax Cut Ad Mention of JFK Is 'Irresponsible,' Kin Say in Letter Demanding That a TV Spot Be Pulled," *Los Angeles Times,* May 9, 2003.

11. Herbert Walzer, "Corporate Advocacy Advertising and Political Influence," *Public Relations Review* 14 (spring): 1988.

12. Peter T. Kilborn, "The Key Democrat," *New York Times,* May 30, 1985, 15; Hedrick Smith, "Analysis of Democrats' Strategy on Tax Reform? Yes—With Three Conditions," *Washington Post National Weekly Edition,* February 18, 1985, 28; and Steven V. Roberts, "A Most Important Man on Capitol Hill," *New York Times Magazine,* September 22, 1985, 44.

13. Mike Allen and Peter Baker, "Hill Takes a Back Seat on Social Security, Administration, Republican National Committee Lead Drive to Add Private Accounts," *Washington Post,* April 6, 2005.

14. Quoted in George C. Edwards III, *The Public Presidency* (New York: St. Martin's Press, 1983), 88.

15. Quoted in Daniel Wise, "The Twilight of a President," *New York Times Magazine,* November 3, 1968, 131.

16. Jimmy Carter, "The President's News Conference of October 27, 1977," *Public Papers of the Presidents of the United States: Jimmy Carter, 1977* (Washington, D.C.: Government Printing Office, 1978), 1914.

17. Fred I. Greenstein, *The Hidden-Hand Presidency* (New York: Basic Books, 1982), 98–99.

18. Fred I. Greenstein, "Ike and Reagan," *New York Times,* January 29, 1983, 19.

19. All of the quoted passages here are drawn from a review of the press in Lawrence R. Jacobs and Robert Y. Shapiro, *Politicians Don't Pander* (Chicago: University of Chicago Press, 2000), 4–5. A variant of this complaint is "waffler." See Jeremy Paul, "Is the President a Waffler?" *Washington Monthly,* April 1996, 36.

20. For examples of Reagan's efforts to restore lost support among women in preparation for the election, see Barbara Bosler, "G.O.P. Starting Campaign to Show 'Reagan Is Terrific on Women's Issues,' " *New York Times,* April 6, 1984, 11; and "Reagan on Women's Issues," *New York Times,* April 6, 1984, 11.

21. Bryce Harlow, in a private interview with Professor John H. Kessel; Kessel, letter to author, October 16, 1985.

22. This analysis follows the procedures employed by Michael S. Lewis-Beck and Tom W. Rice, "Presidential Popularity and the Presidential Vote," *Public Opinion Quarterly* 46 (winter 1982): 534–537.

23. Summarizing her findings, Brandice Canes-Wrone wrote: "The president was found to be most likely to take a popular position when he would soon be facing a contest for reelection and had average approval ratings. When the approval ratings of such a president dropped so that he was relatively unpopular, or when they rose so that he was highly popular, his likelihood of supporting policies favored by the public declined. The likelihood of his taking a popular position was also lower in the earlier part of the term. Finally . . . these effects of presidential popularity and the electoral cycle held only for presidents running for reelection. During the second term . . . a president's popularity seemed to affect his behavior only when he faced a threat of losing office through impeachment proceedings. *Who Leads Whom?* (Chicago: University of Chicago Press, 2006), 182.

24. George Skelton, "Reagan Dip in Poll Tied to Spending Cuts," *Los Angeles Times,* March 19, 1981, 6.

25. Dan Froomkin, "Bush Agenda: Bold but Blurry," *Washington Post,* November 5, 2004.

26. The effects of the pardon on President Ford's defeat in 1976 are documented in Arthur H. Miller and Warren E. Miller, "Partisanship and Performance: 'Rational' Choice in the 1976 Presidential Election" (Paper delivered at the Annual Meeting of the American Political Science Association, Washington, D.C., September 1–4, 1977).

Going Public